explore & discover

A PHOTO-LOCATION AND
VISITOR GUIDEBOOK

ESSEX

VISIT THE MOST BEAUTIFUL PLACES, TAKE THE BEST PHOTOS

BY JUSTIN MINNS

explore & discover
ESSEX
BY JUSTIN MINNS

Copyright © fotoVUE Limited 2023.
Text and Photography: Copyright © Justin Minns 2023.
Foreword Copyright © Paul Forecast 2023.

Justin Minns has asserted his right under the Copyright, Designs and Patents Act 1988 to be identified as the author of this work.

All rights reserved. No part of this book may be reproduced or transmitted in any form or by any means, electronic or mechanical, including photocopying, recording, or by any information storage and retrieval system without the written permission of the publisher, except for the use of brief quotations in a book review.

TRADEMARKS: fotoVUE, the fotoVUE and Explore & Discover wordmarks are the registered trademarks of fotoVUE Ltd.

Publisher: Mick Ryan – fotoVUE Ltd
Edited by Susie Ryder
Layout by Justin Minns
Design by Ryder Design – www.ryderdesign.studio

All maps within this publication were produced by Don Williams of Bute Cartographics. Map location overlay and graphics by Mick Ryan. Maps contain Ordnance Survey data © Crown copyright and database right 2016.

A CIP catalogue record for this book is available from the British Library.

ISBN 978-1-7395083-0-2
10 9 8 7 6 5 4 3 2 1

The author, publisher and others involved in the design and publication of this guide book accept no responsibility for any loss or damage users may suffer as a result of using this book. Users of this book are responsible for their own safety and use the information herein at their own risk. Users should always be aware of weather forecasts, conditions, time of day and their own ability before venturing out.

Front cover: *Boats on the Thames Estuary at low tide. Canon 5D IV, 16–35mm at 20mm, ISO 100, 1.6s at f/16, LEE 0.9 hard ND grad, tripod. Dec.*
Rear cover left: *Epping Forest in spring. Canon 5D IV, 24–70mm at 50mm, ISO 100, 1/40s at f/5.6, LEE polariser, tripod. May.*
Rear cover right: *Thaxted windmill in evening light. Canon 5D IV, 16-35mm at 30mm, ISO 100, 1/8s at f/16, tripod. Sep.*
Opposite: *Ulting church. Canon 5D IV, 24–70mm at 70mm, ISO 100, 1/80s at f/16, tripod. Sep.*

Printed in China on behalf of Latitude Press Limited.

The deepest Essex few explore
Where steepest thatch is sunk in flowers
And out of elm and sycamore
Rise flinty fifteenth-century towers

Essex by John Betjeman.

CONTENTS

Locations overview	6
Acknowledgements	8
Foreword by Paul Forecast – Regional Director for the National Trust (Midlands & East of England)	12
Introduction	14
Getting to and around Essex	18
Where to stay, eat & drink	20
Essex weather and seasonal highlights	24
Essex climate and weather	28
Using this guidebook and getting the best image	30
Camera, lenses and captions	32
Classic Essex locations	34
Access and conservation	36

NORTH ESSEX: THE STOUR TO THE COLNE

	Introduction	40
	Area Map	42
1	Chalkney Woods	46
2	Chappel Viaduct	50
3	Bures	56
4	Hillhouse Woods	62
5	Dedham	68
6	Manningtree	74
7	Wrabness	80
8	Harwich & Dovercourt	86
9	Hamford Water	94
10	Walton-on-the-Naze	104
11	Frinton-on-Sea	108
12	Clacton-on-Sea	114
13	Colne Point	120
14	St Osyth Creek	126
15	Point Clear	132
16	Brightlingsea	134
17	Thorrington Tide Mill	140
18	Alresford Creek	144
19	Fingringhoe	150

CENTRAL ESSEX: THE BLACKWATER

	Introduction	158
	Area Map	160
1	Mersea Island	164
2	Tollesbury	172
3	Heybridge Basin	178
4	Maldon	184
5	Beeleigh Falls	190
6	Hoe Mill Lock	196
7	Sandford Mill	200
8	Danbury Common	204
9	Mundon Oaks	210
10	Stansgate	216
11	Bradwell-on-Sea	218

SOUTH ESSEX: THE CROUCH TO THE THAMES

Introduction 226
Area Map 228
1 Battlesbridge 232
2 South Woodham Ferrers 238
3 North Fambridge 242
4 Burnham-on-Crouch 246
5 Lion Wharf 252
6 Paglesham 258
7 Barlinghall Creek 262
8 The Broomway 266
9 Red Sands Fort 272
10 Shoeburyness 276
11 Southend-on-Sea 282
12 Leigh-on-Sea 286
13 Two Tree Island 290
14 Hadleigh Castle 296
15 Coalhouse Point 300

WESTERN ESSEX

Introduction 306
Area Map (south) 308
1 Warley Place 312
2 Mountnessing Windmill 318
3 Epping Forest 322
4 Temple Hill 328
5 The Stort Navigation 336
Area Map (north) 342
6 Hatfield Forest 346
7 Felsted Mill 352
8 Bocking Windmill 356
9 Finchingfield 358
10 Thaxted 364
11 Saffron Walden 368
12 Bragg's Mill 374

FEATURE PAGES

Towns & Villages 382
Churches 390
Historic Buildings & Gardens 398
Nature Reserves 408
About the Author 412
About fotoVUE 414
Index 416

CONTENTS 5

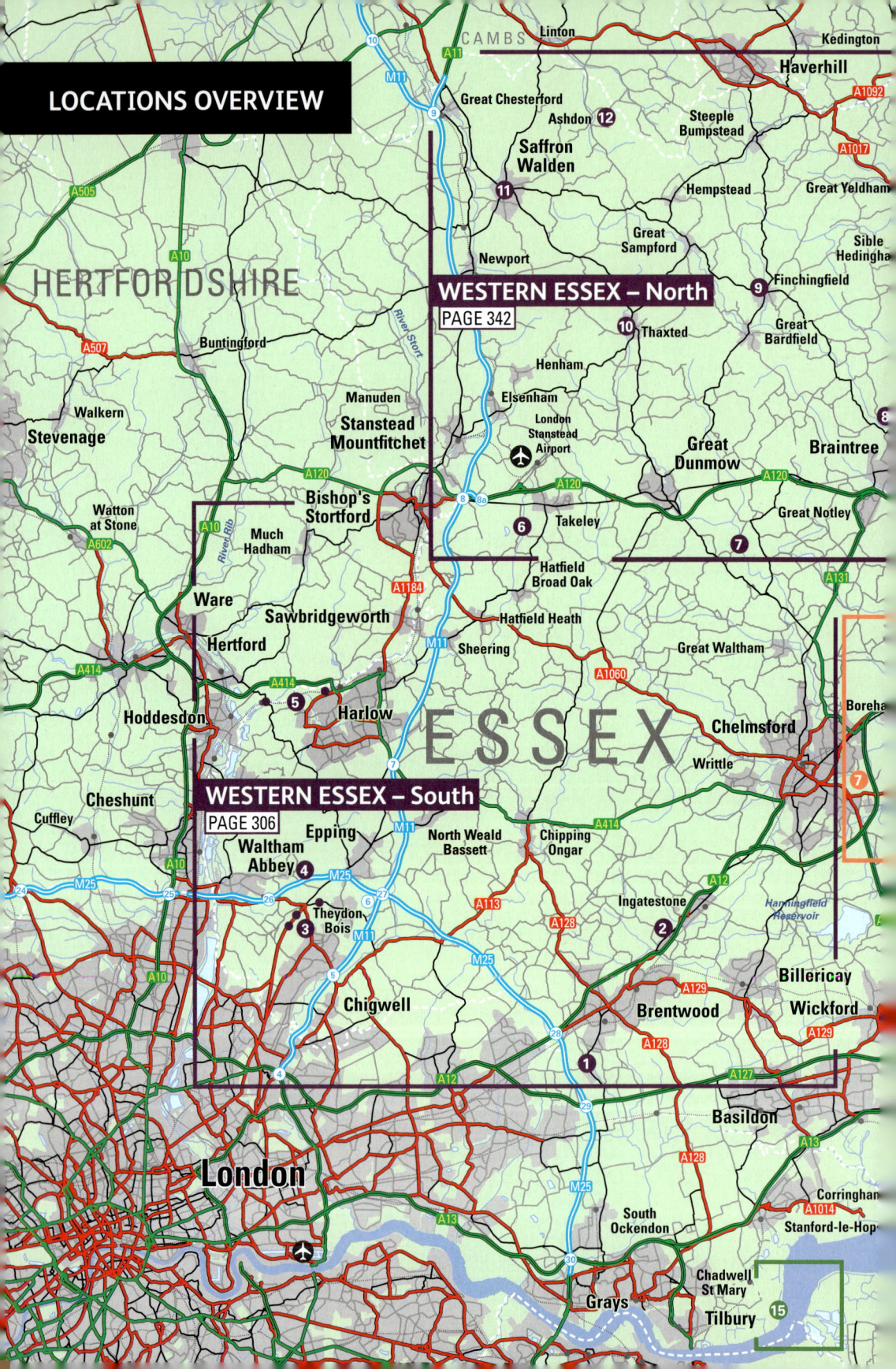

ACKNOWLEDGEMENTS

Although it is my name on the front of this book, these things don't happen without the help and support of a great many other people.

As an Essex boy myself, born and raised in the very north of the county, a stone's throw from the River Stour and the border with Suffolk, it was a delight to be able to spend the last couple of years revisiting old haunts and discovering new ones. So, a massive thanks to Mick Ryan at Fotovue for giving me the opportunity and guidance, and to the rest of the team at Fotovue – Susie, Nathan and Don for all of their hard work turning my ramblings and photos into this wonderful book.

As always, I owe a great deal to my wife, Johanna for her constant help and encouragement, her patience putting up with my last minute decisions to go out chasing the light and especially for always making sure there is coffee and breakfast ready to go. I should also mention our Labrador, Millie for keeping me company and providing motivation to keep exploring further; I really couldn't have done it without you both.

Special thanks also (in no particular order) to the following: everyone at the National Trust in the East of England for giving me the opportunity to photograph the wonderful parts of East Anglia that they care for, and for kindly allowing me to use some of those images in these pages; everyone at LEE Filters and f-stop gear for their valued support over the years, and all the lovely Essex folk I've met and chatted with either while out working on this book or on social media for their help, advice and local stories.

Finally, my parents: my mum, from whom I apparently inherited my creative talents, and my father, who sadly passed away before this book was finished, for passing on his love of the Essex coast and countryside.

Justin Minns
April 2023

Opposite: Sunrise at Walton-on-the-Naze. Canon 7D, 10–20mm at 10mm, ISO 100, 15s at f/16, LEE 0.9 ND & 0.9 hard ND grad, tripod. May.

Blue hour at Dovercourt lighthouse. Canon 5D IV, 24–70mm at 30mm, ISO 100, 30s at f/11, LEE Little Stopper & 0.6 hard ND grad, tripod, Mar.

FOREWORD

Foreword by Paul Forecast

I love Essex. I am thrilled to be asked to write the foreword to Justin's book. His stunning photos capture perfectly for me the county's spirit of place and his engaging and informative writing has added new depth to my own understanding and appreciation of a place that I thought I knew well.

King Aescwine created the Kingdom of East Seaxe in the sixth century. Many of the landscapes which would have been familiar to our Anglo-Saxon forebears can still be seen today and have been captured in Justin's beautiful images. It is a county bounded by water, with the rivers Lea and Stour marking the western and northern boundaries, the Thames Estuary to the south and the North Sea to the East. In between is a patchwork of estuaries and creeks, royal hunting forests, heathland, chalk grassland, meadows, and farmland. These in turn are rich in wildlife.

I have worked for over a decade alongside a committed and talented group of people who have protected and enhanced the landscapes of Essex that hold so much nature, history, and beauty. Justin's photographs could lull you into thinking that work to protect these special places is complete. As with all places in the UK, the landscapes of Essex are under threat from development, intensive agriculture, and inequality of access to green space. Essex is especially vulnerable to the impacts of climate change with a soft low-lying coast which is under threat from sea level rise and being one of the driest counties putting pressure on our rivers and wetlands. I hope that as well as enjoying Justin's photographs they will inspire you to take action to look after what we have, create new places for wildlife, and to provide access to nature for all.

The National Trust looks after some of the places covered in this book, including Hatfield Forest, Northey Island, Constable's Stour Valley and Danbury Common. We hope that Justin's photos inspire you to visit soon. You would be very welcome.

Paul Forecast
Regional Director for the National Trust (Midlands & East of England)
June 2023

Opposite: Dedham church in the mist. Canon 5D IV, 24–105mm at 75mm, ISO 100, 1/5s at f/16, LEE 0.6 med ND grad, tripod. Apr.

INTRODUCTION

To some, the mention of Essex conjures up visions of the brash, fake-tanned stereotypes of TV shows like The Only Way is Essex so the very existence of this book (and indeed its contents) may come as something of a surprise. And Essex is a surprising place – a county of contrasts. Beneath the shallow perception lie depths of history; Britain's oldest town sits just a few miles from its newest city, and a stone's throw from the bustle of the country's busiest motorway you can become lost in the tranquility of an ancient forest.

The Essex coast is the second longest of any English county, meandering for over 350 miles from the Suffolk border in the north to the Thames Estuary in the south and it is here, under the region's famous big skies, that most of the locations in this book are to be found. Passing golden sandy beaches, colourful with piers and beach huts, the coastline takes regular detours inland along broad, silvery estuaries, peaceful but for the cries of birds, the tinkling of rigging and flap of sails. This is where the magic of Essex lies: on the secretive coast that hides over thirty-five islands (the number fluctuates with the tide) and in the capillary-like network of creeks that branch out and get lost in mile upon mile of wonderfully lonely marshland.

There is more to Essex than the coast though. More than 70% of the county is given over to agriculture and you don't have to travel far from the urban border with London in the south to discover the rural heart of Essex – a gently rolling medley of golden farmland and ancient forest dotted with historic towns and sleepy villages, thatched cottages and timber-framed buildings.

The Kingdom of Essex was founded by Saxons in the 6th century but the county's long and rich history goes back much further. Clacton-on-Sea, is one of the oldest known occupied sites in Britain, dating back to 450,000 BC (did I mention Essex was surprising?) Much later, when the Romans arrived, they built their capital at Colchester and – almost a thousand years on – it was on an Essex beach that King Cnut failed to turn back the tide. Hints of this history can be seen throughout the county, from the impressive medieval churches and well-preserved towns and villages (Essex has 14,000 listed buildings) to the string of wartime defences along the Thames Estuary.

Essex is still something of a hidden gem amongst photographers, certainly when compared to its neighbouring East Anglian counties to the north, and I hope those reading this book enjoy discovering its treasures as much as I have. Wherever your own interest lies, I encourage you to use the book as a starting point from which to explore further and find out for yourself just what a surprising place Essex is.

Justin Minns
April 2023

Opposite: Blue hour at Hamford Water. Canon 5D IV, 24–70mm at 35mm, ISO 100, 4s at f/16, LEE 0.6 med ND grad, tripod. June.

Dawn on the River Stort. Canon 5D IV, 24–105mm at 35mm, ISO 100, 1/5s at f/16, LEE 0.6 med ND grad, tripod. June.

GETTING TO AND AROUND ESSEX

Situated on the coast just to the north east of London, Essex is well connected by major roads and rail networks and is easily reached by road, rail, air and even sea.

From London and the south

Visitors from London or the south and west of the country will probably arrive via the M25, from which there are three main routes into the county: the M11 heads northwards into the west of Essex, the A12 is the most central, running north east through the county, and the A127 provides access to the south east of the county.

From the north

The main route for visitors from the Midlands and north (those not arriving via the M25) is the A14, which comes east from the M1, M6 and A1 meeting the M11 at Cambridge on its way into Essex. The main routes from East Anglia are the A12 in the east, A134 in the centre and A11/M11 in the west.

Travelling around Essex

Country Lanes

Essex is well connected by A roads many of them dual carriageways, so getting around is reasonably quick and easy (if you avoid peak times). You don't have to go too far to find yourself in the countryside in Essex and, in the most rural areas, roads become narrow and winding with hedgerows reducing visibility. You never know what's around the next corner so drive carefully and prepare for the unexpected, be it oncoming vehicles, tractors, cyclists, walkers or wildlife.

Peak Times

The Essex coast, estuaries and rivers can become very busy during summer, school holidays and bank holiday weekends, especially if the sun is out. The same is true of tourist attractions. Roads are congested and parking spaces harder to find so allow extra time or, better still, plan your visit for sunrise or sunset when there are fewer people around. Even at the busiest times, beaches empty quickly as sunset approaches and you'll soon have the place to yourself.

Major roads, particularly in the south of the county, can become very busy at rush hour and delays are not uncommon (the M25, A12 and A127 are amongst the worst culprits). They are all much clearer in the early hours for sunrise trips but major roads are occasionally closed between 10pm and 6am for overnight roadworks.

Parking

The parking mentioned in this book ranges from large pay and display car parks to small lay-bys at the side of the road. Official car parks are marked with a blue parking symbol. The informal parking places are marked by a small letter P on the maps – park in these places at your own risk. Always park with consideration, avoid blocking gates or parking in passing places. Pay particular attention when parking at the coast – during spring high tides the car park (and indeed the whole road in some cases) will be flooded. These are mentioned in the location guide so be sure to check the tide times and heights before your visit.

An overgrown bus stop at Dedham. Canon G1 X, 35mm, ISO 800, 1/250s at f/5. Oct.

A cyclist in the Essex countryside. Canon 5D IV, 70–200mm at 200mm, ISO 100, 1/30s at f/16, LEE polariser, tripod. Apr.

Train

Most trains to Essex from around the country connect via London. From the capital the Great Eastern Main Line and Western Main Line run through Essex from London Liverpool Street to Norwich and Cambridge respectively. While the London, Tilbury and Southend line goes from Fenchurch Street to Southend.

The main rail lines within the region, most run by Greater Anglia or C2C are:

Crouch Valley line: Wickford to Southminster.
Gainsborough line: Mark Tey to Sudbury.
Great Eastern Main line: London Liverpool Street to Norwich.
London, Tilbury and Southend line: London Fenchurch Street to Shoeburyness.
Mayflower line: Manningtree to Harwich.
Sunshine Coast line: Colchester to Walton.
Western Main line: London Liverpool Street to Cambridge.

Bus

National Express runs coach services to Colchester, Chelmsford, Braintree and Harlow from around the UK. There are local bus services between towns and villages across the county – First Bus (*firstbus.co.uk/essex*) is the main provider or check Traveline (*traveline.info*)

By air

For visitors from further afield, Essex has two international airports: in the south of the county there's Southend Airport and, further north, London Stansted. This is the larger of the two and it's ideally situated near the M11 for the north and west of the county and the A120 for routes east.

By boat

Ferries run regularly between the Hook of Holland and Harwich International for visitors wanting to drive from Europe.

WHERE TO STAY, EAT AND DRINK

Essex, particularly the coast, is a popular destination so there is a great deal of choice when it comes to accommodation and places to eat.

If you are looking for a central location to use as a base, the Chelmsford area has good road links and nowhere in Essex is more than an hour's drive away. Every area in this book is well provided for in terms of hotels, pubs, B&Bs and holiday cottages so another option is to stay locally and explore each area individually. Essex has good road links (if a bit too much traffic) so choose accommodation fairly close to of one of the main routes and the rest of the county will always be within easy reach.

Accommodation

B&Bs, Hotels & Holiday Cottages

Here are a few recommendations and the best resources to help you find accommodation in Essex.

Useful resources include:
visitessex.com
tripadvisor.com
landmarktrust.org.uk
quirkyaccom.com
pitchup.com
coolcamping.com

- The Blue Boar, Abridge RM4 1UA
- Marygreen Manor Hotel, Brentwood CM14 4NR
- The Rose and Crown, Colchester CO1 2TZ
- Millsoms, Dedham CO7 6HW
- The Swan Inn, Felsted CM6 3DG
- Finchingfield Camping, Finchingfield CM7 4JB
- Pontlands Park, Great Baddow CM2 8HR
- Essex Glamping, Hadleigh SS7 2AP
- High Barn Heritage, Greenstead Green CO9 1RR
- The Pier, Harwich CO12 3HH
- Channels Lodge, Little Waltham CM3 3PT
- Mulberry House, High Ongar CM5 9NL
- Roslin Beach Hotel, Thorpe Bay SS1 3BG
- Five Lakes, Tollshunt Knights CM9 8HX
- Piglets Boutique B&B, Wimbish CB10 2XJ

Eating

When it comes to pubs, Essex has some fabulous ones, ranging from the cosy country kind to gastro pubs, all serving good food and the region's excellent beers. The following are some of my favourites, along with recommendations from the helpful people on my Facebook page.

Pubs

- Cricketers, Clavering CB11 4QT
- Woolpack Inn, Coggeshall CO6 1UB
- Sun Inn, Dedham CO7 6DF
- The New Bell Inn, Harwich CO12 3EN
- The Duke's Head, Hatfield Broad Oak CM22 7HH
- The Peterboat, Leigh-on-Sea SS9 2EN
- Queen's Head, The Hythe, Maldon CM9 5HN
- The Fox Inn, Matching Tye CM17 0QS
- The Plough & Sail, Paglesham SS4 2EQ
- Peldon Rose, Peldon CO5 7QJ
- The Railway Arms, Saffron Walden CB11 3HQ
- The Old Windmill, South Hanningfield CM3 8HT
- The Hoop, Stock CM4 9BD
- The Fox & Hounds, Tillingham CM0 7SU
- Fleur De Lys, Widdington CB11 3SG
- Rose and Crown, Wivenhoe CO7 9BX

Fish and Chips

- Howard's Fish & Grill, Benfleet SS7 5LH
- The Jolly Fryer, Burnham on Crouch CM0 8AG
- Gary's fish and chips, Clacton CO15 2BX
- Young's Other Plaice, Frinton-on-Sea CO13 9RX
- Our Plaice, Maldon CM9 6JE
- Riverside Fish and Chips, Manningtree CO11 1UN
- West Mersea Oyster Bar CO5 8LT
- Henleys, Wivenhoe CO7 9HA

Cafés

- Peaberries, Burnham on Crouch CM0 8AG
- Greensward Café, Clacton CO15 1XB
- Elder Street Cafe, Debden CB11 3JY
- Hall Farm, Dedham CO7 6LS

20 WHERE TO STAY, EAT AND DRINK

Above: The Plough & Sail at Paglesham.
Right: The Hoop at Stock.

- Rainbow Café, Dovercourt CO12 3TA
- Original Tea Hut, Epping Forest IG10 4HR
- The Lock Tea Room, Heybridge CM9 4RS
- Osea View Café, Heybridge CM9 4SA
- Red Dog, Inworth CO5 9SP
- 19 to Go, Kirby-le-Soken CO13 0DA
- Sara's Tea Garden, Leigh-on-Sea SS9 2EP
- Paper Mill Lock Tearooms, Little Baddow CM3 4BS
- Mrs Salisbury's Famous Tea Rooms, Maldon CM9 5EP
- Ocean Beach, Southend SS1 2YG
- Oliver's on the Beach, Southend SS1 1DL
- The Loft – Tea by the Sea, Tollesbury CM9 8SE

WHERE TO STAY, EAT AND DRINK

A calm misty morning on the River Crouch. Canon 5D IV, 16–35mm at 19mm, ISO 100, 2s at f/16, LEE 0.6 hard ND grad, tripod. Feb.

ESSEX WEATHER AND SEASONAL HIGHLIGHTS

Essex oil seed rape fields. Canon 5D IV, 16–35mm at 35mm, ISO 100, 0.6s at f/16, LEE 0.9 med ND grad, tripod. Apr.

SPRING – March, April, May

The season starts slowly, the trees and landscape still bare and uninspiring but the weather is often changeable at this time of year. Its battle with the rear guard of the retreating winter creates brooding skies and dramatic light so it's the ideal time to be out under the big skies at the coast.

At the coast, March and April brings some of the highest tides of the year, so it's the time to visit the wrecks at Maldon, Stansgate, Coalhouse Point and anywhere that works at very high tide.

The countryside starts to come to life around mid-March when native crocuses and daffodils can be seen amongst the ruins at Warley Place. Into April and oil seed rape has added splashes of yellow to the patchwork of fields across the county and the verges are thick with a white froth of cow parsley and the first sprinkling of red campion. When the hedgerows turn white with first blackthorn and then hawthorn blossom, spring has arrived.

By May, wildflower meadows like Hunsdon Mead and Hatfield Forest are dazzling with buttercups but for many photographers the highlight of spring is the sight and smell of a woodland carpeted with bluebells. Essex has many bluebell woods across the county, but with both bluebells and wild garlic, Chalkney Woods is one of the best. Bluebells usually start flowering towards the end of April but early May is often best for a visit, when the woods are lush with fresh lime-green leaves that contrast with the blue flowers.

Summer at Bocking windmill. Canon 5D IV, 24–70mm at 47mm, ISO 100, 1/400s at f/11, LEE 0.9 med ND grad, tripod. June.

The difference in temperature between warmer days and cool, still nights at this time of year causes mist to form in calm weather, providing wonderful conditions in the low river valleys of the Stour, Colne, Stort and Blackwater.

SUMMER – June, July, August

With very long, hot days (sunrise is as early as 4.30am at the height of summer), harsh, shimmering daylight and everywhere teeming with people, summer is traditionally the least popular season with landscape photographers. Unsurprisingly, given that description but for those willing to brave the early alarm calls, the possible rewards that await are deserted locations, golden light and those lovely cool misty mornings that you get before the temperatures start to climb on a hot day. It is a wonderful time to be out and there's usually time to go back to bed again before the rest of the house is awake. For sunset, choose the more remote beaches to avoid the crowds, or time your visit with a high tide a little before sunset to ensure clear beaches and no footprints.

For me, summer is a colourful time full of life – the perfect time for plump rural landscapes. The windmills at Thaxted, Bocking and Ashdon stand like beacons in ripening fields of swaying barley and wheat, perhaps splashed with a smattering of bright red poppies or the blues and purples of linseed or borage. Purple loosestrife, yellow flag iris and the azure flash of kingfishers and dragonflies bring colour to riverbanks. Even at the coast, the miles of saltmarsh shimmer with a haze of lilac as the sea lavender comes into flower in July. It can be found up and down the coast but Wrabness, Tollesbury and Paglesham are particularly good.

ESSEX WEATHER AND SEASONAL HIGHLIGHTS

Epping Forest in autumn. Canon 5D IV, 24–70mm at 70mm, ISO 200, 1/8s at f/8, LEE polariser, tripod. Oct.

AUTUMN – September, October, November

The favourite season of many landscape photographers, autumn brings shortening days, damp misty mornings and, of course, the changing colours of the leaves. The season is slow to start in the mild Essex climate and September can still be warm but, as in spring, the freshening nights can lead to those atmospheric misty mornings.

Again, as in spring, the autumn equinox is a time for the highest of high tides. The weather is becoming changeable again at this time of year and the combination of clouds, passing showers and spells of sunlight makes it a promising time to head to the coast in search of dramatic light.

The trees and woodlands start to change colour in October, with the peak colours usually coming early in November. There are plenty of great locations in Essex for autumn colour: Chalkney Woods, Hillhouse Woods, Hatfield Forest but particularly the beeches in Epping Forest.

WINTER – December, January, February

Winters are mild in Essex and, aside from the occasional storm from the east, snow has become rather uncommon in recent years, but it is still a fantastic time of year for photography.

It's magical to be out with the camera, extremities tingling on a crunchy frosty morning along the River Stour, for example, or photographing the saltmarsh under frozen pastel sunrise skies. When those easterly storms do happen, they bring the rare opportunity to photograph snow-covered beaches under heavy slate skies.

For those not keen on early starts, those sunrise times are much more civilised – as late as 8am – and as the sun stays fairly low in the sky throughout the short days, with the right conditions the light can be decent all day.

The huge expanses of saltmarsh and mud-flat take on a bleak but beautiful feel at this time of year, especially under dramatic dark skies. Winter is a highlight for the county's coastal nature reserves with tens of thousands of wintering geese coming to feed on the marshes along the coast. Abberton Reservoir and Wallasea Island are just a couple of places to see and hear the spectacle.

With the sun rising and setting at its most southerly extent, winter is also the perfect time to photograph south-facing locations, in particular Thorpe Bay, Shoeburyness and others along the Thames Estuary as well as the beaches in the north of the county.

Dedham church on a misty morning. Canon 5D IV, 100–400mm at 400mm, ISO 100, 1/80s at f/11, tripod. Dec.

Snowdrops signal the end of winter; Warley Place and Marks Hall are two of the best places to see swathes of the tiny white flowers.

Preparing for the weather

Don't just venture out with your camera when the sun is shining; one of the best times for images with impact is when the weather is on the edge – the moment when the sun breaks through briefly, lighting the landscape between showers, for example.

Protect your camera

Many modern cameras have some weatherproofing but it's better to be safe than sorry. There are all sorts of rain covers available for shooting in the rain or protecting your gear from sea spray, from the cheap but effective disposable type (which are little more than a clear plastic bag), to the sort of professional rain covers used by sports and wildlife photographers; either one is best used with a lens hood to shield the lens. I generally opt for a carrier bag plonked over the camera and tripod head to keep things dry while waiting for a shower to pass and a large brolly to keep rain off the front of the lens or filters while shooting

Protect yourself

There's nothing more dispiriting than being cold and damp so investing in decent waterproof clothing and comfortable layers to keep you warm and dry will enable you to focus on your photography for longer in bad weather. Wellies are invaluable at the coast and in wet countryside and dew-soaked vegetation on overgrown paths. It's worth investing in a decent pair that will be more comfortable to walk in and longer lasting.

The weather forecast

Landscape photography is all about being in the right place at the right time. Having a basic understanding of the weather can help you to interpret the forecast and spot the signs that might lead to favourable conditions for photography so you can choose a location accordingly – if, of course, the forecast is correct!

Met Office Weather Forecast *metoffice.gov.uk/public/weather/forecast*

Tidal charts

visitmyharbour.com/tides/area/299/east-coast-of-england

ESSEX CLIMATE AND WEATHER

Beach huts at Mersea in winter. Canon 5D IV, 24–70mm at 26mm, ISO 100, 1/250s at f/8. Feb.

'It is the driest county, yet watery-edged, flaking down to marsh and salting and mud-flat.'
J A Baker, The Peregrine

Located in the east of England close to London and with 350-miles of coastline lapped by the North Sea and the English Channel, Essex has temperate maritime climate of warm summers and cold winters with extreme weather being rare. However extreme temperatures do sometimes occur, such as the 'beast from the east' characterised by arctic temperatures and heavy snowfall caused by areas of high pressure over northern Europe that brings bitterly cold air across the UK, especially in the east of the country.

July and August are the hottest months in Essex, late December until March the coldest, with rain spread evenly throughout the year, with March being the driest month and October being the wettest. Being in the south of England, spring (April–June) comes a few weeks early compared to the North and autumn slightly later (September–November).

Essex's estuarine coastline includes the estuaries of the Thames, Crouch, Roach, Blackwater, Colne and Stour rivers often featuring coastal plains of mudflats, saltmarshes and sandbanks (most having protected status), and these areas sometimes experience coastal fog and mist which can be very special for morning photography. Be aware, these coastlines experience rapid tidal changes. Always check tide times before heading out.

Along with neighbouring Cambridgeshire, Suffolk and Norfolk, Essex is a low-lying area. Its highest point is Chrishall Common near the village of Langley, close to the Hertfordshire border, which reaches 482 feet (147 m), the 16774th highest peak in the British Isles! Essex is slightly drier and cooler than neighbouring inland areas including London.

Heavy skies at Dovercourt lighthouse. Canon R5, 24–105mm at 45mm, ISO 100, 1/400s at f/8. Mar.

Met office weather station averages

Shoeburyness, Essex

Location: 51.554, 0.83 **Altitude:** 2m above mean sea level **Station type:** Residential

☀ **SUN /** Average hours of sunshine per month

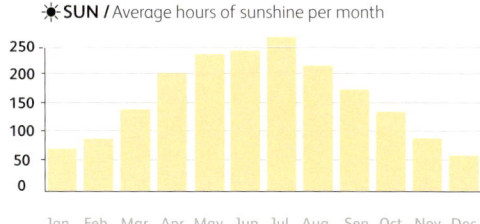

🌧 **RAIN /** Average days rain/month and precipitation in mm

Jan	Feb	Mar	Apr	May	Jun	Jul	Aug	Sep	Oct	Nov	Dec
43 mm	36 mm	32 mm	36 mm	41 mm	44 mm	41 mm	48 mm	42 mm	58 mm	54 mm	49 mm

🌡 **TEMPERATURE /** Average min/max temp per month C/F

22/71 C/F
0/32

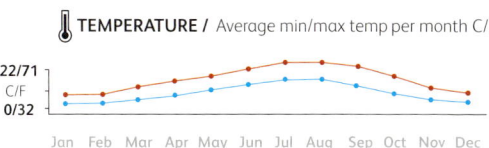

❄ **FROST /** Average days of frost per month

days | 7 | 7 | 4 | 2 | 0 | 0 | 0 | 0 | 0 | 0 | 3 | 7 |

ESSEX CLIMATE AND WEATHER

USING THIS GUIDEBOOK TO GET THE BEST IMAGES

fotoVUE photo-location and visitor guidebooks give you the information and inspiration to get to beautiful locations in the best photographic conditions.

In the right place

Each location chapter has a grey box titled 'How to get here' where there are written directions to the location along with four co-ordinates to the nearest car park or lay-by, including a scannable location QR-code. On the maps are location and sometimes viewpoint pins, and parking symbols.

Main car park

- Lat/Long: 52.05866, 0.32506
- what3words: ///retrieves.streamers.else
- Grid Ref: TL 594 425
- Postcode: CB10 2JA

The QR-code

Using your smart phone camera point the lens at the QR-code and your camera will scan the code that contains the parking location information as a lat-long co-ordinate. On some older phone operating systems you may have to have a QR-code reader app. Once read, your browser will open in Google maps and you can get directions from where you are to the parking spot of your chosen location.

///What3Words

Download the free app at *what3words.com*

Postcodes are great if you are going to a specific building but not ideal for getting to the middle-of-nowhere. Latitude/longitude is precise but it is a hassle to type 16-digits into a navigation app or sat-nav. Better is *what3words*, which assigns each 3m square in the world a unique three-word address that will never change. Download the free *what3words* app then either say, type or scan in the *what3words* of a location, click on navigate, open a map app and you will get directions to the location. You can save locations on your phone, which is useful if you plan on visiting several locations in a day or are on a trip; you can save them all before you set off. The *what3words* app can also take photographs and stamp the *what3words* location on your image as a useful reference source for where your images were taken. In the UK most emergency services use *what3words* so if you get into trouble whilst exploring in a remote location, use the app to help 999 know exactly where to find you.

Ordnance Survey maps

The relevant OS Explorer map (1:25 000) for each location is given at the beginning of each location section next to the introduction. There are several apps that allow you to download the relevant OS maps in return for a subscription. However, it is not recommended to rely solely on a mobile phone or tablet for navigation as batteries can run out and wireless connections can be lost.

Before you set off, study a map so that you know where you are going and give yourself plenty of time to get to your destination. Also, read the accessibility notes to check the distances and terrain to a location's viewpoints.

The fotoVUE maps

Our maps are created by the talented Don Williams of Bute Cartography, then an overlay is added with location and viewpoint pins along with some points of interest and services.

Our map symbols

Our maps are detailed but with few symbols. The symbols that are important are:

A location chapter
A location chapter is marked by a numbered circle or pin and its name.

A location viewpoint
A viewpoint is marked by a small circle sometimes with the name of the viewpoint by it.

Footpaths ----------------
Not all footpaths are marked on our maps, only footpaths that are useful to get to a location and its viewpoints.

Walking man symbol
Paths with a walking man represent longer walks of a few miles, often involving steep uphill walking. These may require navigation and use of map and compass. Sometimes we use them to clarify a right of way.

Old boats on the marsh near Great Oakley. Canon 5D IV, 24–105mm at 32mm, ISO 100, 1/13s at f/16, LEE 0.6 med ND grad, tripod. Jan.

Map Symbols

- ❶ Location chapter pin
- ● Viewpoint pin
- 🅿 Parking
- ⛽ Fuel
- 🚙 Carvanning & camping site
- 🚐 Carvanning site/#vanlife
- ⛺ Campsite/Glamping
- 🌐 World Heritage site/area
- 🏛 Stately Home/Country House
- 🌼 Garden open to the public
- ❋ Popular high viewpoint
- 🌬 Windmill/Windpump
- ⛪ Significant church
- Marsh NR Nature Reserve
- ★ Ancient Site
- 🏰 English Heritage
- 🍺 Pub
- ☕ Cafe
- 🍴 Restaurant
- 🛏 Accommodation
- 🌿 National Trust
- 👣 National Trails
- 🏯 Castle
- ⛳ Golf course
- 🏛 Museum
- 🎪 Country park
- 🚻 Public toilets
- Ⓥ Visitor centre

At the right time

Each location in this book is accompanied by detailed notes on the optimum time of year and day to visit a location to get the best photographic results. Good light can occur at any time, however. Often the best time to visit a location is when conditions are rapidly changing, such as after a storm.

Weather

Check the weather forecast a few days before and the day before a planned outing. Recommended apps are *metoffice.gov.uk* and *yr.no*.

Sun

Topography, sun position and weather determine how light falls on the land. Use the sun position compass on the front flap of this guidebook for sunrise and sunset times, to find out where the sun rises and sets on the compass (there is a big difference between summer and winter) and sun elevation (how high the sun rises in the sky).

Useful websites and apps include **The Photographer's Ephemeris** (*photoephemeris.com*), **photopills** (*photopills.com*) and **Suncalc** (*suncalc.org*).

Exploration

This guidebook will help get you to some of the best photographic locations and viewpoints in Essex. It is by no means exhaustive; use it as a springboard to discover your own viewpoints. Study a map to look for locations or just follow your instinct to discover your own.

CAMERA, LENSES AND CAPTIONS

Equipment

The images in this book are the result of several years' work, during which time I've owned various Canon camera bodies. I currently use the R5 and R7 but the majority of photographs were taken with the Canon 5D Mark IV. I also have an infrared converted X-Pro1, which I love for dramatic black and whites.

Lenses are a similar story, but the lenses usually in my bag are the 14–35mm, 24–105mm and either 70–200mm or 100–500mm, covering a wide range of focal lengths in just three lenses.

Whichever camera and lens I'm using, it is almost always on a tripod as it slows me down and makes me concentrate more on each shot. I use Gitzo tripods with Arca Swiss geared heads for precise control over composition.

For aerial shots I use a DJI Mavic 2 Pro drone, which allows me to put the camera exactly where I need it – invaluable for finding those elusive high viewpoints in this flat part of the world.

Filters are essential in my photography and I have used LEE Filters for over ten years. I use ND filters to control the shutter speed for creative effects, a landscape polariser and – as most of my photography is done around sunrise or sunset – graduated ND filters for controlling the high dynamic range at these times of day. I prefer working with filters as I like to get as much right in camera as possible but occasionally it's necessary to bracket exposures and merge them in post-processing.

All this gear is carried in f-stop bags, which is a modular system so I can tailor it to suit what I need to carry and still have room for all the non-photographic gear required.

Quite a lot of planning and preparation goes into my photography. I'm always aiming to capture the landscape at its most dramatic or atmospheric, so I use various online resources to work out the best time of day and year to visit a location and spend a lot of time studying (and being frustrated by) weather forecasts.

Post-processing is done almost entirely in Adobe Lightroom with just the odd bit, mainly cloning, being finished in Photoshop. I try and process my landscapes for a fairly natural look, with the drama hopefully coming from the conditions.

Equipment list

Camera bodies
- Canon R5
- Canon R7
- Fuji X-Pro1 (infrared converted)

Lenses
- Canon RF 16mm f2.8
- Canon RF 14–35mm f/4 L IS
- Canon RF 24–105mm f/4 L IS
- Canon EF 70–200mm f/4 L
- Canon RF 100–500mm f/4.5-7.1 L IS
- Canon EF 500mm f/4 L IS
- Canon EF 1.4 extender
- Fuji 14mm

Filters
- LEE Filters – ND, graduated ND and circular polariser

Drone
- DJI Mavic 2 Pro

Tripods
- Gitzo Systematic & Mountaineer tripods
- Gitzo monopod
- Arca Swiss P0 hybrid heads
- Lensmaster gimbal head

Bags
- F-stop Tilopa & Ajna backpacks

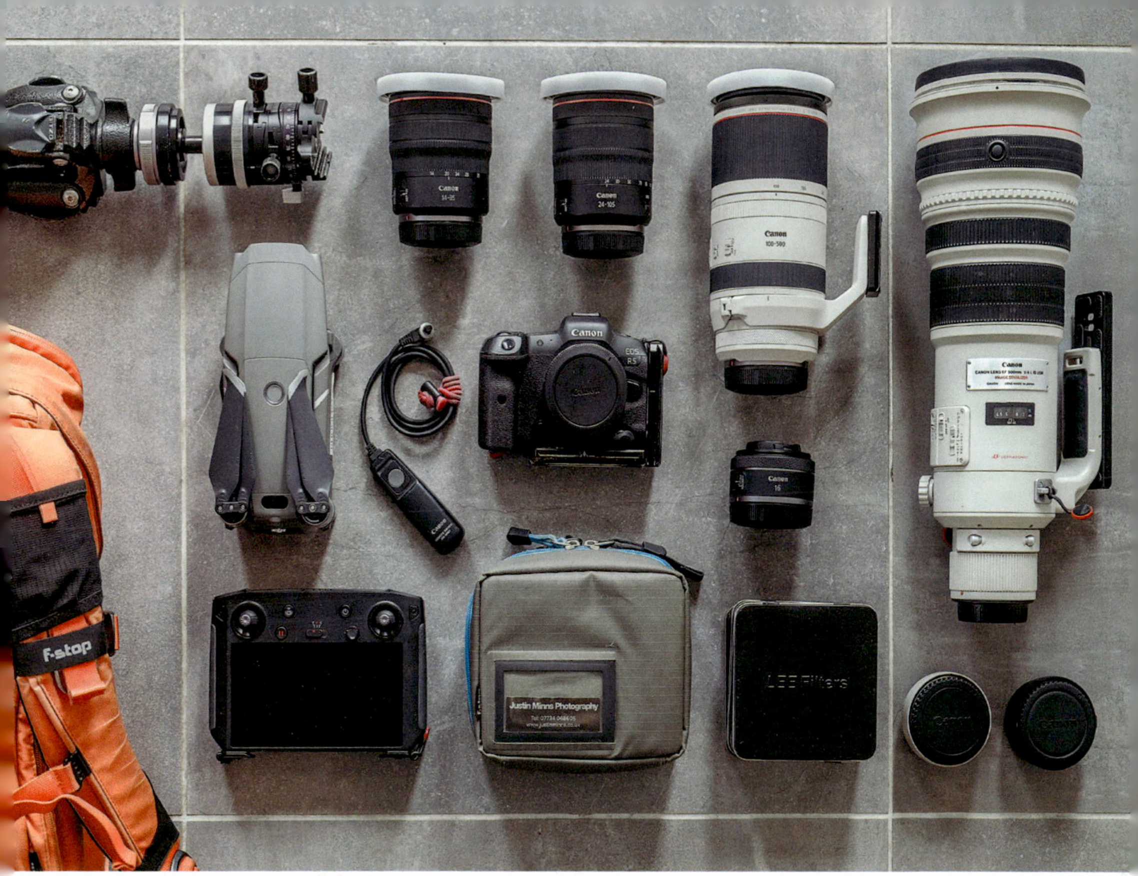

Photo captions

The photo captions in fotoVUE guidebooks are in two parts:

1 Descriptive caption

First is a caption that describes where the photograph was taken, mentioning any references to viewpoints (e.g. VP1) in the accompanying text and any other useful information.

2 Photographic information

The second part of the caption lists the camera, lens, exposure, and the month the photograph was taken. This information is from the Exchangeable Image File Format (EXIF data) that is recorded on each image file when you take a photograph.

Make and model of camera

The focal length of the lens at which the photograph was taken (for non prime lenses).

Tripod or Handheld If a tripod is used, it will say Tripod, otherwise the image was taken handheld.

Canon 5D II, 24–70mm at 20mm, ISO 100, 1/20s at f/11, Tripod. July.

Lens focal length

Light–Exposure information The ISO setting, shutter speed and aperture that the photograph was taken at.

The month taken The month included in the caption enables you to know the (possible) type of weather and state of vegetation at the location.

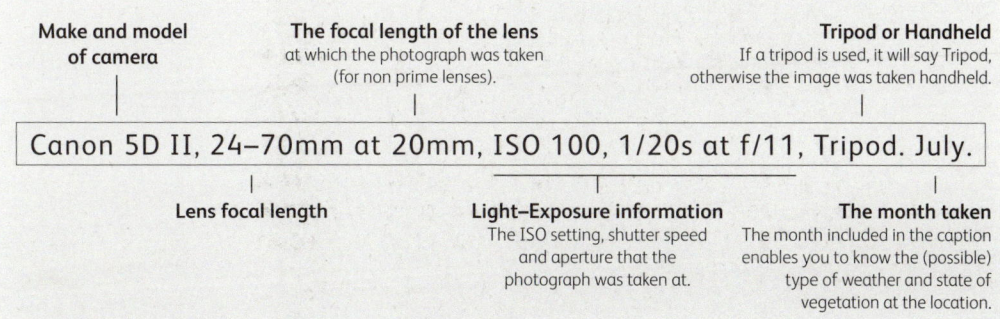

CLASSIC ESSEX LOCATIONS

The locations described in this guidebook are grouped into four sections. The first three sections cover the coast and environs. Starting in the north at the River Stour, where Essex borders Suffolk and divided neatly by the Rivers Colne, Blackwater and Crouch before finishing at the Thames estuary at the southern edge of the county. The final section covers the entire western side of the county. If it's your first time in Essex or you're on a short trip, here is a list of some of the best (or my favourite) locations to visit and photograph:

1	Alresford Creek	The Stour to the Colne	144
2	Harwich & Dovercourt	The Stour to the Colne	86
3	Dedham	The Stour to the Colne	68
4	Hoe Mill Lock	The Blackwater	196
5	Tollesbury	The Blackwater	172
6	Mersea Island	The Blackwater	164
7	Southend-on-Sea	The Crouch to the Thames	282
8	Lion Wharf	The Crouch to the Thames	252
9	Epping Forest	Western Essex	322
10	Thaxted	Western Essex	364

1 ALRESFORD CREEK — P.144

2 HARWICH & DOVERCOURT — P.86

3 DEDHAM — P.68

4 HOE MILL LOCK — P.196

CLASSIC ESSEX LOCATIONS 35

ACCESS AND BEHAVIOUR

Being outdoors means living life to the full and should be enjoyed by all, but we have to share it with others and stay safe. Here is some information and guidelines on accessing the outdoors and looking after yourself.

Public rights of way on maps

Public rights of way are linear routes, which are the legal responsibility of and maintained by Highway Authorities. Details of the routes are held on the Highway Authorities' Definitive Maps. Please stay on public rights of way and don't be tempted to wander into fields. Public rights of way fall into four categories. The following symbols are used on OS 1:25,000 Explorer maps:

Footpaths
For use on foot only.

Bridleways
For use on foot, on a horse or on a pedal cycle.

Restricted Byways
For use on foot, on a horse or pedal cycle, or by horse-drawn vehicle.

Byways
Open to all traffic, on foot, on a horse, on a pedal cycle or motorcycle, or in a motor or horse-drawn vehicle. However, they are mainly for use as footpaths or bridleways and are usually unsealed.

Green Lanes
Unsurfaced rural roads, which have or may have the potential to carry motorised vehicle rights. Green Lanes are ancient routes that have existed for millennia, such as hollow ways, drover's roads, ridgeways and ancient trackways.

Permissive paths are where a landowner gives agreement for public access. There is no statutory legal right to use these routes and permission may be withdrawn. They are shown on OS 1:25,000 Explorer maps as footpaths or bridleways and the agreement may be posted at the start of the path.

Be a respectful photographer

The obvious is always worth stating: do not climb over walls or fences, shut all gates, don't drop litter, pick up litter others have dropped, keep dogs at home or on a lead, drive slowly in rural and urban areas, give way to cyclists, agricultural vehicles and horse riders, park considerately, don't scare livestock and keep quiet (don't play music or fly drones near others) but always say hello to fellow outdoor enthusiasts. In short, follow the **Countryside Code**.

Respect other people

- Consider the local community and other people enjoying the outdoors
- Park carefully so access to gateways and driveways is kept clear
- Leave gates and property as you find them
- Follow paths but give way to others where it's narrow

Protect the natural environment

- Leave no trace of your visit; take all your litter home
- Don't have barbecues or fires
- Keep dogs under effective control
- Bag and bin dog poo

Enjoy the outdoors

- Plan ahead, check what facilities are open, be prepared
- Follow advice and local signs, and obey any social distancing measures

Busy viewpoints

As photography becomes more popular, some accessible locations and viewpoints can become busy in times of good light. In some circumstances this can cause conflict between photographers as they look for the best spot from which to compose their shot. If you arrive at a location and someone is already set up, give them space and don't get in their way. Talking and negotiating helps; they may be OK with you setting up next to them, or with you using their spot after they have finished. There are usually alternative viewpoints, but just make sure you aren't in their line of fire. If there is a crowd at a particular spot, it's often best just to find another viewpoint.

The author & Millie at Shoeburyness.

Mobility ♿

If you can't walk far or up steep slopes, or if you use a wheelchair or have an injury and need to know whether a location is suitable for you, each location chapter has a brief Access Notes section describing the terrain and distance from the road to a viewpoint. Most locations in this guidebook are usually not far from the road and some are roadside.

If a location or viewpoint has the wheelchair symbol, part or all of it will be accessible by wheelchairs. Bear in mind that access for wheelchair users may not be exactly as described in the text, and you should use your own judgment as to how far you proceed at any given location. And don't forget, driving around the countryside will present many superb photographic opportunities; just be careful where you stop – avoid stopping in passing places for more than a quick shot and always be aware of traffic.

Coastal locations

If you or others are in trouble call 999 and ask for the Coastguard. If you don't have a mobile phone, shout for help. Many locations in this guidebook are by the sea, on beaches and on muddy shorelines.

Before you go

- Wear appropriate clothing and footwear.
- Let someone know where you are going and at what time you plan to return.
- Take a fully charged mobile phone with you.
- Check the tide timetables so that you know when high and low tides will be.

Once outside

- Take extra care on rocky beaches that are often slippery and sharp.
- Stay away from cliff edges, especially if it's windy or if the ground is wet.
- Avoid walking below cliffs as many are unstable.
- Obey warning signs and don't climb over fences.
- If you get stuck in mud or quicksand, spread your weight, avoid moving and call for help.
- Always take a head torch with you for night photography.
- If you're taking a selfie, be safe.

NORTH ESSEX: THE STOUR TO THE COLNE

NORTH ESSEX: THE STOUR TO THE COLNE – INTRODUCTION

In the north of the county, much of the border between Essex and Suffolk is formed by the River Stour, which rises in Cambridgeshire, meandering slowly through pretty villages on its way to the tiny town of Manningtree, where it broadens into a tidal estuary, passing Wrabness before meeting the North Sea at Harwich.

The River Stour Valley also forms the backbone of the Dedham Vale Area of Outstanding Natural Beauty, running from Manningtree to Bures passing through a lowland landscape of meadows, farmland and picturesque villages. This is a landscape made famous by the paintings of John Constable, who lived in nearby East Bergholt and reputedly developed his love for this countryside on his daily walk along the river to go to school in Dedham.

Plotting a similar course further south is the River Colne, which winds its way through gentle countryside dotted with pretty villages like Earls Colne and scraps of ancient woodland such as Chalkney and Hillhouse Woods on its way to the historic town of Colchester, Britain's oldest recorded town and the original Roman capital, Camulodunum.

As the Colne nears the sea, it spreads in all directions, filling channels lined with bobbing boats, through nature reserves, creeks and saltmarsh to villages like Fingringhoe, Alresford and St Osyth before reaching the sea at Colne Point.

The stretch of the Essex coast between these two estuaries is the beautiful swathe of golden sand that attracted the seaside towns of Walton-on-the-Naze, Frinton-on-Sea and Clacton-on-Sea. Beyond these towns the coast takes a bit of a detour inland into Hamford Water. A genuine hidden gem, this maze of creeks, saltmarsh and islands is a haven for bird and sailors alike. It's unusual in that it isn't a river or estuary yet at the same time it's an environment typical of the Essex Coast. In fact, the mix of sandy beaches, faded but charming resorts and secret saltmarsh here, captures very well the spirit of the Essex Coast as a whole.

Blue hour at Walton beach. Canon 5D II, 17–40mm at 17mm, ISO 100, 15s at f/16, LEE 0.6 hard ND grad, tripod. Mar.

Previous spread: *The lonely marshes at Hamford Water. Canon 5D IV, 24–70mm at 33mm, ISO 100, 25s at f/16, LEE Little Stopper & 0.9 med ND grad, tripod. Oct.*

Maps

- OS Explorer Map 184 (1:25 000) Colchester
- OS Explorer Map 195 (1:25 000) Braintree & Saffron Walden
- OS Explorer Map 196 (1:25 000) Sudbury, Hadleigh & Dedham

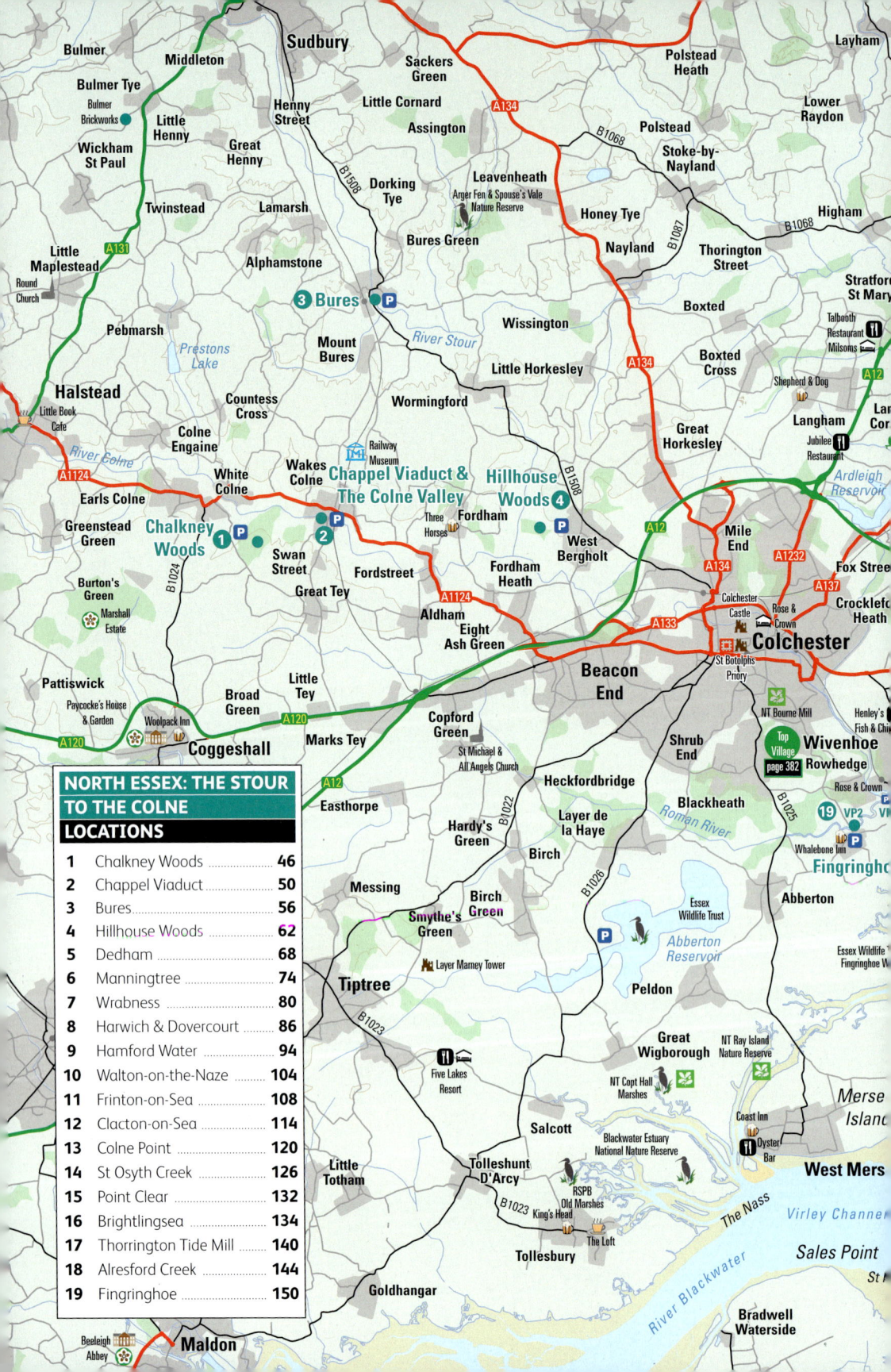

1 CHALKNEY WOODS

An ancient woodland overlooking the Colne valley, Chalkney Woods stands along the path of the old Roman track known as 'Wool Street' which once ran, almost in a straight line, from Colchester to Cambridge.

The track still remains here, so as you walk through the woods in the quiet peace of dawn to photograph the swathes of bluebells that appear in the spring you are walking along a track that has been in use for thousands of years.

What to shoot and viewpoints

Chalkney woods is mainly deciduous woodland and is gradually being reverted to native species including oak, elm, ash, lime, hornbeam and chestnut. Like any woodland location, everyone will be drawn to different things so it is somewhere to explore and there are plenty of paths from which to do so but I can offer a few starting points.

There are patches of bluebells throughout the woods, but they are at their thickest around the edges, one of the best areas being on the south eastern edge where there are also swathes of wild garlic. Much of the wood has been coppiced, which while good for diversity often looks a bit too messy and cluttered for photography, on this side however the trees have been largely left untouched and there is a much more open feel.

The area in question is on the opposite side of the woods to the car park. The most direct route is to follow the main path which runs south east straight out of the car park, as it forks bear left and then shortly afterwards, when it starts to curve left, take the small path on the right and follow it up to the top, passing through an area that is rather good in autumn. When you meet a cross roads go straight ahead and follow that path to the very edge of the woods then turn left where you will pass through a wonderful patch of wild garlic followed by bluebells. It is easier than it sounds and should only take around 15 minutes.

Being on the eastern edge of the woods it is great at sunrise for the classic backlit bluebell shot with long shadows stretching out as the first light streams

A misty autumn morning. Canon 5D IV, 70–200mm at 75mm, ISO 600, 1.6s at f/8, LEE polariser, tripod. Nov.

Previous spread: *First light streaming across the bluebells. Canon 5D IV, 24–70mm at 53mm, ISO 100, 1s at f/22, tripod. Apr.*

1 CHALKNEY WOODS

through the trees. With bright sunlight and dark shadows, the dynamic range can be very high for this sort of shot so it is worth bracketing the exposures to make sure you have captured details in the shadows and the highlights. You could also try creating a sunburst effect as the sun breaks through the trees by hiding all but about a quarter of the sun behind a tree and using a very small aperture. It can be tricky to tell exactly where the sun will break through the trees on your first visit so the augmented reality feature on apps such as Photopills is invaluable. While it is tempting to use a wide angle lens to capture the full glory of the view, longer focal lengths are more effective, their compressing effect intensifies the flowers and enables you to tighten the composition to avoid messy areas of woodland.

Paths make really useful leading lines for woodland photography and the one which meanders it's way around the edge of the woods here is particularly good with some nice curvy sections, overhanging trees and with luck, warm side light. Follow the path north until you meet the main footpath and turn left then take the second path on the left to head back towards the car park.

Light and shadow on the bluebells. Canon 5D IV, 70–200mm at 104mm, ISO 200, 1/13s at f/8, tripod. Apr.

Wild garlic detail. Canon 5D IV, 70–200mm at 126mm, ISO 200, 1/13s at f/8, LEE polariser, tripod. Apr.

How to get here

Chalkney Woods is near the village of Earls Colne, 7 miles north west of Colchester.

Leave the A12 Colchester By-pass at junction 26 and take the A1124 towards Halstead. Follow this road for a little over 6 miles, passing through the villages of Eight Ash Green, Aldham, Chapel and White Colne, then around 100m after passing the Earls Colne village sign turn left into Tey Road (the turning is easy to miss so drive slowly). Stay on Tey Road for around half a mile, shortly after passing the last of the houses turn on to the dirt track on the left on a right hand bend. The small car park for Chalkney Woods is at the end of the dirt track.

Lat/Long:	51.91879, 0.72081
what3words:	///that.pounces.public
Grid Ref:	TL 872 279
Postcode:	CO6 2PR

Accessibility

There are plenty of clearly marked paths through the wood but most are either uneven, strewn with fallen branches or muddy so not ideal for wheelchairs. There are also some gentle slopes.

Best time of year/day

The highlight of the year is spring for the wildflowers and fresh green leaves, the exact time that the bluebells and wild garlic flower will depend on the weather but it's usually mid April to early May. Wood anemones start a month or so earlier. Early morning or late evening are the best times to visit when the low light will be softer and warmer. The bluebells draw quite a few visitors so my preference is early morning when you will probably have the place to yourself. The greens start to fade over summer but the woods come alive again with autumn colour around October and November.

Above: *A path through the bluebells. Canon 5D IV, 70–200mm at 70mm, ISO 200, 1/8s at f/8, LEE polariser, tripod. Apr.*
Below: *Wild garlic on the eastern edge of the woods. Canon 5D IV, 24–70mm at 35mm, ISO 200, 1s at f/22, LEE polariser, tripod. Apr.*

2. CHAPPEL VIADUCT & THE COLNE VALLEY

Built in 1849 using some 7 million locally made bricks, Chappel Viaduct is the longest bridge in East Anglia and one of the largest brick-built structures in England.

The viaduct's thirty-two arches grandly stride across the River Colne valley, a verdant landscape of woodland, meadows and farmland, which provide as much interest for photographers as the viaduct itself.

What to shoot and viewpoints

Viewpoint 1 – The viaduct

The viaduct can virtually be photographed from the car park; the gravel track crunching towards the arches from the car park makes a suitable leading line. A low angle looking up at the viaduct will emphasise its height and add a touch of drama, while in early spring and autumn the sun will rise through the arches. As the footpath passes below the 23m-high arches, it becomes apparent that the legs also have arches running through them and there are some great abstract shots to be found looking through them. There are further views from Millennium Green, a park with a wildlife area on the other side of the viaduct. There's also a pleasant walk around the green to explore and search for foreground interest or overhanging trees to frame views of the viaduct.

Viewpoint 2 – Colne Valley walk

There are several viewpoints around the Colne Valley which can all be taken in on a pleasant 3km circular walk with a couple of optional detours.

From the car park, cross the road and wander down the lane past St Barnabas Church, an attractive 13th-century church. At the end of the lane follow the footpath signs (it is very clearly marked) along the edge of the fields until you reach a pond that sits within a small plantation.

Although surrounded by a fence, it is still possible to photograph the pond, the best spot being at the far end where the raised boardwalk that runs alongside the fence provides a useful vantage point. The evenly spaced trees provide interest on the far side of the lake, in which they're also reflected. The trees also make an interesting subject themselves, particularly in spring/summer when lush and green.

Across the next meadow at a group of rather splendid trees, the path reaches a crossroads. The circular walk heads left but there are a couple of short detours worth exploring first. Following the path straight on, over a rather pointless rickety bridge and through a gate into the next meadow leads to a hedgerow that runs along the lane beyond. From here there are views back along the valley to the viaduct in the distance – a good spot for a telephoto shot or panorama. Incidentally, a 350m walk up this lane brings you to the eastern edge of Chalkney Woods (see page 46)

Alternatively, at the crossroads, taking the path north over the stream, diagonally across the meadow and then

Opposite: A train passing over the viaduct (VP1). DJI Mavic 2 Pro, 28mm, ISO 100, 1/8s at f/8. Sep.

How to get here

Chappel is a village, 5.5 miles north west of Colchester.

Leave the A12 Colchester bypass at junction 26 and take the A1124 towards Halstead. Follow this road for a little over 4 miles, passing through the villages of Eight Ash Green and Aldham. Just after the road passes under the viaduct, turn left onto The Street. The car park is 200m along the road on the left just before the traffic priority sign.

Lat/Long:	51.92129, 0.75392
what3words:	///competing.manager.chill
Grid Ref:	TL 894 283
Postcode:	CO6 2DT

Accessibility

The paths around the viaduct are flat and well maintained and walking distances are short. The path through the valley is across fields and is often muddy so isn't wheelchair friendly. There is usually livestock in the fields here so dogs must be kept on leads.

Best time of year/day

There is something to photograph throughout the year but spring and summer are highlights, when the viaduct is glimpsed amongst clouds of fresh green trees and wildflowers are in bloom in the meadows and woods. Autumn brings colour to the valley and, just like in spring, there is often mist early in the morning. That mist is an incentive to arrive before sunrise but evening golden hour is also a good time for light on the viaduct.

2 CHAPPEL VIADUCT & THE COLNE VALLEY

Top: Wakes Colne church at dawn (VP2). Canon 5D II, 24–105mm at 67mm, ISO 100, 0.8s at f/16, LEE 0.6 hard ND grad, tripod. July.

Above: First light in the Colne Valley (VP2). Canon 5D IV, 70–200mm at 145mm, ISO 100, 1/80s at f/11, tripod. June.

The view down into the Colne Valley on a misty morning (VP2). Canon 5D IV, 70–200mm at 70mm, ISO 100, 1/40s at f/16, LEE 0.9 med ND grad, tripod. Sep.

2 CHAPPEL VIADUCT & THE COLNE VALLEY

Chappel viaduct with sunburst (VP1). Canon 5D IV, 16–35mm at 35mm, ISO 100, 1/80s at f/22, tripod. Sep.

Wakes Colne church from across the valley (VP2). Canon 5D IV, 70–200mm at 170mm, ISO 100, 1/15s at f/16, tripod. Apr.

crossing the bridge over the River Colne brings you to a track. Follow it past the farmhouse to the top of the hill and there is a view of Wakes Colne church, an attractive white-painted wooden church, across the field. This is best photographed in spring or summer when there are crops in the field. It works well at sunrise or at the end of the day for last light on the church.

Back at the crossroads, to continue the circular walk, turn left over the stile and head south up through the copse of trees. After almost 400m there is another crossroads with one path going right out of the woods across a field.

Take the opposite path and go left down into the woods; this is Hickmore Fen, an area thick with bluebells in the spring. Follow the path up the steps and out of the woods, turn left and walk along the field edge alongside the woods. At the end of the woods there is a view of Wakes Colne church across the valley, another view that is best shot with a telephoto lens so don't take it out of your bag to lighten the load on the walk!

The path goes down some steps onto a lane. Turn left and walk down the hill. Just round the corner Chappel Viaduct will come into view across the fields. Take the gate on the

Sheep in the Valley (VP2). Canon 5D IV, 70–200mm at 150mm, ISO 400, 1/50s at f/5.6. June.

The meadows are alive with buttercups in spring (VP2). Canon 30D, 70–200mm at 118mm, ISO 100, 1/50s at f/8, tripod. May.

left opposite the row of cottages and follow the path down across the field. This field has some of the best views of the viaduct, the village and valley and is a good spot when there is mist in the valley below or for evening side light. Again the 70–200mm lens comes into its own here, both for picking out compositions of Wakes Colne church amongst the trees across the valley or Chappel church rising from the early morning mist and for stitched panoramas of the viaduct, which being such a wide subject suits the format rather well. Standard 3x2 format landscape shots can feel a bit empty but work well with an interesting sky and sheep in the field to fill the foreground.

To return to the car park, carry on diagonally down the hill, through the gate then turn right along the field edge. Climb over the style at the end and back onto Chappel Hill. The car park is 150m down on the right.

Top: A panorama of the Colne Valley (VP2). Canon 5D IV, 24–70mm at 70mm, ISO 100, 1/8s at f/11, LEE polariser, tripod. May.

3 BURES

Bures is a pretty village in the Stour Valley Area of Outstanding Natural Beauty. Interestingly, the village is actually two hamlets split by the River Stour, which forms the border between Essex and Suffolk. Bures Hamlet sits on the Essex side of the river, and Bures St Mary across the river in Suffolk.

As such, this community of around 2000 people is served by two county councils, three district councils and two parish councils. It has two members of parliament, two education authorities and the police, fire and ambulance services are also separate.

The village has many historic buildings and is an interesting place to explore with the camera but it is the beautiful stretch of river that meanders through the meadows south of the village that we'll focus on.

What to shoot and viewpoints

Viewpoint 1 – The river
Go through the gate at the back of the car park and the river is a 200m walk along the path straight across the playing field. There are several viewpoints on or around the bridge here, starting with the bridge itself, which is a good place for an unobstructed view along the tree-lined river in either direction but especially to the south, where the view is free from man-made distractions. The bridge does vibrate a bit underfoot so be sure to wait until anyone crossing has done so before taking the shot.

The bridge itself serves as an attractive focal point from either bank but there are a few distractions near the bridge on the northern bank – bins, picnic benches, signs and so on, which are hard to avoid from the southern side. The better option is to walk north along the northern bank where, as well as a wooden jetty there are several fishing spots that provide easy access to the water's edge for views back along the river to the bridge. These works well in winter, when the sun rises along the river.

Top: The mill at sunrise (VP2). Canon 5D IV, 24–70mm at 26mm, ISO 100, 1/40s at f/22, LEE 0.9 med ND grad, tripod. Aug.

The view from the bridge at sunrise (VP1). Canon 5D IV, 24–70mm at 47mm, ISO 100, 1.3s at f/16, LEE 0.9 hard ND grad, tripod. Nov.

How to get here

Bures is a village on the Essex/Suffolk border, 9 miles north west of Colchester.

Take the A12 south from Colchester and turn off at J26 signposted the A1124 to Halstead. At the roundabout turn left onto the A1124 and follow it for almost a mile before turning right just before the petrol station onto Wood Lane, signposted Fordham. Stay on this road for just over 6 miles all the way into Bures. Just after crossing the river, turn right into Church Square, follow the road around the corner and park in the small car park on the right next to the community centre.

- **Lat/Long**: 51.97077, 0.77685
- **what3words**: ///results.outlast.flinches
- **Grid Ref**: TL 908 338
- **Postcode**: CO8 5BX

Accessibility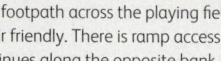

The main footpath across the playing fields is flat, firm and wheelchair friendly. There is ramp access to the bridge and the path continues along the opposite bank. Other paths are all flat but those along the river are grassy and may be muddy. There is no wheelchair access to the mill.

Best Time of Year/Day

The river here is beautiful all year, lush with soft greens in spring/summer, starker but more dramatic in autumn/winter light.

Sunrise is the best time of day throughout the year, and if conditions are good there will often be mist hanging over the river and meadows or a frost during the winter. It's also the time to avoid crowds during the summer, when the river and playing fields are busy and there are often people swimming in the mill pool.

The mill and trees along the river catch the light towards the end of the day from mid autumn to early spring.

3 BURES

The mill looks dramatic in infrared (VP2). Fuji X-Pro1, 14mm, ISO 200, 1/50s at f/8. June.

Viewpoint 2 – The Mill

The mill is a short walk of around 800m from the footbridge. Follow the path south east along the tree-lined Suffolk side of the river, stay on the path as it turns left away from the river past some buildings and then, just beyond, at the edge of the field, go through the gate onto the lane. Turn right along the lane and at the fork bear left through the white gates. Just before reaching the mill, 150m along the lane, look out for the footpath sign on the right. This leads around the mill and out into a field, where just to the left are views back across the pool to the water mill.

There are good views from all along the fence here or go over the style to get closer to the water, where there's a small jetty for foreground interest.

It's worth exploring further; the sun comes up across the field to the right of the mill – a good option early in the morning if there is mist and sheep or cattle in the field.

The view across the meadows in autumn (VP2). Canon 5D IV, 24–70mm at 70mm, ISO 100, 1s at f/16, LEE 0.9 med ND grad, tripod. Nov.

Previous spread: *The bridge on a misty winter sunrise (VP1). Canon 5D IV, 24–70mm at 44mm, ISO 100, 2s at f/16, LEE 0.9 med ND grad, tripod. Nov.*

Opposite: *A frosty morning at the mill (VP2). Canon 5D IV, 24–70mm at 33mm, ISO 100, 2s at f/16, LEE 0.9 med ND grad, tripod. Nov.*

4 HILLHOUSE WOODS

Hillhouse Woods is a beautiful remnant of ancient woodland on the slopes of the River Colne Valley with one of the best displays of bluebells in the area.

What to shoot and viewpoints

Essex is blessed with an abundance of bluebell woods but what makes these woods unusual is that the carpet of bluebells extends out from under the trees and into open glades. The entrance to the woods is a short walk along the track beside the church. After around 500m follow the track as it bends to the left and the woods are another 250m straight ahead.

As always, I'd recommend exploring the woods for yourself, it's big enough to have variety but small enough to easily explore and if you take a photo of the map at the entrance you can use that to guide you. It isn't the clearest map so I'd also have the Ordnance Survey app handy. This will show exactly where you are on the map.

Some of the best areas of the woods are to the east. Head straight into the woods, keep left at the fork then when you meet another path turn left, cross the stream and go straight on at the fork. The path squiggles past a bench which, surrounded by bluebells, makes a nice subject itself, and then opens up into a big patch of bluebells at the edge of the wood. In spring, this is a lovely spot early in the morning when the first light streams through the trees.

Perhaps my favourite spot though is not far from here at the southern edge of the wood. Walk back along the path 50m or so to the fork and take the other path south. This opens up into a glade thick with bluebells and a scattering of trees. There are views from both this end of the glade and the southern end where there are some very old gnarled oaks. Rather than walk through the flowers to the southern end, keep following the path, turn right and follow it back into the glade. If you can tear yourself away from the bluebells, turn to the south and there are also rather good views out from the woods across the Colne Valley, especially in evening light. Continue on the footpath path in a northerly direction and it will loop back to the entrance of the woods.

It's not just about the bluebells here, there are plenty of other wildflowers to include in your wider woodland shots or fill the frame with so don't forget your macro lens.

A carpet of bluebells. Canon 5D IV, 24–105mm at 65mm, ISO 100, 1/3s at f/11, LEE polariser, tripod. Apr.

How to get here

Hillhouse Woods is in West Bergholt, 3 miles north west of Colchester.

Take the B1508 from Colchester and follow the road for 2.5 miles, passing over the A12 and through West Bergholt. After leaving the village, turn left into Hall Road at the brown church sign and after almost half a mile there is a dirt track on the right before the church. Park at the entrance to this track where it is safe to do so.

- **Lat/Long:** 51.91708, 0.8392
- **what3words:** ///credited.obeyed.stiletto
- **Grid Ref:** TL 953 280
- **Postcode:** CO6 3DU

Accessibility

The path to the woods and those inside are uneven and often muddy so not ideal for wheelchairs. There are also some gentle slopes.

Best time of year/day

The highlights of the year are spring for the wildflowers and fresh green leaves, and autumn for the seasonal colour. The exact time that the bluebells will flower in spring depends on the weather but it's usually mid April to early May. October to early November is usually the best time to photograph autumn colours. Early morning or late evening is the best time to visit when the low light will be softer and warmer. The woods will be quieter early in the morning and there is always a chance of mist.

*Top: A path through the bluebells. Canon 5D IV, 24–105mm at 65mm, ISO 100, 1/8s at f/11, LEE polariser tripod. Apr. **Above left**: Greater Stitchwort and bluebells. Canon 5D IV, 100–400mm at 235mm, ISO 100, 1/40s at f/5, tripod. Apr. **Right**: Greater Stitchwort detail. Canon 5D IV, 100–400mm at 400mm, ISO 100, 1/40s at f/5.6, tripod. Apr.*

4 HILLHOUSE WOODS

An atmospheric misty autumn morning. Canon 5D IV, 70–200mm at 90mm, ISO 100, 1/4s at f/8, LEE polariser, tripod. Nov.

Top: An autumnal detail. Canon 5D IV, 70–200mm at 70mm, ISO 100, 1/10s at f/8, LEE polariser, tripod. Nov. **Middle**: Along the lane. Canon 5D IV, 70–200mm at 98mm, ISO 100, 1/25s at f/8, LEE polariser, tripod. Nov. **Bottom**: The view from the edge of the woods. Canon 5D IV, 70–200mm at 78mm, ISO 100, 1/80s at f/8, LEE polariser, tripod. Nov.

5 DEDHAM

Dedham is best known for its location in the very heart of Constable Country – the quintessentially English landscape of beautiful water meadows and pretty villages alongside the River Stour made famous by the work of artist John Constable.

This is a designated Area of Outstanding Natural Beauty which attracts artists and photographers (and tourists by the coach load) but Dedham has more to offer than its location. Clustered around a high street of pretty Georgian facades covering the original medieval buildings and dominated by a 15th-century church built from the wealth of the wool industry, it is a charming village to explore.

What to shoot and viewpoints

Viewpoint 1 – The river ♿
The river is the main attraction for photographers and there are views from the bridge just a few metres from the car park. From spring until autumn a line of pretty wooden rowing boats is moored along the river bank here and the bridge provides an elevated position from which to photograph them. A tight composition works well, zooming in on the boats to avoid any distractions and focusing the attention on the overlapping shapes. The river is overhung here by horse chestnut trees and they tend to die off early in autumn so spring when the trees are in flower or summer are the best times of year.

There are actually two bridges here and the area between the two is a good spot from which to photograph the view across the meadows with the river meandering off into the distance. It's a few metres higher than the river bank and offers better visibility – particularly useful on a misty morning. »

How to get here

Dedham is a village close to the Suffolk border, 5 miles north east of Colchester.

Take the A12 north from Colchester for around 4 miles and turn off at J30 signposted the B1029 to Dedham. At the end of the sliproad turn right onto the B1029 and follow it for a mile into Dedham. The car park is on the right immediately after crossing the river. If it is full, there is another one 100m along the road on the left; both are pay and display.

Lat/Long:	51.96235, 0.99393
what3words:	///bootleg.simulates.soccer
Grid Ref:	TM 057 335
Postcode:	CO7 6DH

Accessibility

The paths along the river aren't wheelchair friendly but the views from the bridge and around the village are all on paved footpaths.

Best time of year/day

The best time to photograph the river are early mornings, when, if conditions are right (and they often are), the low-lying River Stour Valley will be covered by a blanket of mist. It is beautiful throughout the year but for atmosphere, winter is hard to beat, when there can be spectacular frosts to add to the mist. You probably won't be the only photographer there if conditions are good but most tend to head towards Flatford so the Dedham end of the river may be quieter.

I like to photograph the village in spring and summer when the trees and gardens are lush and green but Dedham is a very popular tourist destination, especially in the summer months, so come early in the morning to avoid the crowds.

Top: Sunrise over the riverside meadows (VP1). Canon 5D IV, 24–70mm at 33mm, ISO 100, 1/5s at f/16, LEE 0.9 med ND grad, tripod. Apr.

Above: Rowing boats lining the river bank (VP1). Canon 30D, 17–85mm at 64mm, ISO 100, 1s at f/8, tripod. July.

Previous spread: Sunrise along the River Stour (VP1). Canon 5D IV, 24–70mm at 28mm, ISO 200, 1.6s at f/11, LEE 0.9 med ND grad, tripod. Apr.

Opposite top: The boathouse on a spring morning (VP1). Canon 5D IV, 24–70mm at 33mm, ISO 100, 1/5s at f/16, tripod. Apr.
Bottom: Dedham Mill reflected in the mill pool (VP1). Canon 5D IV, 24–70mm at 35mm, ISO 100, 1/4s at f/16, tripod. Apr.

5 DEDHAM

On the north side of the bridges a public footpath follows the river in either direction. I should mention that the border between Essex and Suffolk runs along the centre of the river here so by crossing the bridge we have actually slipped over the border into Suffolk. It seems a shame to miss out on these views along the river for the sake of a few metres!

The path on the right (signposted Flatford) heads east across the meadows. There are numerous viewpoints waiting to be discovered amongst the reed-lined banks and twisted willows overhanging this stretch of river, but one in particular worth noting is at the first bend. Here, there are interesting groups of trees either side of the watering spot used by the cows that graze the meadows here. These trees add interest to views along the river in either direction and if you are lucky, there may even be cows in the water as well.

Apart from the winter months, there will usually be cows somewhere along the river. They add a timeless quality and look particularly good in views of the misty meadows. They can be over inquisitive at times though so if you are nervous of them, or have a dog with you, give them a wide berth.

The tiny hamlet of Flatford is around 1 mile further along the river path – a walk I would highly recommend – but it takes us well into Suffolk and beyond the scope of this book. (It is covered in *Photographing East Anglia*)

The path heading in the other direction from the main road offers further (though perhaps not as plentiful) river views as well as one or two landmarks. The first stretch passes the mill pond with the mill on the far bank. Dedham Mill was owned by John Constable's father, and although the large brick version we see today is much more recent, it can still make an attractive subject, especially reflected in the calm mill pond. Follow the path as it temporarily turns away from the river and where it returns to the river bank you'll find a rather elaborate boat house. Just beyond this, as the path begins it's journey along the river towards Stratford St Mary, there are views across the river towards Dedham church rising above the trees.

Swans on the Stour (VP1). Canon 5D IV, 70–200mm at 200mm, ISO 100, 1/10s at f/5.6, tripod. June.

Opposite left: *Cows by the river (VP1). Canon 5D II, 24–105mm at 58mm, ISO 100, 0.3s at f/16, tripod. Nov.* **Right**: *A cow reflected in the Stour (VP1). Canon 5D IV, 100–400mm at 200mm, ISO 200, 1/50s at f/8, tripod. May.*

5 DEDHAM

Viewpoint 2 – The village ♿
The village high street, around which the village is centred, is 300m south along the road from the car park. There is a wealth of interesting things to discover and photograph along its length but a good place to start is Royal Square, the small square with the memorial at its centre next to the church. There are good views of the high street from here with the memorial in the foreground (perhaps use it to hide parked cars) as well as the church from the gate; use the path through the churchyard as a leading line.

Leaving the High Street, the path south from Royal Square leads to Duchy Fields, a playing field across which you'll see further views of the church. Try using the trees lining the path to frame the view. The path also continues south beyond the playing field to some attractive beamed cottages at Southfields.

Viewpoint 3 – The church
Another, lesser seen view of the church is from a hill to the south west of the village. Walk or drive southwest along the High Street and halfway up the hill turn right onto Stratford Road (signposted Stratford St Mary) and park in the lay-by 200m on the right. Take care if on foot as the road is fairly narrow and there is no footpath. There are actually lovely views from here across the fields towards Stratford St Mary Church and a bench from which to enjoy them. The footpath to the hill is on the opposite side of the road about 30m further along. Follow the footpath through the trees and the church can be seen from atop the hill to the left.

There is another view of Dedham Church 200m further along the road from the lay-by where, from the entrance to the field, it can be seen above the trees to the east. This view works well in the summer evenings with last light shining across the fields and lighting the tower.

*Opposite top left: Dedham High Street (VP2). Canon 5D IV, 24–105mm at 40mm, ISO 100, 1/15s at f/16, tripod. June. **Top right**: Dedham Church in morning light (VP3). Canon 5D IV, 70–200mm at 140mm, ISO 100, 1/40s at f/11, tripod. Dec. **Middle**: Cottages at Southfields (VP2). Canon 5D II, 16–35mm at 23mm, ISO 100, 1/20s at f/16, tripod. June. **Bottom**: Dedham Church from Duchy Fields (VP2). Canon 5D IV, 24–70mm at 35mm, ISO 100, 1/8s at f/16, tripod. Apr.*

Rowing boats lining the river bank (VP1). Canon 5D IV, 24–105mm at 105mm, ISO 400, 1/100s at f/5.6, tripod. Apr.

6 MANNINGTREE

A small town (the smallest in England it is claimed) on the banks of the River Stour Estuary and a stone's throw from the Suffolk border, Manningtree has a darker claim to fame than its diminutive size...

In the 17th century the town was home to Matthew Hopkins, the self-appointed Witchfinder General. Hopkins lived in Manningtree for three years, during which time he was believed to have been responsible for the execution of over 200 witches, six of which were hanged right here in Manningtree.

What to shoot and viewpoints

Viewpoint 1 – The river
Access to the tiny beach is via the entrance to the slipway next to the parking spaces on Quay Street. The beach itself, so called only because of the presence of sand, offers little of photographic note but the raised walkway along the western side provides a vantage point from which to photograph the sunrise along the river. This is effective both at high tide, when the beach floods and there are often impressive reflections in the broad sweep of calm water, and at low tide, when the end of the walkway has the best views along the channel. A lens in the 70–200mm range works well to compress the distance and emphasise the scattered boats or just to pick out a section of the view.

At low tide there is a host of small boats left scattered in the mud. It is possible to walk out closer to them and use them as foreground interest but stick to the hard path directly in front of the slipway; elsewhere you run the risk of losing your wellies in the deep, clinging mud!

Top: The Stour Estuary at dawn (VP1). Canon R5, 100–400mm at 150mm, ISO 100, 1.6s at f/11, LEE 0.6 med ND grad, tripod. Apr.

The view along the Walls (VP1). Canon R5, 100–400mm at 115mm, ISO 100, 1.6s at f/11, LEE 0.6 med ND grad, tripod. Apr.

How to get here

Manningtree is a small town, 8 miles north east of Colchester.

Take the A137 from Colchester and follow it for just over 7 miles through Ardleigh to Lawford. Turn left at the mini roundabout next to the petrol station, signposted Manningtree, to stay on the A137 then at the roundabout at the bottom of the hill take the 2nd exit onto the B1352 (Station Road). Follow this road into the town centre as it becomes the High Street then as the road bends left and downhill towards the river, turn left into Quay Street and park in one of the free parking spaces on the right.

- **Lat/Long**: 51.94585, 1.06592
- **what3words**: ///truffles.soda.pricier
- **Grid Ref**: TM 108 319
- **Postcode**: CO11 1AU

Nearest Tide Station

Mistley

Accessibility

There are some wheelchair-friendly views from the slipway near the parking spot and from the paved footpath along The Walls, particularly opposite Hopping Bridge and towards Mistley Towers. If you plan on walking on the mud or saltmarsh, bring your wellies. There are no facilities along the river but there are pubs and cafés in Manningtree High Street and in Mistley just past Mistley Towers.

Best Time of Year/Day

There is something to photograph here throughout the year and indeed throughout the day. Manningtree is on the southern bank of the river so for sunrise views out over the estuary, March through to early September is best. There aren't quite as many options for photographing the sunset here but it is a good time for catching the last warm side light.

Mistley Towers faces south so the sun is in a better position for golden hour light from autumn to early spring.

MANNINGTREE

Swans on the Stour at low tide (VP2). Canon R5, 100–400mm at 135mm, ISO 16000, 1/800s at f/11. Mar.

Viewpoint 2 – The Walls

East of the beach there are several viewpoints along The Walls, the oddly named road that runs along the river for around half a mile.

The first is a group of old boats on the marsh around 300m along the road. These are best photographed at high tide when the glassy surface of the water-filled creeks contrasts nicely with the saltmarsh and decaying boats ... try picking out a single boat to keep things simple.

The marshes will flood at high tide so be careful not to step into one of the creeks or pools that will be harder to see.

A little further along the river, at the metal railing, you'll see a creek, which at low tide carves a nice meandering leading line out through the mud towards the river beyond. There will usually be swans feeding here providing an interesting focal point in the creek (or a nuisance, depending on your point of view). Historically, the river here has been home to a huge bevy (the collective term apparently) of around 400 swans that came to feed on grain from the nearby quay. There are still up to 200 here, which makes quite a sight at high tide.

Cross the road and there is an old brick bridge overlooking a pond, known as Hopping Bridge. This, incidentally, is the pond Hopkins was believed to have used to duck witches – the premise being that if they drowned they were innocent but if they didn't drown they were witches and thus executed. Today there are only ducks and a good view across the pond to Mistley Church.

Opposite top left: *The riverside at first light (VP1). Canon 5D IV, 24–70mm at 30mm, ISO 100, 1/8s at f/16, LEE polariser, tripod. May.* **Right**: *Mistley Church from Hopping Bridge (VP2). Canon 5D IV, 24–105mm at 45mm, ISO 200, 1/8s at f/16, LEE polariser, tripod. May.* **Middle**: *Little Egret on the River Stour (VP1). Canon R5, 100–400mm at 400mm, ISO 800, 1/640s at f/5.6. Mar.* **Opposite**: *Old boats along the Walls (VP2). Canon 5D IV, 24–105mm at 35mm, ISO 200, 1/2s at f/16, LEE 0.6 med ND grad, tripod. June.*

NORTH ESSEX – MANNINGTREE

6 MANNINGTREE

Mistley towers in infrared (VP3). Fuji X-Pro1, 14mm, ISO 200, 1/350s at f/8, tripod. May.

Viewpoint 3 – Mistley Towers ♿

Wander around the bend from the pond and Mistley Towers will come into view across the road. This pair of porticoed towers once sat at either end of an unusual 18th-century church designed by Robert Adam but the middle was later demolished leaving just the two towers in a small graveyard.

Due to the close proximity of the road on two of the sides and warehouses and trees on the other two, angles from which to photograph the towers are somewhat limited. One spot is from the path on the opposite side of the road as you approach from the pond. From here trees hide the warehouses and careful composition can reduce the portion of road visible. The other option is to get close

Top: *A black swan amongst the mute swans (VP2). Canon 5D IV, 70–200mm at 90mm, ISO 200, 1/800s at f/5.6. June.*

Above: *Tombstones at Mistley Towers (VP3). Canon 5D IV, 24–70mm at 70mm, ISO 100, 1/2000s at f/2.8. Sep.*

and shoot with a wide-angle lens from within the graveyard (which is always open) or through the fence.

7 WRABNESS

Wrabness is small village overlooking the River Stour Estuary at the very north of Essex. This peaceful place, surrounded by farmland, woodland and nature reserves, feels a million miles away from the busy ports of Harwich and Felixstowe whose cranes are visible on the horizon to the east.

One of this village's attractions (local opinion is very much split on quite how attractive it is) is a *House for Essex* or *Julie's House*, as it is also known, a rather striking conceptual house overlooking the river. Designed by artist Grayson Perry, it is a mausoleum for a fictional Essex woman, built by her husband after a tragic accident … in short, Essex's answer to the Taj Mahal.

What to shoot and viewpoints

Viewpoint 1 – A House for Essex
Whatever you think of a House for Essex, with its copper-clad roof, and walls covered in white and green ceramic tiles, it certainly stands out in the agricultural landscape and makes a fine subject for photographers. If the colour doesn't do it for you, it's a subject that lends itself to mono, infrared, long exposure or any other more creative techniques.

You can reach it from either parking spot but the station car park is nearest, around a 300m walk. From the car park entrance turn left and the house is at the end of Black Boy Lane. The best views are from the other side of the house, where it's possible to shoot it from a dramatic angle, close up with a wide-angle lens or use a longer lens to concentrate on the details. To truly appreciate the full incongruous glory of the house, you need to get a bit further away and include more of the surrounding landscape. There are views from the bottom of the hill looking back up or from the top of the lane that leads down to the river from the Stone Lane parking place. From there, the house is visible across the fields with woodland as a backdrop.

A distant view of the House for Essex (VP1). Canon 5D IV, 24–105mm at 105mm, ISO 100, 1/5s at f/16, tripod. June.

If you continue on the footpath as it moves away from the house, along the edge of the next field to the river, turn left and follow the path along the river, it will lead you to the next viewpoint. It's a pleasant walk and there are views across the river to the Royal Hospital School in Holbrook along the way but to go directly to the river – it is a shorter walk from the second parking place.

Opposite*: A House for Essex in infrared (VP1). Canon 5D IV, 16–35mm at 24mm, ISO 200, 3.2s at f/8, IR filter, tripod. June.*

Overleaf*: The wreck on the marshes (VP2). Canon 5D IV, 16–35mm at 16mm, ISO 100, 1/2s at f/18, LEE 0.6 hard ND grad, tripod. June.*

7 WRABNESS

Viewpoint 2 – The river

To get down to the river follow Stone Lane (a private road but a public footpath), which is on the right just beyond the parking place. There is a rather good view of the river from the parking place, which would explain the bench, depending on what's growing in the field, as it will appear in the foreground. The same goes for the aforementioned views of a House for Essex, which can be seen across the fields from the first stretch of Stone Lane. At the bottom of the hill as the lane bears left, you can either carry on to the shore or take the path on the right onto the saltmarsh.

It's a fairly compact area of saltmarsh to explore but there is plenty to discover. Twisting creeks, scattered pools, a boat wreck and a rather random tree all make interesting subjects and with river views in front and trees behind, you can shoot in almost any direction. It is a flat, open landscape though so a good sky definitely helps. The boat wreck is right next to the tree so is easy to find and photographs well either from the front, jutting up from the marsh or looking across its skeletal remains from the back.

There is also a lot to photograph along the shore. Yachts moored in the river, small boats hauled up onto the sand and an array of beach huts and chalets on stilts lining the top of the beach. I hesitate to call it a beach because although it is sandy around the high water mark, as the tide recedes it reveals its true muddy nature. It's also worth noting that above the high water mark the land is private.

Some of the best views are from where the footpath first heads onto the beach; there is usually a jumble of boats on the shore here which make useful foreground interest for views over the river and with a wider lens it is also possible to include the huts receding into the distance. Explore a bit further and you'll discover the ribs of a shipwreck visible as the tide goes out and under the crumbly cliffs there are often dead trees on the beach.

*Opposite top: A calm morning on the Stour (VP2). Canon 5D IV, 24–105mm at 80mm, ISO 100, 1/5s at f/18, tripod. June. **bottom**: Stormy skies over the marshes (VP2). Canon 5D IV, 16–35mm at 16mm, ISO 100, 1/13s at f/16, LEE 0.6 med ND grad, tripod. June.*

Boats on the shore at sunset (VP2). Canon 5D IV, 16–35mm at 16mm, ISO 100, 30s at f/11, LEE Big Stopper & 0.9 hard ND grad, tripod. June.

How to get here

Wrabness is a village by the River Stour, 15 miles east of Colchester.

Leave the A12 at junction 29 Colchester bypass and take the A120 east towards Harwich. Follow it for around 11 miles then turn right onto Primrose Lane (signposted Wrabness Station). At the crossroads go straight across onto Rectory Road, House for Essex parking is in the station car park half a mile along Rectory Road. For the river parking continue past the station and turn right onto Church Road. After around a quarter of a mile you'll pass a bench on the right, park on the verge (well worn from parking) just beyond it.

Viewpoint 1 and 2 – A House for Essex

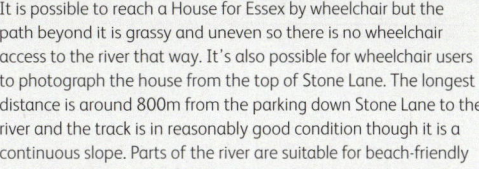

- Lat/Long: 51.93928, 1.17173
- what3words: ///hazelnuts.acclaimed.outer
- Grid Ref: TM 181 315
- Postcode: CO11 2TN

Viewpoint 2 – The river

- Lat/Long: 51.942, 1.1641
- what3words: ///seashell.driveway.recount
- Grid Ref: TM 175 317
- Postcode: CO11 2TQ

Nearest Tide Station

Harwich

Accessibility

It is possible to reach a House for Essex by wheelchair but the path beyond it is grassy and uneven so there is no wheelchair access to the river that way. It's also possible for wheelchair users to photograph the house from the top of Stone Lane. The longest distance is around 800m from the parking down Stone Lane to the river and the track is in reasonably good condition though it is a continuous slope. Parts of the river are suitable for beach-friendly wheelchairs but much of it is muddy and along with the marsh area, unsuitable.

Best Time of Year/Day

With plenty of variety and views in all directions there is something here all year round. It's a great spot for sunset – it's on the southern bank of the river so from spring until early autumn you can catch the sunrise or sunset there and the rest of the year will be good for side light.

A House for Essex looks fantastic in changeable weather with big clouds and splashes of sunlight. Afternoons are the best time to visit, especially in spring and autumn when the sun should be to the side.

Above: Sea lavender on the marshes at sunset (VP2). Canon 5D IV, 16–35mm at 17mm, ISO 400, 0.4s at f/16, LEE 0.6 hard ND grad, tripod. June.

8 HARWICH & DOVERCOURT

If you are of a certain age, the phrase 'Hello campers … hi-de-hi!' will probably ring a bell (if it doesn't, ask your parents). The classic 80s sitcom Hi-De-Hi! was filmed in Dovercourt in the old holiday camp just a stone's throw from the lighthouse. At around the same time, the town's distinctive cast iron landmark was being restored to its former glory.

What to shoot and viewpoints

Viewpoint 1 – Dovercourt Lighthouse ♿

Built in 1863, Dovercourt Lighthouse is actually one of a pair – the high lighthouse and the low lighthouse. When the lights from the two were aligned, the ship was on the correct course into the deep water channel. The one of most interest is the low lighthouse, which is around 150m from the beach at the end of a concrete causeway. The other is at the top of the beach.

At low tide the receding water leaves the beach covered in sand ripples and pools. These make wonderful foreground interest especially when side lit by the rising sun, which further emphasizes the contoured effect. If you have a wide-angle lens, now is the time to use it: try using a low viewpoint to get close to the foreground for maximum impact. The tide here goes out past the lighthouse so it's possible to walk out and shoot from different angles depending on where the light is coming from. Just don't forget your wellies.

Seaweed-draped wooden groynes that line the beach also make interesting lead-in lines, both at low tide surrounded by pools and ripples or at high tide with the sea breaking around them. Using an ND filter to slow the shutter speed to around one second can help convey the sense of motion in the water as it rushes around the groynes, without losing too much detail.

With a shape resembling a moon landing craft, the lighthouse makes an excellent subject for long exposures. This technique is particularly effective at high tide when the causeway is covered by water and the lighthouse appears isolated out to sea. An exposure time of two minutes or more should be enough to turn the water around it flat and milky, adding to the otherworldly look of the place.

For a different angle, take a walk north around the promenade for around 350 metres to where footpaths zig zag up the slope, providing a higher viewpoint.

Sunrise at Dovercourt Lighthouse (VP1). Canon 5D IV, 16–35mm at 16mm, ISO 100, 0.4s at f/22, LEE 0.9 hard ND grad, tripod. Nov.

8 HARWICH & DOVERCOURT

A dramatic sunrise at Harwich Lighthouse (VP2). Canon 5D IV, 16–35mm at 16mm, ISO 100, 30s at f/16, LEE Little Stopper & 0.9 med ND grad, tripod. Dec.

Viewpoint 2 – Harwich Lighthouse ♿

Harwich low lighthouse is a 200m walk south along the promenade from the car park and while this older brick lighthouse is perhaps not as photogenic as its iron neighbour a mile south in Dovercourt, it's definitely an interesting alternative. There are views looking along the promenade towards it or from the grass behind but the better views are from the beach looking up towards it, especially with the tide high enough to reach the sea wall.

Continue along the promenade to the eastern tip where, from below Beacon Hill Fort, a stone breakwater extends out into the entrance of the natural harbour formed by the rivers Stour and Orwell. This is a good spot for sunrise or high tide at any time of day, especially when the sea is rough and waves break over the breakwater. There is a metal railing to deter people from walking out onto the breakwater, but this can be avoided either by standing right behind it or by cloning it out of wider views. The stone surface can be treacherously slippery when wet even by the railing so take care.

Opposite top left: Beach huts at dawn (VP1). Canon R5, 100–400mm at 190mm, ISO 200, 1s at f/5.6, tripod. Mar. **Top right**: The breakwater at dawn (VP2). Canon 5D IV, 16–35mm at 16mm, ISO 100, 60s at f/16, LEE Little Stopper & 0.9 med ND grad, tripod. Nov. **Middle left upper**: The breakwater at dawn (VP2). Canon 5D IV, 16–35mm at 16mm, ISO 100, 30s at f/14, LEE Little Stopper & 0.9 med ND grad, tripod. Nov. **Middle left lower**: A splash of light (VP1). Canon R5, 24–105mm at 105mm, ISO 100, 1/13s at f/11, LEE 0.6 med ND grad, tripod. Feb. **Middle right**: A dramatic sunrise at Harwich Lighthouse (VP2). Canon R5, 24–105mm at 32mm, ISO 100, 1.3s at f/16, LEE Little Stopper & 0.6 med ND grad, tripod. Dec. **Bottom**: A rainbow over Dovercourt Lighthouse (VP1). Canon R5, 24–105mm at 26mm, ISO 100, 1/800s at f/8, LEE polariser. May.

HARWICH & DOVERCOURT

Viewpoint 3 – Ha'penny Pier ♿

Built in 1853, Ha'penny pier is one of the last surviving working wooden piers in the country. Even the original 19th-century ticket booth, where the 1/2d toll would have been paid, survives. Although small, the wooden pier offers a variety of photographic opportunities from detail shots of the fishing nets and boats to wider views of the pier itself as well as an excellent vantage point for views across the mouth of the rivers Stour and Orwell. Wider views work well from last light into blue hour when the lights on the pier and the port of Felixstowe across the river come on. There are views from both ends, either looking north east from the start of the pier to include the lightship or facing west from the far end to include the pier and the sun setting over the River Stour.

A wide-angle lens is useful here so you can include both the pier and the receding line of lamp posts along its centre as well as the sunset sky.

How to get here

Dovercourt is on the Essex coast, 16.5 miles east of Colchester.

From Colchester head eastbound on the A120 for almost 14 miles then at the Ramsey roundabout take the third exit (B1352) up the hill towards the church. Continue for around a mile then turn right at the mini roundabout onto to the B1414 and at the next mini roundabout turn left onto low road. Follow this road for around 1.5 miles, past the boating lake on the right and the lighthouse should come into view. Park on the road in front of the lighthouse.

Viewpoint 1 – Dovercourt lighthouse

- Lat/Long: 51.93038, 1.27505
- what3words: ///regrowth.jaws.decisive
- Grid Ref: TM 078 162
- Postcode: CO12 3SS

Viewpoint 2 – Harwich lighthouse

- Lat/Long: 51.9455, 1.28995
- what3words: ///reliving.glare.spill
- Grid Ref: TM 262 325
- Postcode: CO12 3DT

Viewpoint 3 – Ha'penny pier

- Lat/Long: 51.94787, 1.28584
- what3words: ///stereos.quicksand.squad
- Grid Ref: TM 259 328
- Postcode: CO12 3HB

Nearest Tide Station

Harwich

Accessibility ♿

All parking is close to the locations so very little walking is necessary. There is wheelchair access to Ha'penny Pier and to the beach at Dovercourt Lighthouse (for those with beach-friendly wheelchairs) but it's also possible to shoot both lighthouses and the breakwater from the promenade. Down on the beach at low tide the wet sand is soft and muddy in places so wellies are a must.

Best time of year/day

Dovercourt Lighthouse photographs well at any time of year. Sunrise is usually the best time of day for dramatic skies but evening light works just as well for side light on the lighthouse. Long exposures can be taken at any time – the tide height and cloud cover being more important than the time of day. The same is true of Harwich Lighthouse and breakwater but Ha'penny Pier is better suited to sunset.

The high and low lighthouse (VP2). Fuji X-T10, 18–55mm at 39mm, ISO 200, 1/320s at f/5. Mar.

Opposite top: The lightship from Ha'penny pier (VP3). Canon 5D IV, 16–35mm at 16mm, ISO 100, 15s at f/16, tripod. Oct
Bottom: Blue hour at Ha'penny pier (VP3). Canon 5D IV, 16–35mm at 18mm, ISO 100, 2.5s at f/16, tripod. Oct.

9 HAMFORD WATER

Hamford Water or the Walton Backwaters, as it is known locally, is a peaceful tidal inlet tucked away behind the Naze at Walton. A National Nature Reserve and Site of Special Scientific Interest covering over 2000 hectares, this marvellous maze of mud flats, islands, saltmarsh and twisting creeks is blessed with some equally fantastic names … Skipper's Island, The Twizzle and Bull's Ooze to name but a few.

Anyone who has read Arthur Ransome's Swallows and Amazons series as a child may also recognise this area as the setting for the book Secret Waters. Ransome changed the place names: Kirby Quay became Witch's Quay, for example but little else has changed here since the book was published in 1939.

What to shoot and viewpoints

A public footpath runs 8.5 km along the sea wall all the way from Beaumont Quay to the causeway at Horsey Island. It is a beautiful walk with many photographic opportunities which should take around 2 hours but for shorter visits there are parking options at each end.

Viewpoint 1 – Beaumont Quay

Built from stone blocks from the Old London Bridge, Beaumont Quay is at the very furthest reaches of the backwaters and, like Landermere Wharf, is a relic of the days when Thames sailing barges would have crept up the shallow channels at high tide to these and many other unlikely looking, small and remote docks around Essex.

To reach the quay, go through the gate beside the parking and it is just 50m along the path. All that remains of the buildings that once lined the quay is a single storehouse (and a kiln behind it) but that makes an interestingly remote focal point in views looking east along Beaumont Cut. There are often boats either in the creek or on the quayside providing suitable foreground material, and for views along the cut without the storehouse, there is a short path that goes just beyond the building. Although high tide is a good time to visit, providing reflections on a calm day, at lower tides the curving course of water stands out brightly against the contrasting texture of mud.

Further interest lies slightly west of the quay, at the very end of the creek, where the skeletal remains of an old barge lie half buried in the mud. The sea wall behind it provides some extra height to open up the view over the creeks and beyond.

Old boats on the marsh (VP2). Canon 5D IV, 16–35mm at 20mm, ISO 100, 0.6s at f/16, tripod. June.

Viewpoint 2 – Landermere Wharf

The sea wall footpath runs east from Beaumont to Landermere Wharf but it's worth stopping at a group of old boats lying on the marsh about 900m along the route. They are best photographed at a high tide when some of them will be surrounded by water. Try shooting from a low angle, using the jetty as a dramatic leading line.

A little further along the footpath from the boats, the path turns inland onto a lane. Turn left and Landermere Wharf is around 150m along on the left. There are a couple of points of interest here – the wharf itself and a small jetty a little further along the footpath.

Previous spread: Last light on Landermere Wharf (VP2). Canon 5D IV, 24–70mm at 28mm, ISO 100, 1/4s at f/16, LEE 0.6 hard ND grad, tripod. Apr.

With a row of sturdy wooden posts lining its frontage, the wharf provides an excellent foreground for shots to the west of the nearby house overlooking the river or boats out on the river. From up on the sea wall the wharf itself can make a great subject if there are interesting boats moored there. Further along the sea wall, a small wooden jetty makes a similarly useful foreground for sunrises or sunsets over the river.

Top: Beaumont Quay bathed in warm light (VP1). Canon 5D IV, 16–35mm at 22mm, ISO 100, 15s at f/11, LEE Little Stopper, tripod. July.

Above left: Beaumont cut at sunrise (VP1). Canon 5D IV, 100–400mm at 170mm, ISO 100, 1/2s at f/11, LEE 0.9 hard ND grad, tripod. Mar. Right: Sunset at Landermere Wharf (VP2). Canon 5D IV, 24–70mm at 30mm, ISO 100, 1/4s at f/11, LEE 0.9 hard ND grad, tripod. Apr.

9 HAMFORD WATER

Viewpoint 3 – Saltmarsh
The sea wall footpath carries on beyond Landermere and the next stretch has some particularly good views over the creeks and saltmarsh. After about 300m, a bridge spans one of the creeks, making a useful focal point in an otherwise flat landscape.

The bridge looks like something from an Indiana Jones movie; as though it would collapse as soon as our hero was halfway across, but it is safe and beyond it a plank path heads far out across the marsh. The path itself works well as a simple leading line through the landscape of saltmarsh and twisting creeks and there are usually a few small boats lying around waiting to be incorporated into your composition. Beware of being caught out by incoming tides here; the marsh can flood at high tide so it's safest when the tide is on its way out but never go out without knowing the tide times.

If you want to explore further there is about 3km of sea wall and saltmarsh views to the jetty at Kirby Creek (viewpoint 5), but in the summer this end of the path can be rather overgrown, so it is an easier walk in the other direction starting from Kirby Quay.

How to get here

Viewpoints 1-3
Beaumont Quay is near the village of Thorpe-le-Soken, 14 miles east of Colchester.

Leave the A12 at junction 29 Colchester bypass and take the A120 east towards Harwich. After around 5 miles turn off onto the A133, signposted Clacton and at the roundabout take the first exit to continue onto the A133 towards Clacton. At the next roundabout take the first exit onto the B1033 towards Frinton and follow that road for almost 4 miles then at the mini roundabout in Thorpe-le-Soken, turn left onto the B1414. Follow the B1414 for just over a mile then turn right onto Quay Lane; it's a small road and there are colourful signs advertising businesses there. Follow the lane past farm buildings almost to the end and there is a small parking area on the right just before the gate.

- **Lat/Long:** 51.87215, 1.17931
- **what3words:** ///opposites.bearings.composes
- **Grid Ref:** TM 189 240
- **Postcode:** CO16 0BB

Viewpoints 4-6
Kirby Quay is in the village of Kirby-le-Soken, 14 miles east of Colchester.

Follow the directions above but instead of turning onto the B1414, continue through Thorpe Le Soken then turn left onto the B1034 signposted Walton. Follow the B1034 for 2 miles into the village and turn left just after The Ship pub onto Quay Lane. Park along the road where it is safe to do so.

- **Lat/Long:** 51.853, 1.23106
- **what3words:** ///butterfly.wipes.bumping
- **Grid Ref:** TM 226 220
- **Postcode:** CO13 0DP

Nearest Tide Station
Bramble Creek

Above: Boats on the saltmarsh under stormy skies (VP3). Canon 5D IV, 24–70mm at 24mm, ISO 100, 1/80s at f/11, tripod. Mar.

Accessibility ♿

Beaumont Quay is only a few metres from the parking but the area is often muddy and the ground uneven. The walk to Landermere Wharf is around 1.3km further along an easy, but not wheelchair friendly, path. From the second parking place, the walk to Kirby Quay is around 250m mostly along the road but beyond that it isn't wheelchair friendly. It is an easy 1.5km walk along the sea wall to the jetty at the Twizzle and almost twice that distance in the other direction to Kirby Creek. The paths can be muddy in the winter and sometimes overgrown in summer.

Best time of year/day

There are opportunities here all year – spring and summer are good for wildflowers on the saltmarsh while autumn and winter bring dramatic skies and light. Sunrise is a great time for atmospheric conditions and early side light but the sun position better suits sunsets at most of the viewpoints. In addition to the tips for tides already mentioned, it's worth noting that the highest tides will completely flood the marshes turning the area into a huge body of water – ideal if you want the boats near Landermere or the curved jetty to be surrounded by water but completely submerging everything else.

Top: Rickety plank bridges across the saltmarsh (VP3). Canon 5D IV, 16–35mm at 16mm, ISO 100, 1/4s at f/16, LEE 0.6 hard ND grad, tripod. Apr.

Above: Dramatic light over Hamford Water (VP3). Canon 5D IV, 24–70mm at 24mm, ISO 100, 30s at f/11, tripod. Apr.

9 HAMFORD WATER

Top: Thatched cottage at Kirby Quay (VP4). Canon 5D IV, 24–105mm at 24mm, ISO 100, 1/5s at f/11, tripod. Aug.

Middle: Low tide at the small jetty (VP5). Canon 5D IV, 24–70mm at 24mm, ISO 100, 1/4s at f/16, LEE 0.6 med ND grad, tripod. Mar.

Bottom: Reflections at Kirby Quay (VP4). Canon 5D IV, 24–70mm at 45mm, ISO 100, 1/15s at f/16, tripod. July.

Viewpoint 4 – Kirby Quay

From the parking on Quay Lane, walk down the road. After around 250m you will see the river ahead and, on the right, across a little wooden bridge, a pretty thatched cottage that will likely have you reaching for your camera. Kirby Quay itself is further along the lane, past the next house where the path turns right after the sheds. This is where the best views are to be found – looking out along the creek to the house at the quayside and beyond. With a bit of luck an interesting boat – a sailing barge perhaps – will be on hand to add to the timeless quality that oozes from the Walton Backwaters.

Viewpoint 5 – Kirby Creek Jetty

Kirby Creek is around 2.75 km north west of Kirby Quay. The path is on the left around 75m along Quay Lane from the thatched cottage. Cross the rather wonky bridge over the ditch then follow the path across the small meadow and around the edge of the field where it rejoins the riverbank. If time is short, there is a small jetty here, which at high tide makes a good subject for a long exposure on an overcast day or a foreground at sunset. But if you are heading to Kirby Creek, follow the sea wall path until you reach a curving wooden jetty.

The sea wall provides a higher viewpoint to best show the curve of the jetty though close up with a wide-angle lens is perhaps a more dramatic angle, especially with the jetty sweeping across the frame from one corner. There are usually a few boats scattered on the marsh here and these can be incorporated into compositions of the jetty or isolated as a subject. Unless you like mud, a high tide over 4m is needed to fill the pools in the surrounding marsh with water – considerably higher to flood the marsh. The highest will completely cover the jetty but unfortunately those never coincide with sunset.

There are further views around 250m along the sea wall, where another path and several photogenic rickety wooden bridges span the creeks across the marsh. This path leads out to a causeway across to Skipper Island, an Essex Wildlife Trust nature reserve but access is by prior permission only.

Opposite: Sunset at Kirby Creek (VP5). Canon 5D IV, 16–35mm at 25mm, ISO 100, 1.6s at f/16, LEE 0.9 med ND grad, tripod. June.

9 HAMFORD WATER

Top: The Wade at low tide (VP6). Canon 5D IV, 16–35mm at 30mm, ISO 100, 1/6s at f/16, LEE 0.6 med ND grad, tripod. July.

Middle: The jetty at the Wade (VP6). Canon 5D IV, 16–35mm at 16mm, ISO 100, 60s at f/11, LEE Big Stopper, tripod. Feb.

Bottom: Sunset over the Wade at low tide (VP6). Canon 5D IV, 24–70mm at 30mm, ISO 100, 1/25s at f/16, LEE 0.6 med ND grad, tripod. July.

Viewpoint 6 – The Wade

In the opposite direction to viewpoint 5, The Wade is the name of the wide channel across which a causeway spans the 1km to Horsey Island. Beside the causeway, which is about 1.5km east along the sea wall from Kirby Quay, is the type of worn wooden jetty that photographers love. This is a spot that works best at high tide, certainly for long exposures. A tide over 4m will be enough to surround the

jetty and cover the adjoining slipway, which otherwise has an annoying habit of poking into the corner of compositions. That said, low tide, when the track appears to stretch out across the mud to nowhere can still be an interesting time, especially at sunrise or sunset.

Don't hurry to the jetty though because there are wonderful views along the first 500m of the walk from Kirby Quay. Shoot from the path to look out over the marsh or come down from the sea wall onto the marsh to find creeks or pools to use as foreground interest. As this stretch faces west, it's a good spot for sunset throughout the year.

Above: Sunset at the curved jetty (VP5). Canon 5D IV, 16–35mm at 16mm, ISO 100, 1/20s at f/22, LEE 0.9 hard ND grad, tripod. May.

WALTON-ON-THE-NAZE

With sandy beaches, a pier, amusements and perhaps even kiss me quick hats, Walton-on-the-Naze is a small, traditional seaside town, but its destiny was reshaped dramatically by the power of the sea. Back in the 14th century, Walton was a farming village several miles inland; 400 years of coastal erosion later it was on the coast. Now the original village is nine miles out to sea.

Thankfully the coast – most of it anyway – is now protected by a sea wall. The 'Naze' – an unspoilt area of heath, marsh and crumbling cliffs (from the Old English word Ness meaning headland) is still eroding at a rate of about two metres a year although the Crag Walk Heritage Project is attempting to stop the 86ft-high Naze Tower, which dominates the coastline from its clifftop vantage point, from ending up on the beach.

What to shoot and viewpoints

Viewpoint 1 – The pier
Walton Pier, the third longest in the country, is a little featureless but photogenic nonetheless, thanks to the beautiful beach around it – a perfect stretch of golden sand broken up by various groynes, breakwaters and slipways, all of which work well either as isolated subjects or as foreground interest for shots of the pier.

A good place to start a wander along the beach is the slipway, which is down a set of steps from The Parade, directly opposite the T-junction. At high tide, long exposures and minimal compositions can give breakwaters and slipways that minimal look so don't forget your Big Stopper filter.

The groynes photograph well at low tide when surrounded by pools of standing water, channels and ripples carved into the smooth sand, all of which look fantastic when side lit. For bold compositions, try getting low and close with a wide-angle lens. »

Previous spread: Sunrise at the Naze (VP2). Canon 5D IV, 16–35mm at 16mm, ISO 100, 1/13s at f/22, LEE 0.9 med ND grad, tripod. Feb.

How to get here
Walton-on-the-Naze is a town, 19 miles south east of Colchester.

Leave the A12 at junction 29 Colchester bypass and take the A120 east towards Harwich. After around 5 miles turn off onto the A133, signposted Clacton and at the roundabout take the first exit to continue onto the A133 towards Clacton. At the next roundabout take the first exit onto the B1033 towards Frinton and follow that road for almost 4 miles then, after passing through Thorpe-Le-Soken, turn left onto the B1034, signposted Walton. Stay on the B1034 for just over 3.5 miles then at the T-junction turn left onto Walton High Street. Follow the road to the T-junction facing the beach, turn right onto The Parade and there is parking along the road immediately on the left.

Viewpoint 1 – The pier

- **Lat/Long:** 51.84799, 1.27232
- **what3words:** ///surging.onwards.gambles
- **Grid Ref:** TM 254 216
- **Postcode:** CO14 8AP

Viewpoint 2 – The Naze

- **Lat/Long:** 51.86366, 1.28821
- **what3words:** ///boasted.riverbank.consults
- **Grid Ref:** TM 264 234
- **Postcode:** CO14 8LF

Viewpoint 3 – The Backwaters

- **Lat/Long:** 51.85889, 1.2785
- **what3words:** ///ventures.cape.hairstyle
- **Grid Ref:** TM 258 228
- **Postcode:** CO14 8HZ

Nearest Tide Station
Walton-on-the-Naze

Accessibility
There is wheelchair access to the slipway (and indeed the beach for those with a suitable wheelchair) from further along The Parade close to the pier and there is plenty to shoot along this promenade.

Reaching the beach at the Naze is a bit trickier, as there are steps down the cliffs from the car park, but not impossible. About 200m before the car park there is a small turning on the right – Sunny Point – with a sign reading 'No coaches beyond this point'. From here a path slopes down and runs alongside the beach as far as the rocks.

Best time of year/day
At both beach viewpoints, sunrise is the best time of day all year but it's worth noting for those who like shooting the sunrise that in the summer months it will be rising along the beach rather than out to sea. The Backwaters viewpoint faces north so can be shot at either end of the day, when the boat will be side lit by the rising or setting sun, and in the summer months the rising or setting sun can be included in compositions. For long exposures, high tide at any time of day works well, particularly when it's overcast. If it's not, check the sun calculator to make sure bright sun won't be in your shot.

Sunrise at Walton beach (VP1). Canon 5D II, 17–40mm at 21mm, ISO 100, 4s at f/16, LEE 0.6 hard ND grad, tripod. Mar.

10 WALTON-ON-THE-NAZE

The best view of the pier is from the pier itself, which is only accessible when the entrance to the arcade is open. Walk straight through and then bear right before the pier narrows. Here, the railings provide a good angle for a shot of the nicer looking part of the pier … another excellent long exposure subject.

The beach continues south past the pier where there are more breakwaters and row upon row of beach huts. After a kilometer or so you'll find yourself in Frinton-on-Sea. Walk 2km in the other direction and when the beach huts come to an end, you have reached the Naze.

Viewpoint 2 – The Naze
The more natural Naze beach is 100m from the car park, reached by descending several flights of steps. At the bottom, in front of the newer rocky sea defences, a sloped wooden breakwater, not dissimilar to a huge wooden Toblerone, stretches out to sea. Surrounded by water at high tide this is another very good candidate for the long exposure treatment.

The Naze beach can be a tricky place to find compositions; aside from a couple of Second World War pill boxes (which started life on the clifftop), it is featureless at high tide. At low tide however, all sorts of shapes, patterns and pools are revealed in the sand and clay. Walk out to the water's edge, (taking care as the clay can be slippery) where these shapes can be contrasted against the water. I like to use a wide-angle lens to get close and fill the foreground with an interesting pattern but with such a simple subject a good sky or sunrise is almost essential.

After sunrise, don't forget to look behind you to see the cliffs and the Naze tower visible on the top and bathed in the early morning light.

Sunrise on the Backwaters (VP3). Canon 5D IV, 16–35mm at 18mm, ISO 100, 6s at f/11, LEE 0.6 med ND grad, tripod. Aug.

Viewpoint 3 – The Backwaters

On the western side of the Naze headland begins the network of creeks and channels known as the Walton Backwaters. Most of the Backwater viewpoints are explored in the Hamford Water section (page 94) but being closer to the coast and separated from the rest by the vagaries of the network of public footpaths, it made more sense to include this one here.

Park in the lay-by on the bend of the road and take the public footpath in the corner. It is 400m to the sea wall, where straight ahead you'll see an old rusty boat stuck in the mud. Compositions are limited slightly by the metal fence to the left but there are still several possibilities. Shooting from up on the sea wall opens up the view to the Backwaters beyond, while going down onto the marsh below (steering clear of the soft mud) and looking up at the boat makes for a more dramatic look.

There are also views looking back from further along the sea wall to the right, which shows the boat at the end of the sweeping curve of the channel.

Whichever position you choose, the river is very muddy at low tide so high tide, when the boat will be surrounded by water, or mid tide, when the shape of the channel is revealed, are the best options. High tide is particularly good for long exposures.

Opposite top left: *Minimal long exposure at the Naze (VP2). Canon 7D, 10–20mm at 10mm, ISO 100, 60s at f/11, LEE Big Stopper & 0.9 hard ND grad, tripod. Sep.* **Top right**: *First light on the Naze cliffs (VP2). Canon 5D IV, 16–35mm at 21mm, ISO 100, 1/4s at f/11, LEE polariser, tripod. Oct.* **Bottom left**: *Long exposure from the pier (VP1). Canon 5D IV, 24–70mm at 24mm, ISO 100, 120s at f/16, LEE Big Stopper & 0.9 ND, tripod. Sep.* **Bottom right**: *Beach huts at Walton (VP1). Canon 5D IV, 24–70mm at 70mm, ISO 100, 1/200s at f/11, tripod. Aug.*

11 FRINTON-ON-SEA

An Edwardian seaside resort sandwiched between Clacton and Walton, Frinton has managed to retain an air of the exclusive reputation it had back in the 'Royal Years' of the 1920s and 30s when anyone who was anyone would spend the summer here.

This is the legacy of Sir Richard Powell Cooper, the man responsible for Frinton's development, and who, in the 1890s, put a number of bye laws in place to attract the 'right sort of people': no amusements on the seafront, no pier, no ice cream vendors on the beach, no shorts at the golf club and no public houses. It's an understatement to say that things change slowly here … a century passed before the first fish and chip shop opened in the town in 1992; the first pub followed in 2000 and if that wasn't enough, since 2008 men have been allowed to wear shorts in the golf club!

What to shoot and viewpoints

Viewpoint 1 – The beach ♿

Frinton's long swathe of smooth golden sand that made it a popular resort is also the big attraction for photographers. The beach is lined by beach huts and protected by wooden groynes. It is much the same along its entire length but the curved promenade and concrete breakwater at the northern end provide added interest.

From the parking take the path across the greensward and down to the promenade. Before heading down on to the beach, there are views in all directions from the promenade itself. Looking south along the beach using the curve of the promenade or perhaps the slipway as a leading line works well. Turn east and the concrete breakwater makes a nice subject for a minimal long exposure or, standing on the breakwater (take care as it may be slippery), there are views along the promenade to the north … in my opinion, these all work best at high tide with water breaking against the sea wall.

Down on the beach, the groynes are best shot with a receding high tide when the waves will be breaking over pristine sand. Experiment with different shutter speeds,

Sunrise on Frinton beach (VP1). Canon 5D IV, 16–35mm at 16mm, ISO 50, 25s at f/16, LEE 0.9 hard ND grad, tripod. Jan.

Opposite left: Beach detail (VP1). Canon 5D IV, 24–70mm at 40mm, ISO 200, 1/250s at f/4. Jan. **Opposite right**: Sunrise on Frinton beach (VP1). Canon 5D IV, 16–35mm at 20mm, ISO 100, 30s at f/22, LEE 0.9 hard ND grad, tripod. Jan.

around 1–2 seconds is good here for 'swooshery' – the blurring created by waves washing back down the beach.

At low tide there are often pools of standing water and sand ripples left on the flat beach. These make fantastic foreground interest, especially with a wide-angle lens and low angle to give them extra impact.

11 FRINTON-ON-SEA

Above: Breakwater long exposure at dusk (VP1). Canon 5D IV, 24–105mm at 40mm, ISO 100, 30s at f/16, LEE Little Stopper & 0.6 hard ND grad, tripod. Jan.

Swooshery around the groynes on Frinton Beach (VP1). Canon 5D IV, 24–105mm at 24mm, ISO 200, 3.2s at f/8, LEE 0.6 hard ND grad, tripod. Jan.

Opposite: Sunset at the beach huts (VP1). Canon 5D IV, 24–105mm at 24mm, ISO 200, 0.6s at f/15, LEE 0.6 med ND grad, tripod. Jan.

How to get here

Frinton-on-Sea is a seaside town, 17 miles south east of Colchester.

Leave the A12 at junction 29 Colchester bypass and take the A120 east towards Harwich. After around 5 miles turn off onto the A133, signposted Clacton and at the roundabout take the first exit to continue onto the A133 towards Clacton. At the next roundabout take the first exit onto the B1033 towards Frinton and follow that road for around 7 miles to the roundabout outside Frinton. Take the third exit signposted Frinton town centre, cross the level crossing and then turn left onto Pole Barn Lane. Follow Pole Barn Lane to the end, turn right onto the Esplanade and park in one of the bays along the road, as close to the junction as possible.

- **Lat/Long:** 51.83669, 1.25652
- **what3words:** ///prosper.baths.panel
- **Grid Ref:** TM 244 203
- **Postcode:** CO13 9JD

Nearest Tide Station

Walton-on-the-Naze

Accessibility

The path down to the promenade is short (less than 200m), paved and wheelchair friendly but it slopes, dropping around 20m as it zig zags down to the beach. There are toilet facilities at each end of the greensward.

Best time of year/day

Like most beaches in this part of the world, sunrise is the best time of day but the beach here angles south east so October to March are the best months with summer sunrises good for views north along the promenade. If you're not an early riser then give winter sunset a try. The end of the day is also best for golden hour light on the shelter from autumn to spring. There are options at any tide but the beach will be totally covered at high tide.

11. FRINTON-ON-SEA

The clock tower at first light (VP2). Canon 5D IV, 24–105mm at 45mm, ISO 100, 0.8s at f/16, tripod. Oct.

Viewpoint 2 – The clock tower shelter ♿
On the greensward further south (1.3km to be precise) is a splendid round seaside shelter with a clock tower. If you don't fancy the stroll along the promenade just drive along the Esplanade where there are further parking spaces in front of the shelter.

It's a simple but interesting subject and there are plenty of options in colour or mono. The path makes a useful leading line for a dramatic low angle, perhaps for a long exposure, with blurred clouds streaking past. However you choose to photograph it, thanks to its position, you can almost always choose the perfect angle for the lighting you want,

Top: Winter at the clock tower (VP2). Canon 5D IV, 24–70mm at 24mm, ISO 200, 1/60s at f/8, tripod. Feb.

Middle: A clock tower long exposure (VP2). Canon 5D II, 17–40mm at 17mm, ISO 5, 107s at f/16, LEE Big Stopper, tripod. Jan.

Bottom: The clock tower at night (VP2). Canon R5, 16mm, ISO 1600, 15s at f/2.8, tripod. May.

whether it be side light to highlight the shape or backlight for dramatic sunlight bursting through the shelter. Keep an eye out for distractions though and, for more impact, try to isolate the shelter without other buildings in shot.

12 CLACTON PIER

Built in 1871, Clacton Pier was originally used as a dock for steam ships bringing visitors to the then new resort of Clacton-on-Sea. In its 150-year history it has been extended, widened, damaged by war, fire and storms (several times) but has remained one of the country's most popular pleasure piers, being named Pier of the Year in 2020.

Clacton's history goes back somewhat further than the pier though: in 1911, a wooden spear head, known as the Clacton Spear, was discovered along with several flint tools and the remains of a giant elephant and hippopotamus – all over 400,000 years old.

What to shoot and viewpoints

In the absence of giant prehistoric mammals, the pier remains the main attraction for photographers, the 50ft 1940s helter skelter adding a particularly prominent point of interest.

There are two promenades, one at street level and one down at beach level, and the pier is visible from both for some distance in either direction, but while there are views from these, there are perhaps better compositions from the beach.

The upper promenade is just a few metres from the parking along Marine Parade just cut through any of the paths between the gardens that run between the road and promenade. This is a good spot to shoot from at blue hour when the colourful lights on the pier contrasting nicely with the deep blues in the sky. Try using a long focal length to fill the frame and a slow shutter speed to blur the motion of moving rides or a standard zoom lens for wider views of the whole pier and reflections of the lights in the sea.

Several paths lead down to the lower promenade and the beach. Low tide reveals sand ripples and pools over much of the flat sandy beach, these work well as foreground interest and with a little work on getting the right angle you can usually find some which point towards the pier. Just to the southern side of the pier a concrete breakwater, more attractive than it sounds, can also be used as foreground interest but the various breakwaters and sea defences along the beach are also excellent for minimal long exposures.

The sea defences on the northern side of the pier and further down to the south, are made from piles of granite boulders. They are rather bulky but can still serve as a foreground or a subject in their own right and they have created some nice small curved bays in between them.

Top: Minimal breakwater long exposure. Canon 5D IV, 24–70mm at 70mm, ISO 200, 30s at f/11, LEE Big Stopper, tripod. Aug.

Above: The pier from the north. Canon 5D IV, 16–35mm at 23mm, ISO 200, 20s at f/16, LEE Big Stopper, tripod. Aug.

Opposite: Clacton Pier at sunrise. Canon 5D IV, 24–70mm at 28mm, ISO 200, 1/15s at f/16, LEE 0.6 hard ND grad, tripod. Aug.

Overleaf: Summer fireworks at the pier. Canon 5D IV, 24–70mm at 35mm, ISO 100, 13s at f/16, tripod. July.

12 CLACTON PIER

How to get here

Clacton-on-Sea is a seaside town, 16 miles south east of Colchester.

Leave the A12 at junction 29 Colchester bypass and take the A120 east towards Harwich. After around 5 miles turn off onto the A133 signposted Clacton and at the roundabout take the first exit to continue onto the A133 towards Clacton. Follow this road for 8 miles all the way to the seafront. Turn right onto Marine Parade and continue for around half a mile, passing the pier and park in one of the free parking bays along the left hand side of the road. These have a limit of 3 hours between 9am and 6pm.

	Lat/Long:	51.7861, 1.1515
	what3words:	///trifling.plot.splash
	Grid Ref:	TM 174 144
	Postcode:	CO15 1LA

Nearest Tide Station

Clacton

Accessibility

There is little walking necessary here and ramps provide wheelchair access to the upper and lower promenade and all the way down to the beach for those with a suitable wheelchair.

Best time of year/day

There are opportunities here all year although during the holiday season it's best to avoid the daytime when the town will be very busy with tourists. Throughout the year the sun can be seen rising behind the pier from one side and then lighting the pier from the other. Autumn to spring are the best times as during the summer months the sun rises a little too far north – a good excuse to avoid those early sunrises. Evening is also a good time to catch the last light of the day on the pier followed by the magic blue hour when the lights on the pier come on.

Above: Dusk at the pier. Canon 5D IV, 24–70mm at 24mm, ISO 400, 0.8s at f/11, LEE 0.6 med ND grad, tripod. Aug.

Opposite: The pier from above. DJI Mavic 2 Pro, 28mm, ISO 100, 1/100s at f/8. Aug.

13 COLNE POINT

How to get here

Colne Point is at the mouth of the River Colne, 15 miles south of Colchester.

Leave the A12 at junction 29 Colchester bypass and take the A120 east towards Harwich. After around 5 miles turn off onto the A133 signposted Clacton and at the roundabout take the second exit for the A133 towards Elmstead Market. At the crossroads turn left onto the B1029 towards Thorrington, follow the road for almost a mile then at the right hand bend take the turning to the left. At the crossroads go straight on and turn left at the next junction onto the B1027. Follow the B1027 for 2.5 miles then turn right onto Colchester Road towards St Osyth. Turn right at the crossroads and follow the road for a mile then turn left immediately after the Point Clear signs, onto Lee Wick Lane. Follow it for 2 miles, over the sea wall to the end where an Essex Wildlife Trust sign indicates the parking spaces for the nature reserve on the left just before the gate. There is a gate just before the road goes up and over the sea wall; if it is closed it is OK to open it but be sure to close it after you. This road is narrow and pot holed in places so drive carefully. The car park is liable to flooding at very high tides so check before visiting.

Lat/Long: 51.77054, 1.05385
what3words: ///vets.crossings.jigsaw
Grid Ref: TM 107 123
Postcode: CO16 8ET

Nearest Tide Station

Brightlingsea

Above: Late afternoon light on the tank traps (VP1). Canon 5D IV, 16–35mm at 18mm, ISO 100, 1/25s at f/16, tripod. May.

Situated on the coast beside Lee-over-Sands, Colne Point is a wild area of saltmarsh and meandering creeks, surrounded by a long shingle ridge that loops around the coast and into the mouth of the Colne Estuary. Lee-over-Sands is a tiny community of little more than thirty houses – many on stilts to combat tidal flooding – clustered along the beach road. The feeling of solitude exuded by their remote location on the marsh is irresistibly photogenic.

It's worth mentioning at this point however that access isn't straightforward: Colne Point is a nature reserve owned by the Essex Wildlife Trust (EWT) and open to members or permit holders only. In addition, the only road to Lee-over-Sands (and thus Colne Point) is private with access limited to residents or those visiting the nature reserve. It is possible to walk along the coastal path from nearby St Osyth Beach (2.5km) but, at the time of writing, EWT membership costs as little as £3 per month, so it is well worth joining.

What to shoot and viewpoints

Viewpoint 1 – Tank traps
The first viewpoint is just a few metres from the parking place where a line of concrete anti-tank blocks stretches along the edge of the saltmarsh. They are now quite buried in places but walk back along the road to the fork and you'll find a small path on the right that leads to a row of blocks alongside the creek. The blocks conveniently lead towards a WWII pill box on the marsh. Overgrown by swaying marram grasses, these (let's be honest) ugly concrete defensive structures somehow add to the remote, wild feel of the place and this is a great area to capture that.

While we are in this area there is also a public footpath that runs along the sea wall in both directions from Beach Road. The extra height provides elevated views over the marshes and it is a pleasant walk in either direction.

Accessibility
There are some views from along the road or from the sea wall footpath which are accessible for wheelchair users but the bridge over the creek onto Colne Point is rather rickety and the path leading to and from it is uneven and usually muddy.

Dogs aren't allowed on Colne Point and access is limited to Essex Wildlife Trust members and permit holders. Permits are available from www.essexwt.org.uk/nature-reserves/colne-point

Best time of year/day
This is a location that works all year round. In summer the marshes come to life with wildflowers, while the remote location suits more dramatic 'bad' weather. If you want colour in the sky, the best time is when the landscape is bathed in the first or last light, and that is good all year round.

13 COLNE POINT

Top: Redshanks in the snow (VP2). Canon 5D IV, 24–70mm at 63mm, ISO 100, 1/200s at f/8, tripod. Feb.

Above: Winter at Colne Point. Canon 5D IV, 24–70mm at 70mm, ISO 100, 1/200s at f/8, tripod. Feb.

Viewpoint 2 – The old jetty

Head west along Beach Road and one of the first in an interesting row of dwellings, sitting all alone on the right hand side of the road is an award-winning house called Redshanks. Raised above the marsh on red stilts, it's a fascinating structure to photograph and although tricky to find an angle that isolates it from its surroundings, it's definitely worth spending a bit of time with it particularly at high tide when it is reflected in the water, or in the evening when the windows glow with reflections of the setting sun. There are a host of interesting subjects to discover here on the way towards the jetty at the far end of the nature reserve, though some areas are private so keep an eye out for signs.

Around 100m beyond the last house at the very end of the beach road there is a wooden bridge across Ray Creek to the shingle spit. The bridge isn't the prettiest but still has potential and makes a good leading line towards the hut on the other side of the creek, particularly when side lit by warm morning or evening light.

On the other side, follow the small path that runs north west past the hut for just over 300m and when it opens out onto the shingle and becomes roped in, look for a small path on the right that runs below the embankment. There is a hide 300m along the path (the path can be slippery so watch your footing) and just beyond the hide are the remains of a rather large jetty. This makes a good subject for a long exposure, especially when surrounded by water at high tide, but this marsh can flood at very high tides so avoid spring tides and make sure you always know whether the tide is coming in or going out before setting off.

Please stick to the paths on the shingle, particularly in nesting season as there are ground nesting birds; chicks and eggs are well disguised.

Above: *Long exposure of the old jetty (VP2). Canon 5D IV, 24–70mm at 24mm, ISO 200, 30s at f/11, LEE Big Stopper & 0.6 med ND grad, tripod. May.*

The bridge over Ray Creek (VP2). Canon 5D IV, 16–35mm at 30mm, ISO 100, 1/2s at f/11, LEE 0.6 med ND grad, tripod. Jan.

14. ST OSYPH CREEK

The pretty village of St Osyth is named after Osgyth, wife of Sighere, the first Christian king of the East Saxons. She became a saint after being beheaded by rampaging Danish raiders in AD 653 and her ghost is said to walk along the walls of St Osyth Priory one night every year, clutching its decapitated head.

Little remains of the priory except for the flint gatehouse, which is impressive (with or without wandering headless ghosts) but the twisting St Osyth Creek and ramshackle boatyard are the main attraction for photographers.

What to shoot and viewpoints

Viewpoint 1 – the creek
There are several views from the footpath that runs along the southern bank of St Osyth Creek, the best of which are all within the first kilometre. The path is on the opposite side of the river to the car park on the right hand side, immediately after the track that leads to the houseboats. The first photographic opportunities come before you even reach the path, amongst the wonderful jumble of houseboats you'll pass as you walk across the bridge.

About 100m along the path, just beyond the houseboats, a couple of old barges lie on the edge of the river, the wood of their exposed ribs streaked by rusting nails as they slowly decay into the mud. They look best at high tide with some water around them, when they make a good subject for a long exposure but bear in mind that at very high tides the marsh will flood making access difficult.

Around 700m further along the path are the remains of a wooden jetty clinging precariously to the bank. There are good views looking along the river here in either direction, with the jetty or the small wooden bridges that lead to it providing a suitably interesting foreground.

There is another wreck down on the saltmarsh just before the sea wall bends 90° to the right. Lying completely on its side with limited access around it there are few options

The barge wrecks. Canon 5D IV, 16–35mm at 16mm, ISO 100, 1/13s at f/16, tripod. Feb.

for compositions but it works well shot from the front, especially when side lit by the first or last light. Take care on the marsh here particularly in low light as the path crosses a couple of small creeks.

Incidentally, the unnaturally regular, square-shaped pools in the saltings here, which become more prevalent if you carry on along the path, are disused oyster beds. Oysters have been cultivated here since the 13th century.

Previous spread: Sunset at the wreck on the saltmarsh. Canon 5D IV, 16–35mm at 16mm, ISO 100, 1/5s at f/16, LEE 0.9 med ND grad, tripod. July.

Sunset and sea lavender. Canon 5D IV, 16–35mm at 20mm, ISO 100, 0.4s at f/22, LEE 0.9 hard ND grad, tripod. July.

Sunset on the saltmarsh. Canon 5D IV, 16–35mm at 16mm, ISO 100, 2s at f/22, LEE 0.9 hard ND grad, tripod. July.

14 ST OSYPH CREEK

Viewpoint 2 – The boatyard
A footpath also runs along the northern bank of the creek or at least the first 400m or so, after which it turns away across the fields. The first stretch of the path passes through the boatyard directly behind the car park and there is an interesting jumble of boats both in and out of the water as well as wider views towards the houseboats across the river. Continue along the path for a few minutes away from the boats and views looking back along the river open up. Then, as the path leaves the river, there is a small inlet with what looks like the remains of an old jetty. The row of worn wooden pilings catches the early morning sun and makes an interesting focal point.

How to get here
Point Clear is at the mouth of the River Colne, 15 miles south of Colchester.

Leave the A12 at junction 29 Colchester bypass and take the A120 east towards Harwich. After around 5 miles turn off onto the A133, signposted Clacton and at the roundabout take the second exit for the A133 towards Elmstead Market. At the crossroads turn left onto the B1029 towards Thorrington, follow the road for almost a mile then at the right hand bend take the turning to the left. At the crossroads go straight on and turn left at the next junction onto the B1027. Follow the B1027 for 2.5 miles then turn right onto Colchester Road towards St Osyth. At the crossroads turn right and at the bottom of the hill, just before crossing the river, there is a small car park on the right opposite the water sports centre.

	Lat/Long:	51.79744, 1.06681
	what3words:	///walked.routines.going
	Grid Ref:	TM 115 154
	Postcode:	CO16 8EW

Nearest Tide Station
Brightlingsea

Accessibility
Walking distances are reasonably short and the ground is flat but too uneven for wheelchairs. However, wheelchair access is possible along the path north of the creek.

Best time of year/day
With views in several directions, there is something here throughout the year but first or last light is probably the best time of day for side light on the boat wrecks and marsh, especially in spring and autumn. Winter is good for dramatic skies and the chance of frosty mornings while in summer, wildflowers will add a splash of colour to the saltmarsh and the sun will set over the western end of the creek.

Top: First light at St Osyth Creek (VP2). Canon 5D IV, 16–35mm at 16mm, ISO 100, 1/3s at f/11, LEE 0.6 med ND grad, tripod. Dec.

Middle: Houseboats at sunrise. Canon 5D IV, 16–35mm at 28mm, ISO 100, 1/5s at f/11, LEE 0.6 med ND grad, tripod. July.

Bottom: Beside the creek (VP1). Canon 5D IV, 16–35mm at 24mm, ISO 100, 1/15s at f/11, LEE polariser, tripod. July.

Across St Osyth Creek (VP2). Canon 5D IV, 24–105mm at 40mm, ISO 100, 1/8s at f/16, LEE 0.6 med ND grad, tripod. Oct.

15. POINT CLEAR

A small village at the tip of a peninsular of sand and saltmarsh, Point Clear may not have the remote, wild feel of some areas of the Essex coast, thanks to the large caravan parks that have spread across most of the point, but it does boast wonderful sunset views.

What to shoot and viewpoints

Viewpoint 1 – Point Clear Bay

Strange as it might sound, the attraction of Point Clear Bay is its mud. At low tide, as the sea retreats from the sandy beach, it reveals a muddy expanse carved with pools and deep channels and dotted with the occasional beached boat. It's far more photogenic than it sounds. It works well when shot with a wide-angle lens to emphasise the channels receding into the distance, especially if you can include a boat as a focal point.

The small beach is directly in front of the car park, which provides a good overview of where the boats and best shapes in the mud are to be found. The mud is soft, deep and smelly so if you need to walk out to get the best angle, wear wellies and stick to the channels, which are firmer.

Viewpoint 2 – Stone Point

Following the footpath or shoreline around to the north west will bring you to Point Clear's point or Stone Point, as it is known. There are several views from the point: to the north west, across the mouth of Brightlingsea Creek, is Bateman's Tower, which provides a distant focal point for wider views or a main one for telephoto shots. Wander along the sand bar at high tide and you can look back across the lagoon towards Point Clear, which is often reflected in the sheltered water. Pay attention to the tides though – you don't want to get stuck out there.

The most popular spot here is the row of chunky old posts, which presumably held a jetty in years gone by. It's situated just in front of the chalets on the lagoon side of the beach. The double row of posts makes a great leading line towards Bateman's Tower or an interesting subject themselves, particularly when surrounded by water at very high tides.

Across the lagoon (VP2). Canon 5D IV, 24–105mm at 24mm, ISO 100, 1/3s at f/16, tripod. Feb.

Previous spread: Light and passing showers (VP2). Canon 5D IV, 24–70mm at 30mm, ISO 100, 1.6s at f/20, LEE polariser & 0.6 med ND grad, tripod. May.

How to get here

Point Clear is at the mouth of the River Colne, 15 miles south of Colchester.

Leave the A12 at junction 29 Colchester bypass and take the A120 east towards Harwich. After around 5 miles turn off onto the A133, signposted Clacton and at the roundabout take the second exit for the A133 towards Elmstead Market. At the crossroads turn left onto the B1029 towards Thorrington, follow the road for almost a mile then at the right hand bend take the turning to the left. At the crossroads go straight on and turn left at the next junction onto the B1027. Follow the B1027 for 2.5 miles then turn right onto Colchester Road towards St Osyth. At the crossroads turn right and follow the road for 2 miles into Point Clear, take the second exit at the roundabout and park on the grass car park on the left.

Lat/Long:	51.79574, 1.02681
what3words:	///rotation.infringe.starfish
Grid Ref:	TM 088 153
Postcode:	CO16 8LX

Nearest Tide Station
Brightlingsea

Accessibility
The longest walk is around 1km from the car park on good paths so although both of the main viewpoints here are unsuitable for wheelchairs, it is possible to shoot from the path or car park. Wellies are essential here.

Best Time of Year/Day
The viewpoints here face north or south west so sunset is the best time of day for dramatic skies and good light but the tide is equally important when planning your visit. Stone Point works best at high tide – particularly a spring tide at any time of day – while Point Clear Bay is best at low tide.

Above: Sunset at Stone Point (VP2). Canon 5D IV, 16–35mm at 19mm, ISO 200, 0.4s at f/16, tripod. May. **Below**: Dramatic light at Point Clear Bay (VP1). Canon 5D IV, 16–35mm at 16mm, ISO 100, 1/15s at f/16, LEE 0.9 hard ND grad, tripod. Aug.

16 BRIGHTLINGSEA

Once an island, Brightlingsea has a long history dating back even before the Romans built a fort here as part of the defences of their original capital at nearby Colchester. The town also has the distinction of being the only Cinque Port – a confederation of the five most important ports along the English Channel – outside Kent and Sussex, having been a limb of Sandwich since 1360.

The most popular attractions for photographers lie to the west, at the end of the Western Promenade, where Bateman's Tower – a folly built by John Bateman in 1883 stands at the mouth of Brightlingsea Creek but there is plenty of interest all along the river here.

What to shoot and viewpoints

Viewpoint 1 – Bateman's Tower ♿

The small beach here is a square of sand, tucked into a corner at the end of the promenade, lined on two sides by beach huts and protected from the sea by a promenade and railings on the other two sides. At the very end of the promenade, Bateman's Tower stands on a point overlooking the beach and estuary. For such a small space there is a surprising amount to photograph.

High tide at Bateman's Tower (VP1). Canon 5D IV, 16–35mm at 18mm, ISO 100, 0.8s at f/16, LEE Big Stopper, tripod. July.

At low tide the rippled wet sand makes an interesting foreground for shots of the vibrant beach huts, especially with reflections in the puddles of water often left behind and lit by the low light from the setting sun. Turn around and the same reflective foreground is just as effective for shots of Bateman's Tower and for much of the year the sun sets behind it.

As the tide comes in, the beach floods but the promenade around it provides a vantage point for views across the water to the beach huts. The water is often calm enough to reflect the beach huts, but if it's rough, long exposures using a big stopper filter work well to smooth the water out. Again this promenade is a good vantage point for Bateman's Tower in the other direction, with the railings serving as a useful lead-in line. As the beach-hut-lined promenade turns the corner towards the town, the curve of the path also makes an effective lead-in line, sweeping from the corners of the frame towards the tower in the distance.

It's worth noting that the tower actually leans slightly, so from certain angles the choice between getting the horizon straight and the tower upright is an OCD nightmare!

At high tide, with the beach flooded and railings and steps appearing to rise from the sea, this area is a great location for minimalist long exposures.

How to get here

Brightlingsea is a coastal town at the mouth of the Colne estuary, 9 miles south of Colchester.

Head south east on the A133 from Colchester. At the top of the hill, turn right at the traffic lights on to the B1028 and after around half a mile, turn left on to the B1027 signposted Brightlingsea. Follow this road for just over 4 miles then turn right at the roundabout on to the B1029. Follow the road for 2.5 miles into Brightlingsea then turn right on to Promenade Way. The pay and display car park is at the end of the road on the left.

Viewpoint 1 – Bateman's tower

- Lat/Long: 51.80625, 1.01304
- what3words: ///regrowth.jaws.decisive
- Grid Ref: TM 078 162
- Postcode: CO7 0HH

Viewpoint 3 – Wrecks

- Lat/Long: 51.80885, 1.0361
- what3words: ///confronts.expand.motivations
- Grid Ref: TM 093 166
- Postcode: CO7 0SZ

Nearest Tide Station

Brightlingsea

Accessibility

The car park is just a few metres from the beach at Bateman's Tower and there is a ramp onto the promenade for wheelchair access. The harbour is similarly wheelchair friendly but the track down to the wreck, although hard, is very potholed and there is no wheelchair access to the marsh.

Best time of year/day

The beach at Bateman's Tower faces south west so it's one of the few coastal locations in this part of the world (or Colne Estuary at least) where you can shoot the sunset over the sea. The best time of year for sunset is autumn to spring. In the summer, the sun sets too far north and the beach is more likely to be busy with people using the huts lining the promenade. For colour, the harbour is also best suited to autumn or winter sunsets while the wrecks and marsh work well all year particularly on calm, misty mornings.

16 BRIGHTLINGSEA

Viewpoint 2 – The Hard ♿
A short walk east along the promenade is a small harbour known as The Hard, an area busy with boats and jetties to explore. While there is plenty of potential for wider sunrise or sunset shots, particularly around the landing jetty or using the wooden kiosk as a foreground, it is also great place to wander in search of nautical details. My favourite area is the small dock clustered with boats at the end of the road past the Colne Yacht Club. Some areas are private though so keep an eye on the signs.

To reach the harbour, follow the promenade east from Bateman's Tower all the way to the end where it meets Fieldgate Dock road. Walk along the road to the corner then go right, around the brick wall, up the ramp and between the swanky new apartment buildings that surround the marina. The Hard is on the opposite side. It's an easy 1km walk on a flat paved surface but there is also a car park by the harbour at Tower Street (CO7 0AP).

It's worth stopping on the way to photograph the marina and discover the hidden viewpoint at the very end of the first row of apartments. It has views out over Brightlingsea Creek to Point Clear, Mersea Island and Bateman's Tower, and is often a good option for sunset.

Viewpoint 3 – Wrecks
On the eastern side of Brightlingsea is an interesting area of saltmarsh, scarred by the shapes of disused oyster pits. These pits are best appreciated from above but along with the creeks carved through the marsh, they also make useful lead-in lines to views of the wrecks stuck in the mud on the edge of the marsh. Parking is a small dirt lay-by next to a row of cottages on Mill Street. There is a track on the right, just past the cottages, which leads down to the marsh. Stay on the track until you are almost at the boat yard and then take the small path out onto the marsh to the shoreline in front of the wrecks. A creek divides the marsh in front of the wrecks so to shoot from the other side, take the bigger path about 50m back along the track.

The wrecks are well positioned to catch the sidelight from the rising or setting sun but they also make a good subject for long exposures, especially when surrounded by water. An hour or so either side of high tide is the best time but be careful at spring tides when the marsh can completely flood. If in doubt, arrive at high tide and go out on a receding tide.

The wrecks from above (VP3). DJI Mavic 2 Pro, 28mm, ISO 100, 1/25s at f/5, LEE polariser. Jan.

Above: A calm sunrise at the wrecks (VP3). Canon 5D IV, 16–35mm at 19mm, ISO 100, 2s at f/11, LEE 0.9 hard ND grad, tripod. Jan.
Below: Bateman's Tower at sunset (VP1). Canon R5, 24–105mm at 35mm, ISO 250, 30s at f/8, LEE Big Stopper, tripod. May.

16 BRIGHTLINGSEA

Top: The beach huts in dramatic afternoon light (VP1). Canon 5D II, 17–40mm at 17mm, ISO 50, 1/13s at f/11, LEE 0.6 hard ND grad, tripod. Feb.

Changeable weather at Brightlingsea (VP1). Canon 5D IV, 24–105mm at 24mm, ISO 100, 1/15s at f/11, LEE polariser, tripod. July.

Above: The Marina in evenign light (VP2). Canon 5D IV, 16–35mm at 16mm, ISO 100, 1/20s at f/11, LEE polariser, tripod. Mar.

Top left: Boats at blue hour (VP2). Canon 5D IV, 16–35mm at 33mm, ISO 100, 1/4s at f/11, tripod. Mar.

Top right: Boats and aprtments in the fog (VP2). Canon 5D IV, 24–70mm at 70mm, ISO 100, 1/5s at f/11, LEE polariser, tripod. July.

Above: Bateman's Tower under the stars (VP1). Canon R5, 16mm, ISO 1600, 1/4s at f/2.8, LEE polariser, tripod. May.

17 THORRINGTON TIDE MILL

The current wooden mill was built in 1831 but there has been a mill in this spot at the very end of Alresford Creek for much longer. One is even listed (although without any specific details) in the Domesday Book.

Now the only remaining working tide mill in Essex, Thorrington Tide Mill was used to grind flour using the power of the tide until 1926. Although no longer used, it was restored in 1999 and can be seen working on open days. The main attraction for photographers though is the opportunity to capture views of the mill in the landscape.

as you walk down to find the best angle. It's a bit of a juggling act because the path to the mill and beyond up to the river is a public footpath crossing private land so you also have to watch the signs to avoid wandering off the path. As you get closer there are some interest close up shots, especially of the water wheel on the far side. If details are your thing it might be worth coming along on an open day when you can get interior shots (see accessibility below).

What to shoot and viewpoints

Viewpoint 1 – The tide mill ♿

The entrance to the tide mill is on the right, around 250m south along the road from the parking spot. It's then another 150m walk down the lane to the tide mill itself. As you approach along the lane, there are views of the tide mill with the mill pond to one side and the creek beyond; the gravel lane can make a nice curved leading line echoing the curves of the river beyond. Pay attention to the relationship between the mill and the river beyond

Tide mill detail (VP1). Canon 5D IV, 24–70mm at 70mm, ISO 100, 1/25s at f/4, tripod. Mar.

Top: *The view across the creek to All Saints Church (VP2). Canon 5D IV, 24–70mm at 35mm, ISO 100, 1.3s at f/16, tripod. Aug.*

Opposite top: *The tide mill from the lane at sunset (VP1). Canon 5D IV, 24–105mm at 24mm, ISO 100, 2s at f/16, tripod. Oct.*
Bottom: *Thorrington Tide Mill at last light from along the river (VP2). Canon 5D IV, 24–105mm at 32mm, ISO 100, 1/3s at f/16, LEE 0.6 med ND grad, tripod. Oct.*

How to get here

Thorrington Tide Mill is by Alresford Creek, 6 miles south east of Colchester.

Leave the A12 at junction 29 Colchester bypass and take the A120 east towards Harwich. After around 5 miles turn off onto the A133, signposted Clacton and at the roundabout take the second exit for the A133 towards Elmstead Market. At the crossroads turn left onto the B1029 towards Thorrington, follow the road for just over a mile passing over the level crossing. At the mini roundabout take the 2nd exit onto the B1027 and then at the following mini roundabout take the 1st exit onto the B1029. Park in the lay-by, which is on the left on the first bend about half a mile along the road. If you start to go downhill you have missed it.

- **Lat/Long:** 51.83567, 1.02613
- **what3words:** ///life.incisions.spoil
- **Grid Ref:** TM 085 195
- **Postcode:** CO7 8JJ

Nearest Tide Station

Brightlingsea

Accessibility

While the path along the river isn't wheelchair friendly, the lane leading to the tide mill from the road is and it's possible to photograph the mill from there. I should mention there is a bit of a slope to contend with but if you visit when it's open, there is parking available by the mill (visit www.accessable.co.uk/venues/thorrington-tide-mill for more information).

Best time of year/day

When shooting from the river, afternoon or last light is my favourite time of day as, bathed in light, the mill will stand out from the surroundings. Early mornings are still a good time to visit though for the conditions: there's always a chance of mist over the marshes, particularly in spring or autumn and even a frost in the winter.

17 THORRINGTON TIDE MILL

Viewpoint 2 – Along the river

Perhaps the better viewpoints are from along the river, looking back with the tide mill as part of the landscape. Continue on the track past the mill and bear left to take the footpath along the river. The reeds are usually too dense on the first stretch to get close to the water but as soon as the reeds come to an end it's possible to reach the riverbank for views along the creek to the mill. Wellies are a must here and watch your step when walking on the marsh as there are lots of overgrown small creeks and holes that are easy to fall down or trip into.

Even from the first available view of the mill it is a little distant so a standard zoom lens such as a 24–70mm is ideal (rather than a wide-angle lens which may make the mill appear a bit small). High tide is good for reflections on a calm day but it is also good with a lower tide when the curved shape of the creek carved through the mud is clearer.

Carry on along the footpath away from the mill (it's actually only around a mile along the creek to Alresford – see page 144) and just after you cross a small footbridge, as the river starts to curve south towards the church, there are great views back along the river to the mill. From here a telephoto lens such as a 70–200mm or 100–400mm will come into its own.

The impressive church, up on a small hill overlooking the river, makes another good subject so it's worth carrying on along the path a little further. As with the tide mill, look for curves in the river to act as leading lines.

Top: Sunset along the creek (VP2). Canon 5D IV, 24–105mm at 55mm, ISO 100, 1.3s at f/16, LEE 0.9 hardND grad, tripod. Oct.

A distant view of the tide mill at sunset (VP2). Canon 5D IV, 100–400mm at 105mm, ISO 400, 1/60s at f/11, LEE 0.6 hard ND grad, tripod. Mar.

Opposite left: Last light on vines beside the river. DJI Mavic 2 Pro, 28mm, ISO 100, 1/120s at f/8. Aug. **Right**: A drone view along the creek from above the reeds. DJI Mavic 2 Pro, 28mm, ISO 400, 1/60s at f/8. Aug.

18 ALRESFORD CREEK

Alresford Creek is a fairly short and rather muddy tributary of the River Colne but it does manage to pack in a surprising amount of photographic interest as it twists its way the 3km or so through the marshes from Thorrington Tide Mill to join the Colne.

What to shoot and viewpoints

There is plenty to photograph along the creek in an area around 500m in either direction. Every photographer will be attracted to something different so this is definitely a place to explore but these are a few starting points.

Viewpoint 1 – To the east

The first viewpoints are literally a few metres from the car. Carry on walking along the track towards the river and from the shoreline there are good views of the boats in the creek, especially looking west. A range of different focal lengths are effective here; from a wide-angle lens to include one of the small boats on the shoreline in the foreground or a telephoto lens to zoom in and isolate boats in the creek or to make more of the setting sun. At the very end of the track there is a smaller creek on the left – a good place from which to photograph the white cottage back at the edge of the marsh particularly towards sunset, when the last rays will light the building. The creek makes an effective leading line and there is often an assortment of boats scattered on the marsh here for foreground interest.

Just across this smaller creek to the east is the sort of rickety-looking wooden jetty that landscape photographers can't resist. To get to it, head back along the lane and turn right at the public footpath sign into what looks like the driveway to the house. The footpath bears right just before the house and the jetty will be straight ahead. For shots looking along the jetty, try getting down low so the posts break the horizon; if you are too high the shape of the jetty can get a bit lost in the far bank. A low angle may also serve to hide any boats at the end of the jetty.

There are some great areas of marsh to explore to the east just past the house with plenty of interesting little inlets and pools to incorporate into the foreground of shots of boats in the creek or side-on views of the jetty.

Carry on along the path which runs along the sea wall and eventually you'll come to Thorrington Tide Mill (see page 140) a mile or so away but if you don't want to walk quite that far, just 100m or so along the path, as the angle along the creek changes, it leads up towards Brightlingsea church in the distance. This is a good position from which to photograph the view of the creek and distant church with a telephoto lens.

Opposite: The cottage beside the marsh (VP1). Canon 5D II, 24–105mm at 32mm, ISO 100, 1/3s at f/16, tripod. Apr.

Overleaf: Low tide on a winter morning (VP1). Canon 5D IV, 16–35mm at 35mm, ISO 100, 0.4s at f/16, LEE 0.6 med ND grad, tripod. Aug.

Looking along the creek to All Saints Church at sunrise (VP1). Canon 5D IV, 24–70mm at 67mm, ISO 100, 0.8s at f/11, tripod. Mar.

18 ALRESFORD CREEK

Viewpoint 2 – To the west

Returning to the parking spot and heading west along the footpath are the remains of an old landing stage, once used by the nearby quarry to transport sand. This is best photographed from down on the shoreline where, because of the lower position, much of the structure breaks the horizon and stands out against the sky. It also means you can use the grasses and the posts close to the shore in the foreground. At high tide this works well as a long exposure – the smooth water helps to emphasise and contrast with the shape of the jetty. The only issue with a long exposure is that if there are boats in the shot they will probably blur as they move with the tide.

Something else that works best at high tide, when it is surrounded by water, is the old shed by the river on the end of the point around 300m further west. This was the site of a railway bridge that used to cross the river here until it was demolished in the 1960s and you can still see the bridge supports next to the shed. It is possible to walk out to it by following the path west then, as you pass the point, look out for a path on the left and follow it to the end. There isn't much space there though, especially at high tide, so compositions are limited. Perhaps a better view is from the shoreline before you get to the point, where at sunset the shed and the point are nicely silhouetted.

Another sunset view is from the area of marsh just past the point that faces roughly west across the River Colne. There are plenty of interestingly shaped pools and inlets to use as a foreground, which at high tide will be full of calm, reflective water. It's easy to reach – just look out for the path down next to the bench.

Top: A long exposure highlights the shape of the abandoned landing stage (VP2). Canon 5D IV, 16–35mm at 26mm, ISO 100, 30s at f/11, LEE Big Stopper, tripod. Oct.

Middle: Looking west at sunset across the River Colne (VP2). Canon 5D IV, 16–35mm at 20mm, ISO 100, 1/125s at f/16, LEE 0.9 hard ND grad, tripod. Dec.

Bottom: A rusty wreck on the shore of the creek (VP2). Canon 5D IV, 16–35mm at 20mm, ISO 100, 30s at f/11, LEE Big Stopper & 0.6 med ND grad, tripod. Oct.

How to get here

Alresford Creek is just to the south of Alresford, 6 miles south east of Colchester.

Leave the A12 at junction 29 Colchester bypass and take the A120 east towards Harwich. After around 5 miles turn off onto the A133 signposted Clacton and at the roundabout take the second exit for the A133 towards Elmstead Market. At the crossroads turn left onto the B1029 towards Thorrington, follow the road for just over a mile passing over the level crossing. At the mini roundabout take the 2nd exit onto the B1027 and cross the next mini roundabout, stay on this road for just over a mile and turn left at the Alresford village sign onto Wivenhoe Road. After half a mile turn left onto Church Road and follow it all the way to the river and park on the right along the roadside where there is space to do so.

- **Lat/Long**: 51.83789, 0.9937
- **what3words**: ///nerve.confusion.hesitate
- **Grid Ref**: TM 063 197
- **Postcode**: CO7 8BB

Nearest Tide Station

Harwich

Above: A long exposure of the old shed (VP2). Canon 5D IV, 16–35mm at 18mm, ISO 100, 120s at f/11, LEE Big Stopper & 0.9 ND, tripod. Oct.

Accessibility

The longest walk is around 500m but although the ground is flat, the paths are narrow and often muddy so wellies are recommended and options for wheelchair users are limited to the lane that leads down to the shore. Beware though: this lane floods at high tide and can be muddy at times.

It's also worth mentioning that although the road to the creek is called Ford Lane and there is a ford marked on the map, the track is covered by an awful lot of mud so don't even think about fording it!

Best time of year/day

Most of the views here look roughly south so the best times to visit are between autumn and early spring (during the summer months the sun will rise and set behind you). As always, the light will be better at the start or end of the day but with views in several different directions there will be something to shoot whichever end of the day you visit.

Don't forget to check the tide. Most views work whatever the water height but they change quite drastically between tides so I'd recommend visiting at different times. High tide is good for reflections (providing the water is calm) and long exposures of the structures, while at low or mid tide there is more interest in the marshes with channels in the mud and boats scattered in the creek.

19 FINGRINGHOE

A rural village centred around a duck pond on the village green with an old church, traditional pub and even a red phone box, Fingringhoe feels a million miles from the busy sprawl of Colchester which lies only a couple of miles to the north.

The village name, which appears prominently in lists of Britain's rudest place names and is the cause of much sniggering in local playgrounds, comes from its location on a point of land between the River Colne and the Roman River. It is these rivers that are the main attraction for photographers but for lovers of wildlife, just south of the village is Fingringhoe Wick, considered one of Essex's best nature reserves.

What to shoot and viewpoints

Viewpoint 1 – The River Colne

The River Colne and a view of Wivenhoe on the opposite bank are just a few steps from the parking at the end of Ferry Lane. Wivenhoe waterfront is a pretty jumble of boats and pastel cottages with the church tower dominating the skyline. Although the view is obvious, using different focal lengths for a mix of tighter compositions of houses and boats across the river and wider views incorporating the near bank offers variety. And there is plenty of variety in terms of foreground interest for those wider shots in the shape of boats pulled up on the shore, old posts, even patterns in the mud. A mid to high tide is best to avoid too much mud and for reflections in the river.

This isn't a one trick pony though; walk along the sea wall to the left and around the corner and there are views across to Rowhedge and along the Roman River towards Fingringhoe Tide Mill. The latter works well with a telephoto lens to make more of the distant mill. You can't go too far as the wall abruptly ends at a breach. It is also rather overgrown and uneven so walking along the edge of the marsh can be easier going.

The view to Wivenhoe on a misty dawn (VP1). Canon 5D IV, 24–105mm at 28mm, ISO 100, 1.3s at f/16, LEE 0.6 med ND grad, tripod. Oct.

Opposite left: Perfect reflections of Wivenhoe (VP1). Canon 5D IV, 24–105mm at 105mm, ISO 100, 1/13s at f/16, LEE polariser, tripod. Oct. **Right:** The view along the Roman River to Fingringhoe church and mill (VP2). Canon 5D IV, 100–400mm at 100mm, ISO 100, 1/15s at f/11, LEE polariser, tripod. June.

19 FINGRINGHOE

Wildflowers o the marsh (VP2). Canon 5D IV, 24–70mm at 30mm, ISO 100, 1/180s at f/11, LEE 0.9 med ND grad, tripod. June.

Top: The view towards Rowhede on a calm morning (VP2). Canon 5D IV, 24–70mm at 57mm, ISO 100, 1/13s at f/11, LEE 0.6 med ND grad, tripod. June.

Above: The Roman River on a mist morning (VP2). Canon 5D IV, 24–105mm at 65mm, ISO 100, 1/8s at f/16, LEE 0.6 med ND grad, tripod. Oct.

19 FINGRINGHOE

How to get here

Fingringhoe is a village on the River Colne, 5 miles south of Colchester.

From Colchester town centre head south on Military Road. Continue straight on after half a mile, where the road becomes Old Heath Road. After a further mile it becomes Fingringhoe Road. Continue for two miles then, at the crossroads in Fingringhoe, turn left onto Church Road. Around a half a mile further, turn left again onto Ferry Road. Drive to the end of the road and park on the road where it widens.

Viewpoint 1 – The River Colne

- **Lat/Long:** 51.85305, 0.95847
- **what3words:** ///cave.progress.roosters
- **Grid Ref:** TM 038 213
- **Postcode:** CO7 9BU

Viewpoint 3 – The Roman River

- **Lat/Long:** 51.84497, 0.94548
- **what3words:** ///harp.glitz.debate
- **Grid Ref:** TM 029 203
- **Postcode:** CO5 7BN

Nearest Tide Station

Brightlingsea

Accessibility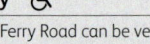

The marsh at Ferry Road can be very muddy and wellies are recommended. It isn't wheelchair friendly but there are views across to Wivenhoe from the lane. The footpath down to the mill, although down a gentle slope, is paved and suitable for wheelchairs.

Best time of year/day

The views across to Wivenhoe are best from autumn to early spring when the village is bathed in the first or last light of the day. Calm early mornings are especially good as there is often a mist hanging over the marsh and river.

The Roman River wo choose your view to suit the time of day (or vice versa). The front of the tide mill will be lit in the afternoon/evening light and the back in the morning.

Top left: The view to Wivenhoe on a misty dawn from Rowhedge (VP2). Canon 5D IV, 24–70mm at 70mm, ISO 100, 1/6s at f/11, LEE 0.6 med ND grad, tripod. June.

Middle left: A misty sunrise on the marshes (VP2). Canon 5D IV, 24–70mm at 57mm, ISO 100, 1/180s at f/11, LEE 0.9 med ND grad, tripod. June.

Opposite: Wivenhoe church reflected in a calm river (VP1). Canon 5D IV, 24–105mm at 55mm, ISO 100, 1/13s at f/16, LEE polariser, tripod. Oct.

Viewpoint 2 – The Roman River

Walk east for around 100m from the church and take the signposted public footpath on the left down to the back of Fingringhoe Tide Mill, where there are views looking along the meandering curves of the Roman River as it carves its way through reedbeds and saltmarsh towards the Colne. High tide tends to smooth out the shape of the river a little so a mid tide works better.

Beyond the mill, the footpath splits. Turn left and walk to the end of the mill's driveway for a good view back along the Roman River to the front of the mill. Continue straight on and it's a pleasant walk of around 1km to Rowhedge with glimpses over the marsh and reedbeds along the way. There are more opportunities around the bend past the new houses where the two rivers meet. From here you can see the Rowhedge waterfront to the left and a different angle of Wivenhoe across the water to the right.

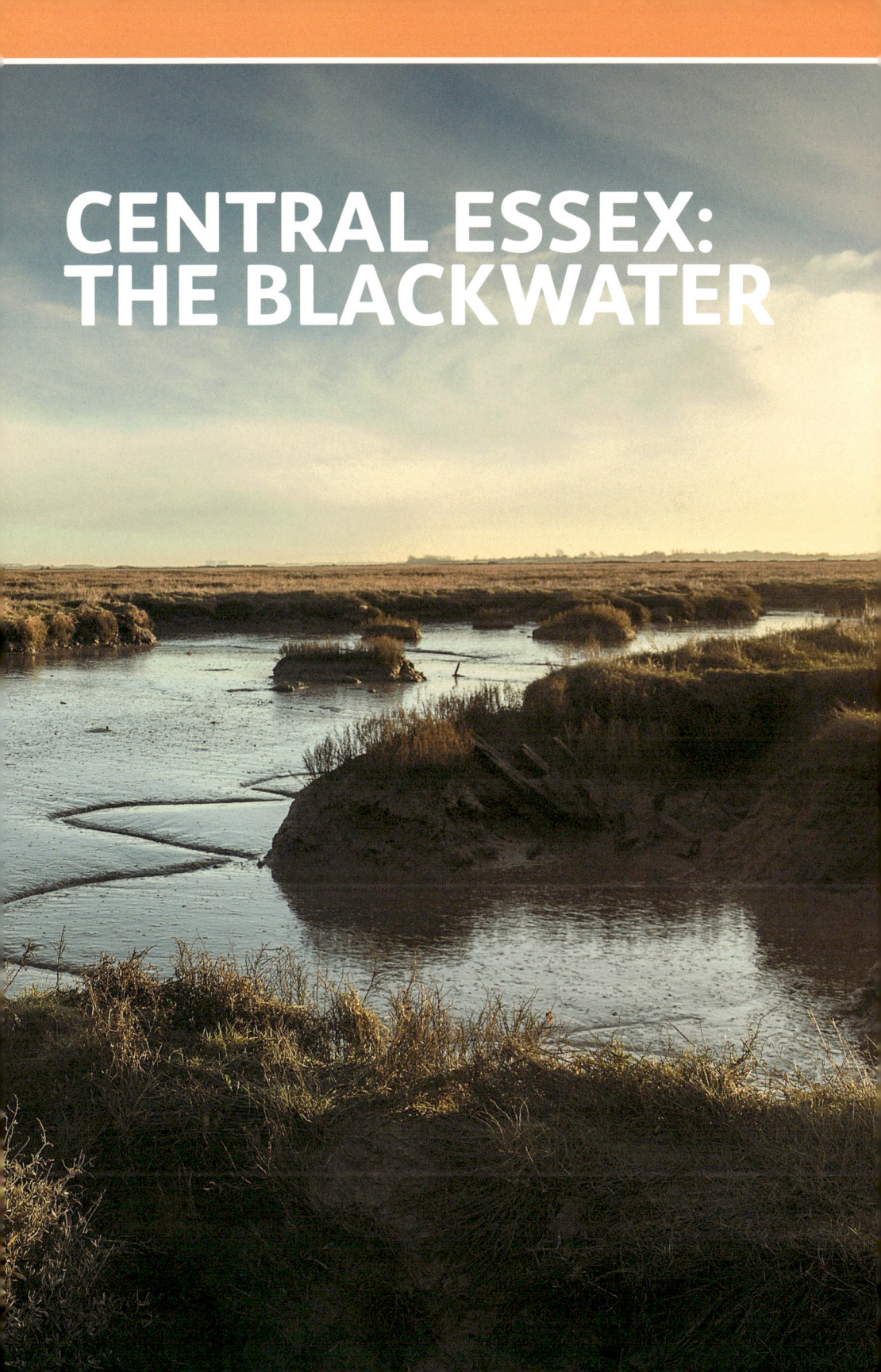

CENTRAL ESSEX: THE BLACKWATER

CENTRAL ESSEX: THE BLACKWATER – INTRODUCTION

Some of the best locations on the Essex coast are to be found in the wide mouth of the Blackwater Estuary as it opens to the North Sea at around the midpoint of the coastline. To the north is Mersea Island, famed for its oysters and on the mainland close by, tucked away in a beautiful area of saltmarsh is Tollesbury. Across the river to the south on the remote tip of the Dengie Peninsular is historic Bradwell.

There is a feeling of remote isolation along the outer reaches of the river apparent at Stansgate and the dead trees at Mundon as well as Bradwell before the estuary returns to the bustle of the 21st century at the charming old town of Maldon. With its abundance of history and old boat wrecks, Maldon along with nearby Heybridge, home of the now iconic Osea beach huts on stilts, are two more classic Essex locations.

Heybridge is also the start of the Chelmer and Blackwater Navigation, which, overhung by trees, winds its way serenely west through a wide peaceful valley to Chelmsford. Along a route dotted with picturesque locks and narrow boats, it also passes the unusual confluence of the tidal and non-tidal rivers Chelmer and Blackwater at Beeleigh Falls.

South of all this is Danbury Common, a large area of heath and woodland along the Danbury Ridge, one of Essex's highest hills.

A misty morning on the Blackwater. Canon 5D IV, 100–400mm at 220mm, ISO 200, 1/30s at f/8, LEE polariser, tripod. Mar.

Previous spread: Old wrecks on Northey Island. Canon 5D II, 24–105mm at 28mm, ISO 100, 1/100s at f/8, LEE 0.6 hard ND grad, tripod. Jan.

Maps

- OS Explorer Map 176 (1:25 000) Blackwater Estuary
- OS Explorer Map 183 (1:25 000) Chelmsford & The Rodings
- OS Explorer Map 184 (1:25 000) Colchester

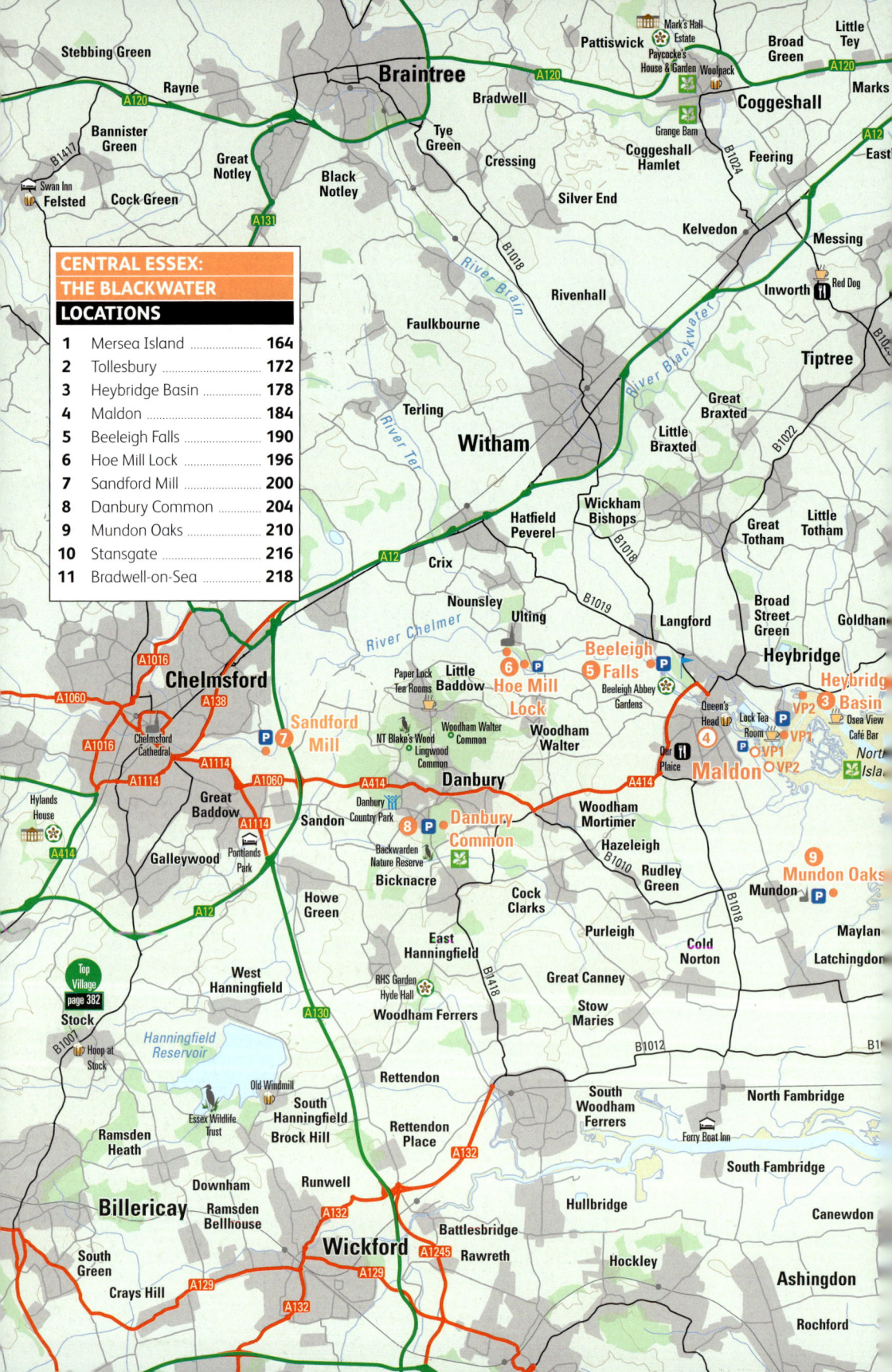

1. MERSEA ISLAND

Situated in the muddy mouth of the Blackwater and Colne river estuaries, Mersea Island is the most easterly inhabited island in the UK. Famous, at least around Essex, for its oysters, the island is a popular destination for lovers of seafood and sailing but tourists have been crossing the causeway to the island ever since the Romans started visiting (from the then-capital city of Colchester a few miles north) nearly 2000 years ago.

Going back even further to a time when the climate was somewhat warmer, the eroding cliffs here have revealed hippopotamus bones, elephant tusks and sharks' teeth dating back 300,000 years.

What to shoot and viewpoints

Mersea Island is divided into east and west, the former being mainly farmland and wild coast, the latter more developed. For photographers, the island is full of interest from sunset views (a rarity on the east coast) across the mudflats, to quirky details like the ramshackle jetties, old oyster beds and rows of brightly painted beach huts. These viewpoints should serve as a starting point; if you would like to explore further, there's a 13-mile footpath around the whole island.

Viewpoint 1 – East Mersea

At Cudmore Grove Country Park on the southern coast of East Mersea, lines of old posts stretch out into the water. These are part of a polder scheme designed to trap sediment, providing somewhere for saltmarsh to grow and hopefully slow down erosion. An additional benefit is that they make an interesting subject for sunrise or long-exposure shots.

To reach the beach here, turn left at the fork after crossing the causeway, signposted East Mersea and follow the road for almost 3 miles before turning left on to Broman's Lane signposted Cudmore Grove. There is a car park at the end of the lane; if you are visiting at sunrise this will probably be closed but there are places to park just outside the gates. To reach the beach, climb the stile and follow the

Polder posts at sunrise (VP1). Canon 5D IV, 16–35mm at 16mm, ISO 100, 8s at f/16, LEE 0.9 hard ND grad, tripod. Feb.

lane on the left, bearing left after around 50 metres on to a track that leads directly to the slope down to the beach. The rows of posts stretch west along the beach from here.

Tide height is key here: low tide reveals hundreds of posts and an awful lot of clay and mud, while high tide covers them completely. Arriving an hour or so after high tide and waiting for the receding water to gradually reveal the posts

is best for simple uncluttered compositions. Wellies are essential here to wade a little closer to the posts for wide-angle shots, but take care where you walk as the clay can be slippery and the mud treacherous.

There are often fallen trees on the beach here, due to cliff erosion. Surrounded by water, these provide some foreground interest for a sunrise or long exposure.

They are usually higher up the beach, so they're perfect to shoot if you arrive too early and the posts are still underwater.

Previous spread: *First light on the marshes at Tollesbury. DJI Mavic 2 Pro, 28mm, ISO 100, 1/40s at f/5.6. July.*

Overleaf: *Sunset on the saltmarsh (VP3). Canon 5D IV, 16–35mm at 16mm, ISO 200, 0.4s at f/22, LEE 0.9 reverse ND grad, tripod. July.*

1 MERSEA ISLAND

How to get here

Mersea is an island, reached by causeway, 7 miles south of Colchester.

Take the B1025, Mersea Road, south from Colchester and follow the road all the way on to Mersea Island. Just after crossing the causeway (the Strood) on to the island, the road forks: turn left for East Mersea and continue right for West Mersea.

Please note: the causeway often (but not always) floods for a short period at high tide, depending on the height of the tide. If visiting for a spring tide, get there well before high tide.

Viewpoint 1 – East Mersea

Lat/Long:	51.79219, 0.99307
what3words:	///centuries.bags.atlas
Grid Ref:	TM 065 146
Postcode:	CO5 8UE

Viewpoint 2 – West Mersea beach huts

Lat/Long:	51.774237, 0.932213
what3words:	///placidly.writings.compounds
Grid Ref:	TM 023 124
Postcode:	CO5 8DE

Viewpoint 3 – West Mersea marina

Lat/Long:	51.779294, 0.898937
what3words:	///headliner.then.gave
Grid Ref:	TM 000 129
Postcode:	CO5 8PB

Nearest Tide Station

West Mersea

Accessibility

Most of the locations on the island are just a short walk along flat and even footpaths from the parking spot. Beaches are generally accessible for wheelchair users who have suitable wheelchairs.

Best time of year/day

The locations around the island face a variety of directions from north west to south east so the best time of year varies. For East Mersea and the beach huts, early mornings from October through to March are the best times to photograph the sun rising over the water or lighting the subject. Sunset is the best time for West Mersea's viewpoints. The island can be busy in the summer but the crowds are largely day-trippers so they thin out in the evening. The most important consideration is the tide: most of the viewpoints here are at their best at or near high tide.

Above: Mersea beach huts in the snow (VP2). Canon 5D IV, 24–70mm at 35mm, ISO 100, 1/200s at f/8, tripod. Feb.

Opposite top: Boats scattered on the beach edge from above (VP3). DJI Mavic 2 Pro, 28mm, ISO 100, 1/40s at f/5.6. Apr.
Middle: Beach hut detail (VP2). Canon 5D IV, 24–105mm at 45mm, ISO 100, 1/180s at f/8, tripod. Aug. ***Bottom:*** *Summer sunset from the beach at West Mersea (VP3). Canon 5D IV, 16–35mm at 19mm, ISO 100, 1/15s at f/22, LEE 0.9 hard ND grad, tripod. July.*

Viewpoint 2 – West Mersea beach huts

There are several viewpoints on the west of the island, reached from a couple of car parks along a 2–3 mile stretch of coast.

To reach the first West Mersea car park, take the right hand fork after the causeway, towards West Mersea, then after around 1 mile turn left on to East Road, signposted East Mersea. After almost half a mile, turn right on to Seaview Avenue and park in the car park at the end of the road on the right.

Lining the beach across the road is a row of rather fancy beach huts, painted in an assortment of pastel shades. Both wide-angle and telephoto shots work well here; the former to exaggerate the perspective of the receding beach huts and the latter to compress the line of huts, thus emphasising their number

During the summer months, the sun will rise behind the huts, while in winter it will rise out to sea and light the fronts of them. Possibly the best times of year are around March and September, when the sun will rise at the end of the huts. Check the sun position compass or an app such as SunCalc for exact timings.

1 MERSEA ISLAND

Sunset at West Mersea (VP3). Canon 5D IV, 16–35mm at 16mm, ISO 100, 0.6s at f/16, LEE 0.9 hard ND grad, tripod. July.

Viewpoint 3 – West Mersea marina

To reach the second West Mersea car park, take the right-hand fork after the causeway, towards West Mersea. Follow that road as it becomes the High Street and then the Coast Road. The car park is just under 2.5 miles along the road on the left, just before the large jetty.

This stretch of waterfront is packed in both directions with boats old and new and all the paraphernalia that comes with pleasure and fishing craft. As such, it's a great place to explore, camera in hand, looking out for interesting details. A couple of places in particular are worth seeking out. The first is a ramshackle jetty, a few minutes walk to the north of the car park. Follow the Coast Road to the end then take the path around the back of the sailing club and along the shore where you will see the jetty stretching out over the saltmarsh. This is best shot either around high tide when it is surrounded (for a short period) by water. This wooden jetty consists of a patchwork of repairs and is well suited to long exposures – the simplified water highlighting

the textures of the wood – but take care when walking here as it's uneven and slippery when wet. Late spring/summer is a good time to visit when the sun sets at the end of the jetty. Around the next corner of the path are more of the polders. These ones, stretching north west into the causeway, (known as the Strood) are perfect for sunset shots.

Walk along the Coast Road in the other direction, past the boatyards and the houseboats moored on the saltmarsh at the end of long jetties, and a wooden boardwalk stretches out over the marsh to a sandy point. Littered with small boats that serve as foreground interest for views over the river, this is a great sunset spot throughout the year or for sunrise during the winter months.

Top: Sunset along the river (VP3). Canon R5, 70–200mm at 113mm, ISO 100, 1/3s at f/16, LEE 0.9 hard ND grad, tripod. Apr.

Above: Sunset at the end of the jetty (VP3). Canon 5D IV, 16–35mm at 18mm, ISO 800, 1/8s at f/16, LEE 0.6 hard ND grad, tripod. July.

2 TOLLESBURY

Mentioned in the Domesday Book of 1086, Tollesbury sits by a pretty creek close to the mouth of the River Blackwater estuary. The name is believed to mean 'The place where toll was paid by ships coming up this bay', which most likely dates back to a toll charged here by the Romans. Today, the river still brings money to the village but from its oysters and the popularity of sailing in the area, demonstrated by a marina full of shiny yachts.

Far more interesting to photographers than Tollesbury's marina, is the maze of small inlets cutting through the saltmarsh flanking the creek that winds it's way out to the Blackwater estuary. A network of paths and boardwalks leads across the marsh to rickety wooden jetties, where a variety of boats are moored. Dominating the view is the Trinity, an out of service lightship that has been permanently anchored here and used as a centre for outdoor activities since the 1990s.

What to shoot and viewpoints

Viewpoint 1 – Sail lofts and old buildings ♿
The row of distinctive wooden buildings that greet you as you walk east from the car park towards the quay, are known as the sail lofts. These have been recently restored but although not quite as photogenic now, they have retained their charm and make an attractive subject, especially looking along the road towards the rather more weathered structure at the end.

The lofts are raised from the ground on short legs and being only a few metres from the water's edge, it's not difficult to guess why. Turn up at high tide and there's a good chance the lofts will be neatly reflected in the flooded road.

Viewpoint 2 – Boats on the saltmarsh ♿
The marsh here is a fascinating place to explore, changing drastically between high and low tide and with enough creeks, jetties and boats to keep you busy for days. On the subject of tides, parts of the marsh will flood at high tide

The sail lofts at dawn (VP1). Canon 5D IV, 24–105mm at 24mm, ISO 200, 30s at f/11, tripod. July.

so make sure you check tide times and go when the tide is going out to avoid being stranded.

There are several paths on to the marsh but the main one to mention is the one leading to the lightship. Walk down the road from the car park and, with the sail lofts on your left, cut between the first and second sail loft – the path is straight ahead. As it branches off to the right there are good views of the lightship with meandering creeks and old posts in the foreground. There are plenty of old wooden jetties and interesting boats to photograph on the saltmarsh but pay attention to the signs as some of the paths are private.

The other side of the creek is rather less 'maintained' and doesn't have the same restrictions, leaving you free to explore. The paths need a little care as they can be muddy and slippery with plenty of old posts lurking amongst the vegetation to trip over. To access this side of the creek, climb up on to the raised path facing the sail lofts (there are steps behind the old wooden boat shed), then follow the path south, past the restaurant and marina to the marsh. There are several paths down on to the marsh, all of which are worth exploring but the path opposite the lightship leads out to an old wreck with great views down the river and it's a good place to start.

Opposite: The lightship at sunrise (VP2). Canon 5D IV, 16–35mm at 19mm, ISO 100, 1.3s at f/22, LEE 0.9 hard ND grad, tripod. July.

2 TOLLESBURY

Viewpoint 3 – Dead trees

To the north east of the quay, in an area of marsh, stands a row of dead trees. Presumably this marsh was once fields, until a breach in the old sea wall turned it into wetland. The result is that at high tide these trees are, rather photogenically, surrounded by water.

As is often the case with unusual places like this, the trees work well in mono. Similarly, using a long exposure to blur the water and clouds highlights the unusual nature of the scene. As well as the dead trees, there is a larger, single tree around 100m along the sea wall but for all these shots, timing is everything; the water recedes quickly after high tide and the effect is soon lost so aim to arrive before high tide to avoid missing high water.

It is possible to walk to the dead trees from the quay – the footpath is just north of the sail lofts and is around 1.5km along the sea wall. If time (or energy) is short then park at the end of Station Road and walk the 600m down the track to the sea wall instead. If you decide to walk along the sea wall there is a lovely area of saltmarsh, devoid of boats or any human interference except for the odd plank bridge spanning one of the capillary-like network of creeks. These bridges make excellent focal points but take care if crossing them and observe the warning signs. And don't wander on to the marsh on a rising tide unless you are sure of the tide height.

Previous spread: *The saltmarsh from the air (VP3). DJI Mavic 2 Pro 28mm, ISO 100, 1/40s at f/5.6. July.*

How to get here

Tollesbury is on the Essex coast, 6.5 miles south east of Tiptree.

Take the B1023 south from Tiptree, following the road for about 3 miles into Tolleshunt D'Arcy. At the triangle junction in the village centre, turn right on to the B1026 then take the next left on to the B1023 Tollesbury Road. Follow that road for around 2.5 miles, all the way into the village centre, then turn left on to Woodrolfe Road, signposted Tollesbury Marina. After around quarter of a mile you'll find a free car park on the left.

Viewpoint 1 & 2 – Quay & saltmarsh

- **Lat/Long**: 51.759934, 0.843575
- **what3words**: ///treetop.grid.brass
- **Grid Ref**: TL 963 106
- **Postcode**: CM9 8RY

Viewpoint 3 – Dead trees

- **Lat/Long**: 51.761924, 0.833775
- **what3words**: ///clustered.surfed.used
- **Grid Ref**: TL 957 114
- **Postcode**: CM9 8RR

Nearest Tide Station

Bradwell Waterside

Accessibility ♿

None of the viewpoints is more than around a 10–15 minute walk from the car but most of the paths are uneven and muddy, particularly on the marsh where the tide covers them. The main path out towards the lightship however is flat and wheelchair friendly.

Best time of year/day

With such a variety of things to photograph, there's never a bad time to visit Tollesbury, except perhaps during the summer peak season, when it will inevitably be busy during the day. There are views of the boats on the saltmarsh in all directions so there are always options, wherever the light is coming from. Likewise, the dead trees can be shot from different angles, either towards the light at sunrise or sidelit in the afternoon. The only place that is less flexible time-wise is the sail lofts, which are best shot in the afternoon or evening when the light will be on them.

Tollesbury is very muddy at low tide so a mid to high tide is best, parts of the marsh will start to flood with high tides of over around 4.6m (Bradwell Waterside tide station).

*Opposite top: The dead trees at sunrise (VP3). Canon 5D IV, 24–105mm at 24mm, ISO 100, 1.3s at f/16, LEE 0.9 hard ND grad, tripod. Aug. **Left**: A plank bridge across the saltmarsh (VP3). Canon 5D IV, 16–35mm at 16mm, ISO 100, 0.6s at f/22, LEE 0.9 hard ND grad, tripod. July. **Right**: Low tide at Tollesbury (VP1). Canon 5D IV, 24–105mm at 24mm, ISO 100, 1s at f/11, LEE 0.9 hard ND grad, tripod. Mar.*

Top: The old granary at high tide (VP2). Canon 5D IV, 16–35mm at 24mm, ISO 100, 25s at f/11, LEE Little Stopper, tripod. July.

Above: One of many photogenic boats in the creeks (VP2). Canon 5D IV, 16–35mm at 16mm, ISO 100, 1/500s at f/11, tripod. July.

3 HEYBRIDGE BASIN

Heybridge Basin is a village that has grown around the entrance to the Chelmer & Blackwater Navigation on the northern bank of the Blackwater Estuary. The 'basin' refers to a wider area of water at the start of the canal where large boats can be moored and turned. Built in the 18th century, the canal stopped being used commercially in the 1970s but these days it is still busy, though now with pleasure craft.

What to shoot and viewpoints

Most photographers are drawn to the distinctive line of beach huts raised up over the beach but there's a lot more to point a camera at along the 3.5 kms of shoreline, especially as you have to pass most of it on the walk around the sea wall to reach the huts.

Viewpoint 1 – Around the Basin

At the far corner of the car park is a path through to the canal. Turn left and walk 200m or so along the bank to meet the footpath that runs along the seawall around the Blackwater. If boats are your thing, you might want to pause here as the canal is usually packed with all manner of craft to photograph.

To head south, use the wooden boardwalk that runs along the lock gates to cross the canal. This stretch of river is a great place to shoot the sunrise and there is abundant subject matter in the jetties, wrecks and boats spread out along the water's edge. Some jetties are private however so please observe any signs. »

Boats around the Basin (VP1). Canon 5D IV, 24–70mm at 70mm, ISO 100, 10s at f/8, tripod. Aug.

How to get here

Heybridge is a village on the Blackwater Estuary, 10 miles east of Chelmsford.

From the A12 at Chelmsford (junction 18), take the A414 east towards Maldon. Follow the A414 for 6 miles to Maldon, then at the Morrison's roundabout take the 1st exit to stay on the A414 north around Maldon. Follow the A414 for almost two miles and then at the roundabout take the first exit onto the B1018 towards Heybridge. At the next roundabout take the 2nd exit onto the B1022, signposted Colchester and then the 2nd exit at the following roundabout onto the B1026 signposted Heybridge Basin. After three quarters of a mile, for the Heybridge Basin parking, turn right onto Basin Road, follow the road into the village and park in Daisy Meadow free car park on the right. The entrance to the car park is on a left hand bend and is a little hard to see. If you get to the Jolly Sailor pub you've missed it – turn around and it's on the next corner.

- **Lat/Long:** 51.72945, 0.70652
- **what3words:** ///knees.royally.hazel
- **Grid Ref:** TL 870 068
- **Postcode:** CM9 4RW

Top: Boats along the canal (VP1). Canon 5D IV, 24–70mm at 28mm, ISO 140, 1/10s at f/16, LEE polariser, tripod. Aug.

Opposite: Sunrise on a calm morning (VP1). Canon 5D IV, 16–35mm at 21mm, ISO 200, 2s at f/8, LEE 0.9 hard ND grad, tripod. Aug.

Nearest Tide Station

Osea Island

Accessibility

It is a 2.5km walk around to the beach huts from the parking. The paths are generally flat and mainly paved so wheelchair access is good with a few exceptions: the boardwalk across the lock gates is narrow, the first section of the path heading north from the lock is flanked on the river side by a concrete wall and the section between the two sailing clubs is uneven and narrow in places.

Best time of year/day

With one viewpoint facing roughly south and the other east, there will always be something to photograph here at any time. You can catch the sunrise or sunset from the Mill Beach viewpoints from late autumn to early spring or catching the first and last light at just about any time. The basin viewpoints on the other hand are better at sunrise all year.

At low tide there is a lot of mud on display so a calm high tide or mid tide, when there is a variety of textures, is my preference here. To catch the beach huts surrounded by a lot of water tide height is more important. Look for tides of around 6m or above (Osea Island tide station). The water surrounds the huts at tide heights lower than 6m but not for long. Barring freak weather, these highest tides only happen during the spring and autumn months.

3 HEYBRIDGE BASIN

A good place to start is right there at the entrance to the lock, where the view across to the sheds and moored boats works equally well with a nice calm, reflective high tide or just a channel of water cutting through the mud at low tide. Use a wide-angle lens and either include the open gates as leading lines or just make the most of the reflections.

The first 400m or so is probably the best; beyond that, as the path bends around to the right, although still a nice walk, there is less to photograph unless you carry on for some distance towards Heybridge, where you'll find views across the river to Maldon.

Heading north, the seawall passes another glorious nautical jumble before opening out to clearer views across the estuary on its way towards the Blackwater Sailing Club and the second viewpoint. A 70–200mm lens is useful here

Top: A long exposure of the beach huts on a spring high tide (VP2). Canon 5D IV, 16–35mm at 24mm, ISO 100, 120s at f/22, LEE Big Stopper, tripod. Mar.

Above: Chalets towards Mill Beach at first light (VP2). Canon 5D IV, 24–105mm at 47mm, ISO 100, 1/5s at f/16, LEE 0.6 med ND grad, tripod. Dec.

for picking out compositions amongst the old boats and jetties and for shots of boats out in the estuary. The longer focal length will compress the distance making the boats appear closer together.

Viewpoint 2 – Around Mill Beach ♿

Continue along the path from Blackwater Sailing Club as it loops lazily around towards Salcote Sailing Club. Just beyond this is a row of old huts. In contrast to the neat, modern and far more celebrated huts a kilometre or so further along the beach, these are a mismatched, ramshackle row of chalets but no less attractive to photograph in my opinion.

The star attraction on this side of the river though is the line of beach huts raised on stilts, which look out across the river from the water's edge. They photograph well in the early or late light but the classic shot is when they are surrounded by water at high tides; they make a wonderful subject for long exposures. Apart from at the highest spring tides, the tide turns quickly leaving only a small window to photograph them in the water. Plan your visit carefully and arrive in plenty of time to make the most of the opportunity. Try isolating a single hut or group of three, or look along the line from either end to see them receding into the distance. Shooting from down on the beach gives a slightly different look to shooting from the sea wall so take your wellies and experiment with both.

Continue along the path to the west and there are views across to Osea Island.

4 MALDON

If you have more than a passing interest in cuisine then you will probably be familiar with the ancient town of Maldon for its world-famous sea salt.

The dry climate makes the water in the shallow tidal creeks of the Blackwater Estuary particularly saline and with an abundance of these creeks, this corner of Essex is the perfect place for harvesting salt from the sea. Indeed, it has been produced here in the same way, by evaporating sea water, for thousands of years.

There's more to Maldon's history than condiments though. Just to the east of the town is the site of the Battle of Maldon – the oldest battlefield in England, in fact – where in 991 Saxons defended the town from Viking raiders. The Saxons lost the hard-fought battle but at such a cost to the Vikings that they left without completing their raid.

What to shoot and viewpoints

Viewpoint 1 – The promenade ♿
There is plenty of interest for photographers all along the length of the promenade. To get there walk along the tree-lined lane to the south of the car park and after around 250m it opens out with kiosks on the right and a lake to the left with the river and promenade straight ahead.

The classic view of Maldon is from along the promenade here; head east a little and the sweeping curve of the river leads nicely to the quay with the church above. The tide height makes a big difference here: too high a tide and the curve gets a bit too wide; too low and the reflections get lost – somewhere in between is just right. The promenade is a convenient place to shoot from and the height helps show the curve of the river but for something different try getting down to the shoreline and using the grasses or boats for foreground interest. Be sure to wear wellies, especially if the tide is higher and tread carefully on the mud. »

The view of Maldon from the promenade on a misty morning (VP1). Canon 5D IV, 24–70mm at 50mm, ISO 100, 1/60s at f/11, tripod. Nov.

Black-tailed godwits on the Blackwater (VP2). Canon R5, 500mm + 1.4 converter at 700mm, ISO 3200, 1/1600s at f/5.6. Mar.

How to get here

Maldon is a small town on the confluence of the River Chelmer and Blackwater Estuary, 8 miles east of Chelmsford.

From the A12 at Chelmsford (junction 18), take the A414 east towards Maldon. Follow the A414 for 6 miles to Maldon, then at the Morrisons roundabout take the 3rd exit onto the B1018 and continue on this road for just over a mile, crossing two roundabouts. The road becomes Park Drive after the 2nd roundabout, continue to the end of Park Drive, turn right and there is a pay & display car park immediately on the right before the no entry signs.

- **Lat/Long:** 51.725, 0.69288
- **what3words:** ///tactical.caressed.braved
- **Grid Ref:** TL 860 063
- **Postcode:** CM9 5UR

Nearest Tide Station
Osea Island

Previous spread: *The statue of Byrhtnoth through the mist at sunrise (VP1). Canon 5D IV, 70–200mm at 98mm, ISO 100, 1/8s at f/16, LEE 0.6 med ND grad, tripod. Nov.*

Accessibility

Promenade Park, where all of the first viewpoints are located, is completely wheelchair accessible. The barge graveyard can be photographed from the lane above but this may be muddy at certain times of year. There are toilets, including disabled toilets and refreshment kiosks in the park.

If you are going to shoot from the shoreline anywhere here you will need wellies as it is very muddy.

Best time of year/day

There's something here all year. The barge graveyard faces east so sunrise is good all year round; an early afternoon visit will be necessary to catch the highest tides. Similarly, the statue of Byrhtnoth is best at sunrise but it faces south east so September to March are best. Tide isn't too important here but calm water will reflect the colours of the sunrise and so low tide is best avoided. The view of the quay from the promenade looks north west so you could shoot it with the sun setting behind the town during the summer months. I prefer it however at sunrise any time of year with the first light hitting the quay, or the hint of dawn colour that often appears in the sky opposite the sunrise. Another bonus is that the park will be quieter early in the morning.

4 MALDON

At the very eastern end of the promenade, looking across towards Northey Island, stands a statue of Byrhtnoth, hero of the battle of Maldon. With sword raised, the statue looks particularly good silhouetted at sunrise but there are benches all along the promenade here so choose your position carefully to hide them.

Getting quite close works well so you are looking up a little at it but it also looks good from further back. If you walk along the path between the boating lake and the river you can shoot across the marsh towards the distant statue.

Of course, if sword-wielding Saxons aren't your thing, the end of the promenade is also a good spot from which to photograph the sunrise across the river. It looks wonderful on a calm misty morning.

Back towards the town at the opposite end of the promenade is Hythe Quay, where you can photograph up close the Thames sailing barges. In the past, they would have transported cargo to and from London.

Viewpoint 2 – The barge graveyard

Hidden away on the eastern side of Promenade Park is the final resting place of several old sailing barges. Having come to the end of their useful life, they've been left to the elements to rot – just the sort of subject to interest photographers.

The 'barge graveyard' as it is known is just a short walk from the promenade. Walk along the prom towards the statue and turn right at the boating lake. Cut through the car park and walk south straight across the field to the viewing platform and the track just beyond it. Cut across the verge and it's a slight scramble down to the shoreline. If you don't feel up to that, shoot from the top of the bank.

The obvious subject here is the one boat that is still relatively intact and from the shoreline you will be fairly close to it so a wide-angle lens works well. The challenge is excluding all of the bits of decaying boat you might not want in your composition so the longer end of that wide-angle lens is often more effective.

The problem is solved at very high tides (above 5m) when virtually everything bar the main boat disappears beneath the water. This is a great time for minimal long exposures or, on calm days, reflection shots. At lower tides, the decaying remains of the boat in front of the main boat provide useful foreground interest, as do the grasses covering the marsh.

For the close-up lovers amongst you, bring a longer lens too for some interesting, textured detail shots amongst the wrecks.

It's also worth exploring the footpath to the south of the wrecks, which stretches along the marshes to the Northey Island causeway and beyond where there are some good sunrise views across the saltmarsh. Access to Northey Island is limited (see page 408).

Local colour

Annual events provide further photographic opportunities at Maldon. If sailing is your thing, every June there is an opportunity to photograph up to a dozen Thames sailing barges racing from Maldon along the Blackwater Estuary.

Somewhat quirkier and typically British is the Maldon Mud Race – a charity event in which 300 participants, run, wade and slither their way the 400 yards across the very muddy river and back at low tide. A feat apparently harder than it sounds, especially as many are in fancy dress! It's a great opportunity for colourful photography but the event attracts thousands of spectators so arrive early to claim a good spot.

Previous spread: Sunrise at the barge graveyard (VP2). Canon 5D IV, 16–35mm at 21mm, ISO 100, 10s at f/11, LEE 0.9 hard ND grad, tripod. Nov.

Opposite top left: The statue of Byrhtnoth under the stars (VP1). Canon 5D IV, 16–35mm at 16mm, ISO 3200, 20s at f/4, tripod. Apr. *Top right*: Thames barges at Hythe Quay on a misty morning (VP1). Canon 5D IV, 70–200mm at 70mm, ISO 200, 1/50s at f/8, tripod. Nov. *Bottom*: Wrecks at the barge graveyard at high tide (VP2). Canon 5D IV, 24–70mm at 38mm, ISO 100, 30s at f/11, LEE Big Stopper, tripod. Feb.

5 BEELEIGH FALLS

Just before reaching Maldon and heading onwards to the sea, the rivers Chelmer and Blackwater meet in an elaborate arrangement of falls, locks and weirs know as Beeleigh Falls.

The weir is designed to keep the water level of the freshwater Chelmer and Blackwater navigation canal constant in times of high water, when the flood waters cascade down to meet the tidal River Chelmer below. The purpose of some of the other falls isn't quite so apparent but they all provide an abundance of attractive rushing water that has photographers reaching for their ND filters.

What to shoot and viewpoints

Viewpoint 1 – The Chelmer and Blackwater Navigation ♿

The first viewpoint is just beyond the car park from the small hump-backed bridge. The Chelmer and Blackwater Navigation is the river flowing beneath it and there are views along its tree-lined length to the south east from atop the bridge. A wide-angle lens allows for the flood gates in front and the sun rising over the fields to be included. It is also worth walking the 650m along the canal to the next bridge, which doubles as an attractive focal point and an alternative vantage point.

Another view of the canal is in the opposite direction from the hump-backed bridge. Walk over the footbridge across the weir to the lock gates and then across the footbridge and through the gate to the other bank. From this position you can look back south east along the river towards the bridge and even use the gate as foreground interest. Again it is a pleasant walk north west along the river from here.

Top: Beeleigh Falls in autumn (VP2). Canon 5D IV, 24–70mm at 24mm, ISO 100, 25s at f/16, LEE Big Stopper, tripod. Nov.

Detail of the falls beneath the bridge (VP2). Canon 5D IV, 24–70mm at 70mm, ISO 100, 30s at f/16, LEE Big Stopper, tripod. Nov.

How to get here

Beeleigh Falls are on the River Chelmer and Blackwater, 3 miles west of Maldon.

Take the A414 north from Maldon and at the roundabout turn left onto the B1018 Heybridge Approach Road, signposted Colchester A12. At the next roundabout take the first left onto the B1019, follow the road for just over half a mile, past the church on the right, then take the next turning on the left along the single track road signposted Maldon Golf Club. If the gate is open go through and park in the small car park just before the bridge; if it's locked park by the side of the road and walk (the car park is around 700m).

Lat/Long:	51.74396, 0.66404
what3words:	///roughness.polishing.painted
Grid Ref:	TL 840 083
Postcode:	CM9 6LL

Nearest Tide Station

Osea Island

Accessibility

There isn't very much walking needed here and the main paths are wheelchair friendly, especially along the Chelmer and Blackwater Navigation. The paths to get closer to the falls and weir aren't wheelchair friendly and both caution and wellies are advised at those spots. It can get very muddy and slippery.

Best time of year/day

Mornings are probably the best time of day as the sunrise will be visible along the river followed by the first light shining across the falls. Spring and autumn when the trees are fresh green or golden brown are attractive times of year. You're also more likely to get misty mornings, which aren't uncommon here. Tide is also a consideration: low tide will be very muddy while high tide almost covers the falls so somewhere in the middle is preferable.

5 BEELEIGH FALLS

Viewpoint 2 – The Weir
Before crossing the aforementioned footbridge over the weir, take the path on the left into the trees and almost immediately take the path on the right, which leads down to the river bank next to the weir. From here, depending on the tide, it is possible to get close enough to the side of the weir for a dramatic wide-angle view of the rushing water. A mid tide is ideal when the water is high enough to cover the rocks below the weir but low enough not to restrict access. Viewpoints 2 and 3 are perfect for experimenting with different shutter speeds to create different blurring effects on the water using different strength ND filters. An exposure of something like 1 or 2 seconds should be enough to add a silky look to the water, which will get progressively smoother with slower shutter speeds.

Viewpoint 3 – The Falls
Cross the footbridge over the weir and the falls are visible across the reeds to the south west, there are also views along the River Chelmer to the south east from here. The falls are reached via the small path on the left shortly before the lock gates. Follow it for about 100m until you see the falls in front of you then leave the path to get to the shore.

It's worth mentioning that if you're expecting to hear the rumble of water and feel the spray of mist from water plunging down a rock face you may be disappointed; these falls are a series of low, manmade shelves. Get as close to the falls as safely possible for dramatic shots but take care as it can be slippery and uneven. As with the weir, the tide needs to be high enough to conceal rocks around the bottom of the falls but not so high as to reduce the height of the falls themselves or worse, submerge the shoreline you need to stand on.

If you head back to the footpath and proceed along it, there are further views of the falls below the footbridge. Cross the bridge and it's a 1km walk to Beeleigh Abbey.

Top: The canal is atmospheric on a misty morning (VP1). Canon 5D IV, 70–200mm at 200mm, ISO 100, 1/5s at f/16, tripod, May.

Middle: A long exposure of the weir (VP2). Canon 5D IV, 24–70mm at 24mm, ISO 100, 8s at f/16, LEE Big Stopper, tripod, Feb.

Bottom: A misty sunrise at Beeleigh Falls (VP2). Canon 5D IV, 70–200mm at 122mm, ISO 100, 1/180s at f/16, tripod, Nov.

Above: Looking along the canal at sunrise (VP1). Canon 5D IV, 24–70mm at 24mm, ISO 100, 1.3s at f/16, LEE 0.9 med ND grad, tripod, May.
Below: The view from the lock gates (VP1). Canon 5D IV, 24–70mm at 50mm, ISO 100, 4s at f/16, LEE 0.9 med ND grad, tripod, May.

A glorious sunrise at Hoe Mill Lock (VP1). Canon 5D IV, 24–70mm at 35mm, ISO 200, 1/2s at f/11, LEE 0.9 med ND grad, tripod, Dec.

6 HOE MILL LOCK

Named after the nearby water mill (demolished over 100 years ago), Hoe Mill Lock is one of twelve locks spread along the Chelmer and Blackwater Navigation, a 14-mile river canal that connects Springfield Basin in Chelmsford to the sea lock at Heybridge Basin near Maldon.

The waterway runs through a beautiful part of the Essex countryside and Hoe Mill Lock is one of several particularly photogenic places along the public footpath running its entire length.

What to shoot and viewpoints

Viewpoint 1 – The lock and river

To join the public footpath that runs along the river, cross the road from the parking, walk back over the bridge and through the kissing gate.

There are numerous views to photograph here, starting with the classic view looking along the river from the side of the lock itself. It is a bit 'busy' here with buildings, picnic tables and so on by the river so compose your image carefully and pay extra attention to the edges of the frame for distractions. Late spring to early autumn is probably the best time for this shot when the thicker vegetation will hide more of those distractions.

As you wander along the river, you'll see a variety of boats, some more attractive than others, moored along the opposite bank usually all the way until the footbridge. The position of these boats and thus the best spots to photograph may change over time so I'll leave it up to you to find them. My favourite section is towards the footbridge where there are fewer boats and, as it follows the curve of the river, the path and over-hanging trees make a good leading line.

Another favourite spot is from the reeds on the other side of the footbridge, where there's a different angle looking across or along the river at the boats.

Either a standard zoom or wide-angle lens, depending on your preference, will probably be all you need here but I'd bring something longer, like a 100–400mm for detail shots of boats or a possible wildlife encounter.

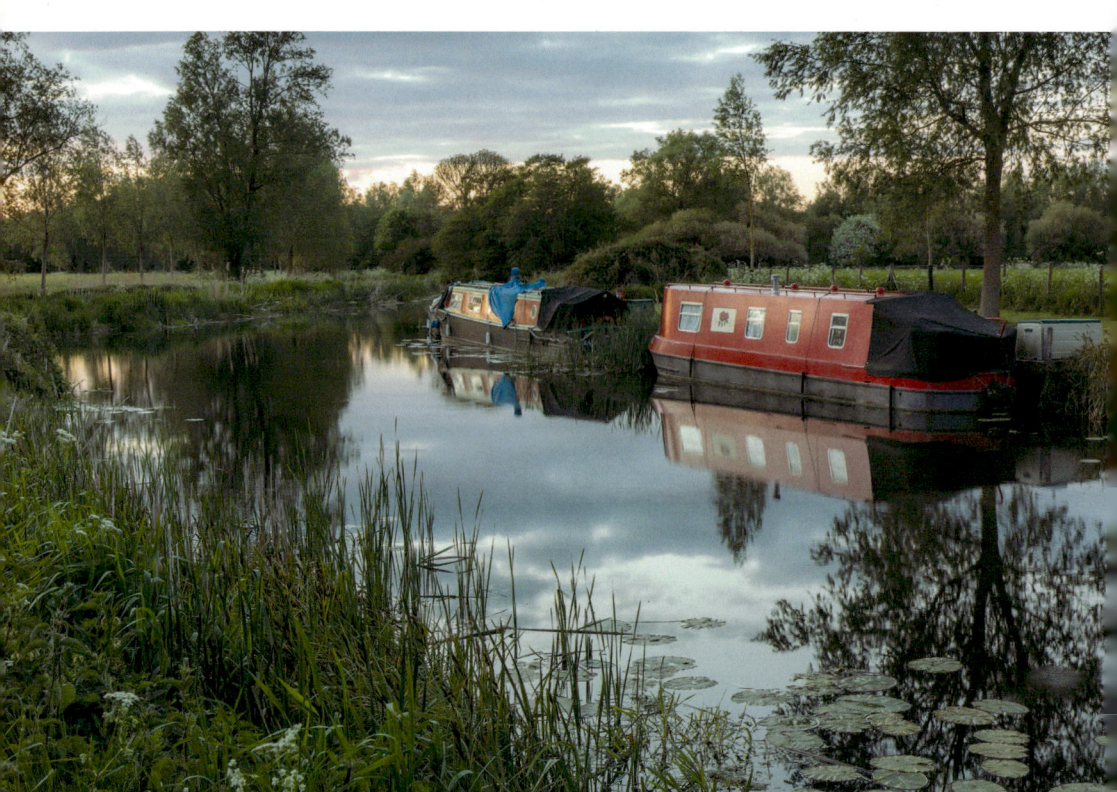

How to get here

Hoe Mill Lock is on the River Chelmer, 5.5 miles east of Chelmsford.

From the A12 at Chelmsford (junction 18), take the A414 east towards Maldon. Follow the A414 for just over 3 miles through Danbury then turn left onto Herbage Road (signposted Woodham Walter). Follow the road for almost 2.5 miles, passing through the village of Woodham Walter until eventually the road crosses the River Chelmer at Hoe Mill Lock. Park in the lay-by on the right immediately after the bridge or if that's full, on the road where it's safe to do so.

	Lat/Long:	51.74382, 0.61728
	what3words:	///onwards.headlight.searched
	Grid Ref:	TL 807 082
	Postcode:	CM9 6RA

Accessibility

The kissing gate entrance is too small for wheelchairs but there is a locked gate a few metres further along which can be used by arrangement with the campsite. The path is flat and firm along the first stretch of the riverbank and the footbridge has a ramp rather than steps so is wheelchair friendly but beyond that the path becomes a bit more narrow and uneven.

Best time of year/day

I enjoy photographing Hoe Mill Lock all year round and early mornings are always a good time to visit. If the weather is calm there will be deep reflections in the water and a chance of mist hanging over the water and fields. The position of this stretch of the river means it is never a particularly good place to see the sun rise or set but from mid autumn to mid spring you will be able to see any sunrise colours. Summer evenings are a little busier but they are a good time to shoot the church in warm side light. The banks look best at this time of year too as they're lush with vegetation but it makes it harder to get close enough to the river for reflections.

Top: Autumn by the river (VP1). Canon 5D IV, 24–70mm at 50mm, ISO 100, 1/5s at f/11, LEE 0.6 med ND grad, tripod, Dec.

Above left: Mist and reeds at dawn (VP1). Canon 5D IV, 24–105mm at 105mm, ISO 200, 4s at f/11, tripod, Apr. *Right*: Cow parsley and canal boats (VP1). Canon 5D IV, 24–105mm at 45mm, ISO 200, 1/8s at f/11, tripod, May.

Opposite: A calm spring morning (VP1). Canon 5D IV, 24–70mm at 45mm, ISO 200, 1/2s at f/16, tripod, May.

6 HOE MILL LOCK

Top: Rushes lock from the air (VP2). DJI Mavic 2 Pro, 28mm, ISO 100, 1/50s at f/5.6. Sep.

Middle: Ulting Church through the trees (VP2). Fuji X-Pro1, 18–55mm at 30mm, ISO 200, 1/320s at f/8, May.

Bottom: Rushes lock at sunset (VP2). Canon 5D IV, 16–35mm at 16mm, ISO 160, 1/8s at f/16, tripod, May.

Viewpoint 2 – Ulting Church

Around 600m further along the path you'll find Ulting Church standing peacefully (and providing a rather attractive focal point) on the opposite bank of the river.

For the best angle, go past the church and then look back from near the bend in the river. The church will stand out

Ulting Church across the river (VP2). Fuji X-Pro1, 14mm, ISO 200, 1/1500s at f/5.6, May.

between the surrounding trees and from this angle it's also possible with a wide-angle lens to include the path and trees leading off into the distance.

To make the most of reflections of the church in the river, try flipping the camera to portrait orientation and getting down low by the water's edge with a wide-angle lens.

The tree-lined path along the riverbank here makes a good subject with or without the church, especially on a misty morning when the receding row of trees vanishes into foggy gloom. It's worth wandering a little further along the path for the river views … carry on for around 800m and you'll come to Rushes Lock but don't forget you'll have almost 2km walk back to the car by then.

7 SANDFORD MILL

There was a wooden water mill on the River Chelmer here for around 900 years (nobody is quite sure of the date). It was replaced in the 1920s by a large brick pumping station, itself made redundant in the 1980s which is now part of Chelmsford Museum and only open on occasional open days.

The interest for photographers though is the lock on the Chelmer Blackwater Navigation; a short stretch of canal lined with boats between two pretty arched brick bridges, tucked away on a surprisingly quiet stretch of river within easy walking distance of Chelmsford city centre.

What to shoot and viewpoints

Viewpoint 1 – Sandford Mill Lock ♿

Walk down the lane onto the first bridge and there are views looking along the river in either direction. To the east, the sun will be rising behind the boat-lined river but unfortunately the car park and pylons limit the options somewhat and there are perhaps better compositions to be found in that direction by going down to the riverside where the lower angle better hides the background.

Turn in the other direction and beyond the lock gates boats line the river on both sides with the second bridge acting as a distant focal point. Try zooming in a bit to make the boats appear closer together and the distant bridge a little more prominent. Walk west along the river (keeping an eye out for interesting boats to photograph) to the second bridge, which can be a better spot looking back the way you came at sunrise. From the other side of the bridge, its arch can be used as an interesting frame for the boats.

Top: The canal framed by a bridge arch (VP1). Canon 5D IV, 24–105mm at 28mm, ISO 100, 1/2s at f/8, tripod. Sep.

Above: A family of swans on the river (VP2). Canon 5D IV, 70–200mm at 200mm, ISO 800, 1/500s at f/5.6. June.

Opposite top: The view along the canal at dawn (VP1). Canon 5D IV, 24–70mm at 70mm, ISO 100, 1/5s at f/16, LEE 0.6 med ND grad, tripod. Feb. **Bottom**: Sandford Mill lock on a misty morning (VP1). Canon 5D IV, 24–105mm at 50mm, ISO 100, 1.6s at f/8, LEE 0.6 med ND grad, tripod. Sep.

How to get here

Sandford Mill is on the River Chelmer, 2.5 miles east of Chelmsford.

Follow the A1060 south east from the centre of Chelmsford and at the Army & Navy roundabout (recognisable from the flyover) take the first exit onto the A138. At the next roundabout take the 2nd exit onto Chelmer Village Way, cross the next roundabout to stay on Chelmer Village Way and half a mile on, turn right onto Sandford Mill Road. Park by the side of the road just before the bridge.

Lat/Long:	51.72902, 0.51759
what3words:	///above.lend.speak
Grid Ref:	TL 739 063
Postcode:	CM2 6NX

Accessibility

The tow path along the river is flat, even and appears wheelchair friendly, certainly during dry weather. There are a couple of steps up to cross the lane at the bridge at the end of Sandford Mill Lock but a path also goes along the river under the bridge.

There are no facilities here but there is a pub, The Fox and Raven, a short walk from Barnes Mill Lock. Alternatively, the busier Paper Mill Lock a few kilometres along the river to the east has tearooms.

Best time of year/day

Spring/summer, when the trees and riverside vegetation are lush and green is a great time to visit, particularly on a misty morning. This is a good spot for atmospheric misty conditions so early mornings are best, especially from spring to autumn when cool, calm nights and warmer days create the ideal conditions.

7 SANDFORD MILL

Top: Misty dawn views at Barnes Mill lock (VP2). Canon 5D IV, 70–200mm at 44mm, ISO 400, 1/250s at f/5.6. June. **Above**: Misty dawn views at Barnes Mill lock (VP2). Canon 5D IV, 24–70mm at 44mm, ISO 100, 1/30s at f/11, LEE 0.6 med ND grad, tripod. June.

Viewpoint 2 – Barnes Mill Lock

Beyond this second bridge and around the first bend, the river quickly reverts to nature, leaving the boats and canal behind. It's a pleasant riverside walk of just over 1km from here to Barnes Mill Lock with photographic opportunities along the way. Barnes Mill itself is tucked away on a loop of river almost out of sight but this is a pretty stretch of river overhung with willows. Notable points of interested are a couple of footbridges, one of which makes a great subject, the other, at the lock makes an excellent mid-stream vantage point for photographing the river in either direction.

Continue west along the north bank of the river from here and less than 1km across the meadows is Chelmsford city centre.

Barnes Mill lock on a misty morning (VP2). Canon 5D IV, 24–70mm at 44mm, ISO 100, 1/15s at f/11, LEE 0.6 med ND grad, tripod. June.

8 DANBURY COMMON

One of the largest areas of common land in Essex, Danbury Common is a patchwork of heath, gorse and ancient woodland. Home to rare flora and fauna, it is a Site of Special Scientific Interest.

Its elevated position on the Danbury Ridge saw it turned into a defensive position during the Napoleonic Wars. In fact, going back much further, Danbury was the site of an Iron Age hill fort. And even though at 107m high the Ridge, formed by retreating glaciers in the Ice Age, is one of the highest hills in the county, it ranks a paltry 3874th highest in England.

What to shoot and viewpoints

With over 200 acres criss-crossed with footpaths, Danbury Common is a wonderful place to explore with the camera. Here are a few pointers to get you started.

Viewpoint 1 – South of the car park ♿
The area south of the car park is largely an area of open heathland amongst deciduous woodland with an easy looping route (start at the car park) from which to explore it. Head out onto the heath and turn right to pick up the path that runs south across an area of heath splashed with wildflowers and heather in summer. Pass through a thin line of trees into another area of heath, eventually reaching a bench at a crossroad of paths. Generally, a short telephoto lens (something in the 70–200mm range) is probably the most useful lens at Danbury Common to isolate areas of interest but with several lone trees and a clear path running across the heath, this is a good area for wider views, particularly at sunrise.

The path continues south before looping round to the left or right, both these routes eventually turn back north the way you came. If you turn right here and follow the path west until you reach the road, on the opposite side is Backwarden Reserve, another 250 acres of woodland, heath, pond and marsh to explore.

On the way back to the car park, try skirting around the right hand edge of the heath to explore paths passing through areas of twisted trees.

The last of the autumn colour on a misty morning (VP1). Canon 5D IV, 70–200mm at 140mm, ISO 100, 1/125s at f/8. Dec.

Above: A frosty start on the common (VP1). Canon 5D IV, 16–35mm at 16mm, ISO 100, 1/2s at f/16, LEE 0.9 med ND grad, tripod. June.
Below: Heather in late summer (VP1). Canon 5D IV, 24–70mm at 28mm, ISO 100, 1/40s at f/11, LEE polariser, tripod. Aug.

8 DANBURY COMMON

A panorama in the woods (VP2). Canon 5D IV, 24–70mm at 50mm, ISO 200, 0.8s at f/4, LEE polariser, tripod. July.

Viewpoint 2 – North of the car park
As it gently slopes up to the north, Danbury Common is covered in ancient woodland sprinkled with the colours of wildflowers in spring. A favourite area of mine is to the east where space is created between clusters of trees by steep gullies. To get there, take one of the paths north from the car park, turn right onto the path you meet and follow it for around 350m. Turn left and up the slope when you see the entrance gates to a house on the right. There's a host of paths and slopes overhung with trees to explore here as well as the occasional rather dark and sinister-looking pond. When you've finished, either follow the same path back or work your way through the trees in a south westerly direction; it's not a huge wood so you're never far from a footpath back to the car park.

Explore further
Danbury Common is just one of several areas of wood and heath to explore here. A little over 1km north east of Danbury Common is Danbury Country Park. The 45 acres of lakes, ancient woodland and wildflower meadows set in the remains of the 13th-century Danbury Palace is a good choice for accessibility.

A similar distance north on the other side of the village are Lingwood Common and Blake's Wood, two more areas of ancient woodland and heath also looked after by the National Trust.

How to get here
Danbury Common is 6 miles east of Chelmsford.

Take the A114 Essex Yeomanry Way south east from Chelmsford for one mile then turn left onto the A414 towards Maldon. Follow the A414 for 3.5 miles into Danbury and at the mini roundabout by the Bell Pub turn right onto Well Lane. At the end of the lane turn left onto Woodhill Road (becoming Bicknacre Road) and the National Trust car park is just over half a mile away on the left – it is along a small dirt track and easily missed. The car park is closed overnight but there is space to park on the verge by the gate and there's another car park 400m back along Bicknacre Road.

- **Lat/Long:** 51.70971, 0.57733
- **what3words:** ///sculpting.successor.fitter
- **Grid Ref:** TL 781 043
- **Postcode:** CM3 4JJ

Accessibility
Danbury Common is accessible from the car park and some paths are firm and even, In wet weather it does get boggy, particularly in the woods.

Best time of year/day
As the seasons change there is always something to photograph. As well as the changing colours of the trees, gorse adds a splash of colour in the spring and can be in bloom from winter to summer when the heather comes into flower. Early mornings can be a good time to catch the mist that forms in pockets around the Common – look for calm, clear conditions and a drop in temperature at night.

Opposite top left: Spring at Backwarden reserve (VP1). Canon 5D IV, 24–70mm at 50mm, ISO 200, 1/200s at f/5.6, LEE polariser, tripod. May. Top right: Autum colour on Danbury Common (VP1). Canon 5D IV, 24–70mm at 60mm, ISO 100, 1/8s at f/8, tripod. Nov. Middle: Greater stitchwort detail (VP2). Canon 5D IV, 70–200mm at 122mm, ISO 200, 1/100s at f/8. May. Bottom: Summer dawn at Danbury Common (VP1). Canon 5D IV, 24–70mm at 50mm, ISO 100, 1/8s at f/22, tripod. Aug.

Twisted oaks in the mist. Canon 5D IV, 24–70mm at 42mm, ISO 100, 1/5s at f/16, tripod. Dec.

9 MUNDON OAKS

Tucked away in the flat landscape of this lonely corner of Essex, their twisted, skeletal shapes bleached almost white by the sun, is a rather mysterious group of dead trees known as the Mundon Oaks.

The origin of the Mundon Oaks is unknown. Mundon Furze, the last surviving section of a large ancient forest that once covered much of this peninsula, is only half a mile away so there's a good chance these trees were part of the same ancient woodland. The most likely explanation is that they were killed by salt water flooding from the nearby Mundon Creek, perhaps from a channel that was cut to allow access to the farm by boat.

What to shoot and viewpoints

Viewpoint 1 – The dead oaks
The dead oaks are just a short walk from the parking place but to add to the eeriness, a sunrise visit will involve a walk through a graveyard in the half light of dawn, so bring a torch! Walk through the churchyard keeping left of the church, through the gate at the far side and then follow the public footpath straight across the field. At the gate, turn right and follow the path; as it curves to the left the trees will be straight ahead. This section of footpath is actually part of St Peter's Way, a pilgrimage route to St Peter's chapel in Bradwell (see page 218).

The trees are on private land so views of them are actually quite limited, restricted to just the stretch of path alongside the field but there is still plenty of scope for interesting compositions. As well as wider shots of the trees (which can work well as a panorama), look for interesting groups or relationships between trees and try to isolate them. To find the perfect spot, try walking along the path watching the trees to see how the space between them changes as you change position. The shapes are much stronger if the trees are separate from each other so pay close attention to overlapping branches.

Opposite: Silhouted trees at sunrise. Canon 5D IV, 24–70mm at 65mm, ISO 100, 1/8s at f/16, tripod. Aug.

To get the best from a dramatic location like this look to add some atmosphere into your images, whether that comes from the conditions – early morning mist for example, shooting moody monos or (on a sunny day) using an infrared filter or converted camera to add impact to those mono shots. If there are clouds blowing past on a windy day, try using a 10 stop Big Stopper filter to do a long exposure and blur the passing clouds into streaks.

Viewpoint 2 – The church
Partly hidden by trees, the timber-framed Church of St Mary is an added bonus that's well worth photographing while you are here. Unfortunately, at sunrise (the best time to photograph the trees) the light will be behind the church which isn't ideal, but it is still possible to shoot it by bracketing the exposures and blending them into an HDR image. A better option is to shoot the church during the afternoon or evening when the light will be hitting the front.

How to get here
Mundon Oaks are on farmland east of Mundon village, 3 miles south of Maldon.

From the A414/B1018 south west of Maldon roundabout, head east on the B1018 and continue on this road for just over a mile, cross the first roundabout and then at the next roundabout take the third exit onto the Mundon Road and follow it to the end. Turn left onto New Hall Lane then take the first right onto Vicarage Lane. At the end of the lane, when it seems like you are approaching a farmhouse, take the fork to the right, past the pond and park at the end in front of the church.

- **Lat/Long:** 51.69106, 0.71783
- **what3words:** ///beginning.hoot.bookshelf
- **Grid Ref:** TL 879 026
- **Postcode:** CM9 6PA

Accessibility
Although the walk is short (less than 250m) and on flat ground, the path is small and often muddy so not ideal for wheelchair access.

Best time of year/day
The trees are east of the path so sunrise is the best time of day. Visit in the summer months if you want the sun rising behind them. For atmospheric images aim for a misty or foggy morning – spring or autumn are often good times for this or on a frosty morning in winter. Afternoon is a good time for mono photography when the light will be hitting the trees from the side.

[9] MUNDON OAKS

Top: The oaks in infrared. Fuji X-Pro1, 14mm, ISO 200, 1/280s at f/8. Aug.

Above: Shapes in the mist. Canon 5D IV, 24–70mm at 70mm, ISO 100, 13s at f/16, tripod. Dec.

Opposite: St Mary's church at first light. Canon 5D IV, 16–35mm at 35mm, ISO 100, 1/10s at f/22, tripod. Aug.

10 STANSGATE

Stansgate is a tiny hamlet in a remote and rather idyllic spot on the southern banks of the River Blackwater overlooking the even more secluded Osea Island.

During the two world wars, being opposite Osea Island, which served as a secret naval base, was an important strategic position, signs of which can still be seen today in the form of a gun emplacement.

What makes this place along the river in particular of interest to photographers is the white wooden hut on the riverbank. During the 19th century a coastguard watch vessel was permanently moored here and this was one of three wash houses built for the officers' families to use.

What to shoot and viewpoints

It's around a 1.5km walk from the parking to the river. Follow the road (which is a public footpath) to the sailing club at the end, go through the kissing gate and follow the footpath through the sailing club to the sea wall where you'll see the wash house.

For images with impact try shooting from close to the hut using a wide-angle lens to also include the view beyond. There are views from either side of it, the best angle will depend on which side the light is coming from but keep an eye on the background to avoid including too much of the nautical clutter that is bound to be lying around. While you have the wide-angle lens on, the jetty in front of the hut makes a great subject in itself.

With its gleaming white paintwork, the wash house also works well as a focal point in wider views from along the sea wall with Osea Island in the background.

How to get here

Stansgate is a hamlet near the village of Steeple on the Dengie Peninsular, 10 miles east of Maldon.

Take the B1010 Fambridge Road south from Maldon for almost 3.5 miles then at the roundabout take the 1st exit onto the B1018. Follow this road for around 1.5 miles then at the roundabout by the church take the first exit towards Bradwell-on-Sea. Continue on this road for 4 miles, pass through the village of Steeple and then just after the national speed limit signs, turn left onto Stansgate Road. After around a mile Stansgate Road becomes a private road so park in the lay-by just before the small turning on the right and walk the last mile along the road to the river.

- **Lat/Long**: 51.70456, 0.80157
- **what3words**: ///remaking.smaller.hello
- **Grid Ref**: TL 936 343
- **Postcode**: CM0 7LQ

Previous spread: The wash house at sunrise. Canon 5D IV, 16–35mm at 16mm, ISO 100, 1/8s at f/16, LEE 0.9 med ND grad, tripod. June.

Opposite top: Boats in the Blackwater at dawn. Canon 5D IV, 24–70mm at 63mm, ISO 100, 1.3s at f/16, tripod. June. **Bottom**: The wash house from along the sea wall. Canon 5D IV, 24–70mm at 65mm, ISO 50, 30s at f/22, LEE Little Stopper, tripod. June.

Nearest Tide Station

Osea Island

Accessibility

The walk to the river is an easy one along a flat road. The pedestrian entrance to the sailing club is through a very narrow kissing gate, which would make wheelchair access impossible but there is also a gate that seems to be unlocked. The path on to the sea wall is a little steep but short.

Best time of year/day

The view is facing north so for sunrise or sunset colours the summer months are the best time of year though first or last light in spring or autumn to side light the hut are also good. For long exposures, anytime of day or year will work (use the sun planner to make sure the sun won't be directly behind you or in your shot), the tide height is the most important consideration. High tide is my preferred time, when there is water around the jetty. A tide height of more than 5m should see the water up to the near end of the jetty but only the highest spring tides will reach the hut.

Above: A calm dawn at Stansgate. Canon 5D IV, 24–70mm at 27mm, ISO 50, 5s at f/16, tripod. June.

BRADWELL-ON-SEA

For a tiny village on a remote and windswept peninsular at the mouth of the River Blackwater estuary, Bradwell-on-Sea has a long and interesting history.

The Romans built a sea fort here with walls 12 feet thick. Then in 653AD, long after the Romans had left, Saint Cedd was sent by Pope Gregory to found a monastery and bring Christianity to Essex. Built on the site of the Roman fort, the monastery now survives as the chapel of St Peter-on-the-Wall, one of the oldest churches in England and a place of pilgrimage.

During World War II Bradwell was home to a fighter base for twenty-five different squadrons and what's left of the runways, control tower and shelters can still be seen. Today the village is in the shadow of a hulking, now decommissioned, nuclear power station but this does little to spoil the views.

What to shoot and viewpoints

Viewpoint 1 – The church
The church is a short walk through the gate at the end of the car park and along a path that would have been walked by thousands of pilgrims, visitors and Roman soldiers. The church stands in an open meadow so it's possible to photograph it from different sides, depending on the light. It has to be said that the church isn't the most visually inspiring building; the interest lies more in its remote location and historical significance than any particular architectural qualities so it benefits from nice warm side light or a dramatic sky. Try shooting from a low angle from across the field so the church stands out against a big sky.

Viewpoint 2 – Sales Point
At its eastern edge, the field meets the coast where a slowly deteriorating wooden lookout tower, once part of nearby RAF Bradwell, stands stark against the endless horizon. The tower looks good as a long exposure with clouds blurring past or as a silhouette against the sunrise or sunset looking back from the marshes (if walking on the marsh, stick to the footpath as this area is a nature reserve).

Sales Point is just to the north along the coastal path. Leave the path at the concrete pill box and walk down to the beach. Here, the mudflats are the attraction for photographers. Mud may sound like an unlikely attraction but as the tide goes out it reveals hundreds of ridges and channels shaped from the clay-like mud. These look fantastic photographed with a wide-angle lens. The lines of posts you'll see stretching across the mud just to the north are actually the remains of Saxon fish traps.

Viewpoint 3 – Waterside
Bradwell Waterside is a hamlet on the western side of the point, you can reach it by continuing on the coastal path from Sales Point but it's a walk of nearly 5km so if you don't fancy that, use the information below to drive there.

Parking is along Waterside Road or – if you're stopping for a drink or a meal – in the Green Man pub car park. Walk along the road towards Bradwell Creek and then take the public footpath heading north, where there's an area of marsh, which facing wet across the Blackwater Estuary, is good at sunset. If you've brought your wellies, head down on to the marsh and look for wrecked boats amongst the pools and creeks. There is also a view north from here towards the nuclear power station if hulking blocks of concrete are your thing.

The other option is to keep walking down to the slipway, which makes an interesting subject itself especially looking across to the boats in the channel at sunset. Just to the right there are also some weathered old posts that look particularly good surrounded by water at high tide. The background can be a bit 'busy' so compose carefully to try and avoid boats clashing with the posts or brush up on your cloning skills.

Opposite: Sunrise at Sales Point (VP2). Canon 5D IV, 16–35mm at 24mm, ISO 100, 13s at f/16, LEE 0.6 hard ND grad, tripod. Mar.

Overleaf: A distant view of the church along the lane (VP1). Canon 5D IV, 24–70mm at 50mm, ISO 50, 1/25s at f/16, LEE 0.9 med ND grad, tripod. June.

11 BRADWELL-ON-SEA

How to get here

Bradwell-on-Sea is on the Dengie Peninsula, 15 miles east of Maldon.

Take the B1010 Fambridge Road south from Maldon for almost 3.5 miles then at the roundabout take the 1st exit onto the B1018. Follow this road for around 1.5 miles then at the roundabout take the first exit towards Bradwell-on-Sea. Continue on this road for 8.5 miles as it winds its way through several villages and then, beside an old petrol station, turn right towards Bradwell Village (there is also a brown sign for St Peter's Chapel). After 3/4 of a mile turn right at the church onto East End Road and follow that road for 1.5miles until it ends in a small car park.

Viewpoint 1 & 2 – The church & Sales Point

	Lat/Long:	51.73279, 0.92988
	what3words:	///noisy.mallets.spotty
	Grid Ref:	TM 024 078
	Postcode:	CM0 7PN

Viewpoint 3 – Waterside

	Lat/Long:	51.73411, 0.88716
	what3words:	///craftsmen.parks.divide
	Grid Ref:	TL 994 078
	Postcode:	CM0 7GQ

Nearest Tide Station

Bradwell Waterside

Accessibility

The church is a 700m walk from the car park and the shoreline is 300m further. The ground is flat but too uneven for wheelchairs, though wheelchair access is possible at the slipway area of Bradwell Waterside. Wellies are essential for photographing the mudflats at Sales Point and at Bradwell Waterside.

Best time of year/day

With a variety of views there is something here throughout the year. Sales Point is best at sunrise any time of year, avoiding high tide when the mudflats will be covered. The church can similarly be photographed at any time of year preferably in the golden hours of first or last light but as this is one of the darkest areas in Essex, night photography is also an option. Sunset is the better time to photograph the west-facing Bradwell Waterside, the sun will be in the best position during spring and summer and high tide would be my preference there.

Top: A distant view of Bradwell power station (VP3). Canon 5D IV, 16–35mm at 16mm, ISO 100, 0.6s at f/16, LEE 0.6 med ND grad, tripod. Aug. **Middle**: The slipway at Bradwell Waterside (VP3). Canon 5D IV, 16–35mm at 19mm, ISO 100, 1/2s at f/16, LEE 0.6 hard ND grad, tripod. June. **Bottom**: St Peter's church at sunset (VP1). Canon 5D IV, 16–35mm at 18mm, ISO 100, 3.2s at f/16, LEE 0.6 med ND grad, tripod. Aug.

Opposite: Star trails over St Peter's church (VP1). Fuji X-T10, 14mm, ISO 1600, 30s at f/2.8 (110 images stacked), tripod. Apr.

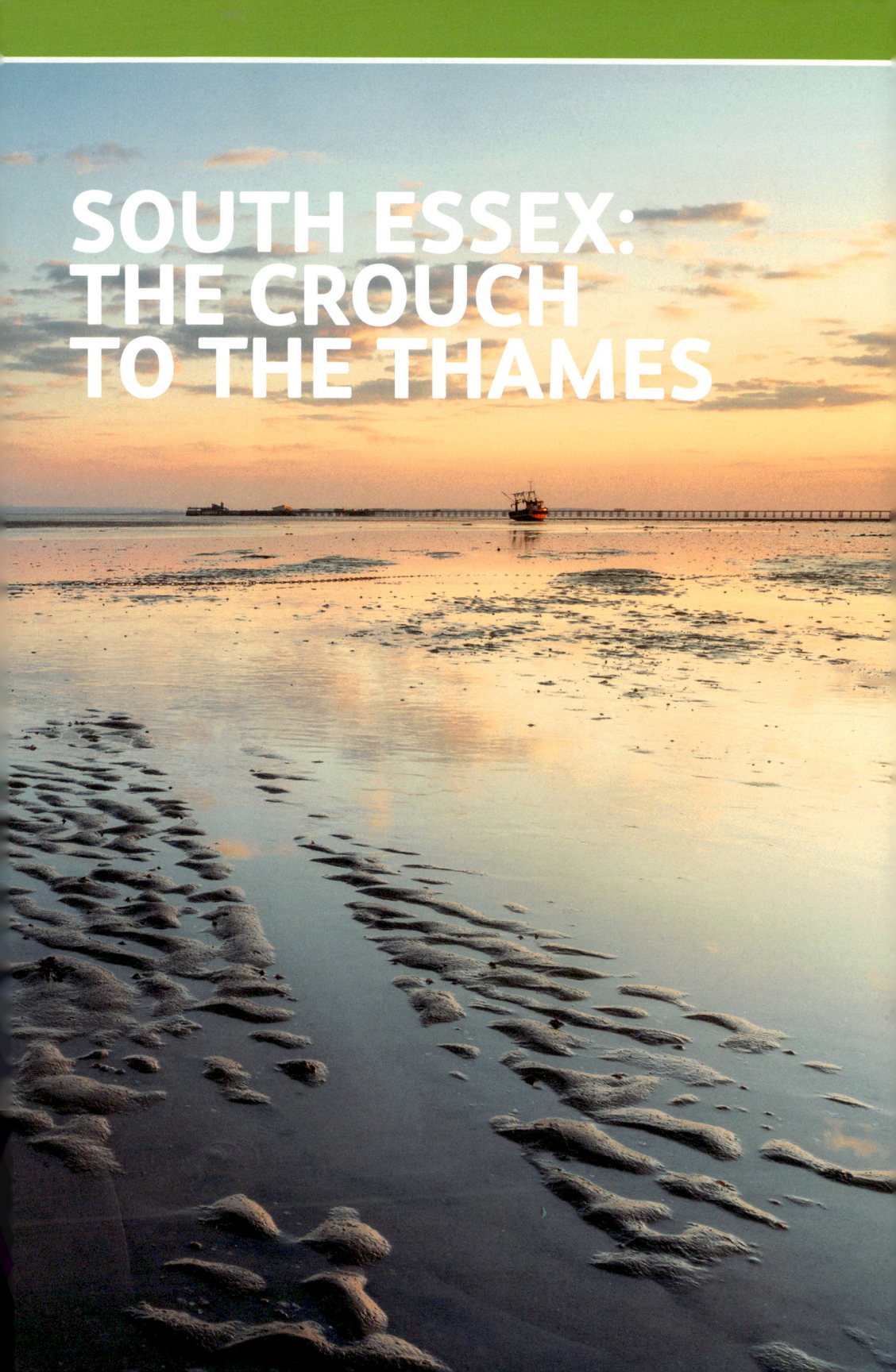

SOUTH ESSEX: THE CROUCH TO THE THAMES

SOUTH ESSEX: THE CROUCH TO THE THAMES – INTRODUCTION

This section of coast, between the estuaries of the rivers Crouch and Thames is full of contrasts, which is what makes it one of the most interesting corners of Essex to photograph.

The Crouch flows lazily through 17 miles of peaceful Essex countryside from the tide mill at historic Battlesbridge, past the new town of South Woodham Ferrers and the ramshackle riverfront cottage at North Fambridge before reaching the pretty sailing town of Burnham-on-Crouch, where red brick and gleaming white weatherboard buildings line the banks.

The River Thames, in complete contrast, is busy with industry, ports and home to the largest town in Essex (Southend-on-Sea) yet no less attractive to photographers. Undoubtedly, the view has changed much since King Henry III built a castle overlooking the Thames at Hadleigh in 1215 but the ruins are every bit as attractive as when Constable painted them 600 years later. There lies much to draw photographers in the remains of the Thames' military and maritime past (and present) too. The old radar tower at East Tilbury and wartime defences at Shoeburyness, for example or the fishing boats in the channel at Leigh-on-Sea or scattered across the endless mudflats at Thorpe Bay.

North of Southend, between the two rivers, you soon find yourself in one of the most secluded parts of the Essex coast. A forgotten landscape of marshy wilderness (or as close as you are likely to get to wilderness in Essex, at least) where a series of islands: Foulness, Wallasea, Rushley, Havengore, Potton and New England float among the twisting creeks which spread from the River Roach; creeks where smugglers once thrived in the lonely outposts of Paglesham and Barling. It is sometimes bleak but always beautiful and one of Essex's hidden charms.

Swans in the mist on the River Crouch. Canon 5D IV, 70–200mm at 200mm, ISO 400, 1/640s at f/8. Sep.

Previous spread: *Last light on the Thames Estuary with Southend pier in the distance. Canon 5D IV, 24–70mm at 24mm, ISO 100, 1/8 at f/16, LEE 0.6 hard ND grad, tripod. Apr.*

Maps

- OS Explorer Map 163 (1:25 000) Gravesend & Rochester
- OS Explorer Map 175 (1:25 000) Southend-on-Sea & Basildon
- OS Explorer Map 176 (1:25 000) Blackwater Estuary

Sunrise over the River Crouch marshes. Canon 5D IV, 16–35mm at 18mm, ISO 100, 0.6s at f/22, LEE 0.9 hard ND grad, tripod. Aug.

1 BATTLESBRIDGE

Despite its warlike sound and claims that King Canute fought Edmund Ironside here over 1000 years ago, Battlesbridge is actually named after the medieval Battaile family who built a bridge across the river here. The aforementioned battle actually happened further along the river at Ashingdon.

Today, it is a sleepy hamlet clustered around the river crossing but there is a lot going on here: it's a centre for the antique trade, with more than sixty dealers working from historic buildings such as the Old Granary. The village also has a craft centre, a motorcycle museum, old pubs and tea-rooms – plenty to keep a photographer busy. But it is the river and the tide mill, restored in the late 1970s, that provide the main attraction for landscape photographers.

What to shoot and viewpoints

Cross the road from the car park and the tide mill will be visible from anywhere along the wall on the other side. The view across the river to the brick tide mill tucked away on the far bank is timeless but it can be frustrating to photograph as access to the river and thus compositional options are somewhat limited. Your position along the wall does make some difference though –moving around to the right makes it easier to include the old lock gates while also hiding the modern buildings in the distance. In the winter, when the vegetation has died back, it is possible to climb over the wall and walk along the bank, which opens up more options. The ground is uneven here though and can be muddy so proceed with caution, especially in low light.

Wander onto the bridge and from the opposite side of the road are views along the river, lined with old boats and barges. It's even possible with a wide-angle lens to include the old granary looming over the river. It can be very atmospheric at sunrise particularly on a misty morning but with retail units to the right and cars often parked near the river on either side, careful composition is needed so keep an eye on the edges of the frame for unwanted distractions. For a lower angle cross the bridge and on the left just before the fence is a gap in the hedge which takes you down to a small jetty in front of the bridge. It can be slippery so take care.

How to get here

Battlesbridge is a hamlet of the River Crouch, 10 miles south east of Chelmsford.

From the A12 Chelmsford bypass take the A130 south and after 5.5 miles take the exit onto the A132 signposted Wickford. At the roundabout take the second exit onto Hawk Hill and follow the road into Battlesbridge. Park in the car park at the Battlesbridge Antiques Centre next to the Barge Inn just before the bridge. Please note, the car park is for customers only and although this won't be a problem at sunrise or sunset, for visits during opening hours either visit one of the shops or the pub here (or along Maltings Road) or park at the railway station about 500m back along the road.

- **Lat/Long:** 51.62299, 0.5708
- **what3words:** ///poorly.twins.ramble
- **Grid Ref:** TQ 780 947
- **Postcode:** SS11 7RF

Nearest Tide Station

Hullbridge

Opposite: Battlesbridge on a misty dawn. Canon 5D IV, 16–35mm at 30mm, ISO 100, 1/10s at f/16, LEE 0.6 med ND grad, tripod. Feb.

Accessibility

Views of the river and mill are easily accessible just a few metres from the car park on paved footpaths but this is a busy stretch of road so take care when crossing. The wall, vegetation and bridge railings may reduce visibility for wheelchair users in places.

Best time of year/day

Sunrise is probably the best time to visit. The River Crouch is often veiled by early morning mist and the mill is lit by first light for most of the year so not only is it more atmospheric but the traffic will be quieter. Around high tide is the best time to visit to catch reflections of the tide mill and avoid the copious amounts of mud at low tide.

Above: The old tide mill under dramatic skies. Canon 5D IV, 24–70mm at 40mm, ISO 100, 1/20s at f/11, LEE 0.6 med ND grad, tripod. May.

Overleaf: The tide mill on a misty morning. Canon 5D IV, 16–35mm at 26mm, ISO 100, 1/8s at f/16, LEE 0.6 med ND grad, tripod. Feb.

A misty dawn on the River Crouch. Canon 5D IV, 70–200mm at 113mm, ISO 400, 1/500s at f/8. Sep.

2. SOUTH WOODHAM FERRERS

South Woodham Ferrers is a modern 20th-century new town built around a central square like a traditional Essex village. As pleasant as the town is, for photographers it is the town's position on the marshland beside the River Crouch estuary that is the attraction.

What to shoot and viewpoints

From the parking it is just a few metres' walk down the lane to the river where you will see a variety of yachts moored along its length. On a calm morning these look very graceful reflected in the still waters, especially if you are lucky enough to catch them in misty conditions. You can photograph the boats in the river from anywhere along the footpath that follows the sea wall and I would recommend exploring it for different views but right here, in front of the sailing club, where you can safely get down to the water's edge for a better, lower view along the river, is the best place to start. The sailing club slipway is private but you can walk on the firm muddy shingle to either side of it.

A 70–200mm lens or something in that range is ideal for isolating groups of boats; look for an interesting boat as a focal point in the group. There are quite a few swans that live along the river so a 24–70mm lens will also come in handy for wider shots if you can manage to coax a swan or two into the foreground.

High tide will increase the reflections but there will be some reflections at any tide and the boats can look attractive scattered in the mud. At low tide you may have to walk out across the mud to get close to the water. If you do so, please stick to the hard shingle area in front of the slipway and tread carefully to avoid any soft mud, which is deep and people have been known to need rescuing from it. As you can imagine, wellies are essential here.

Opposite: Sunrise along the River Crouch. Canon 5D IV, 70–200mm at 150mm, ISO 100, 1/25s at f/8, LEE 0.6 med ND grad, tripod. Sep.

How to get here

South Woodham Ferrers is a town on the River Crouch, 8 miles south east of Chelmsford.

From the A12 Chelmsford bypass take the A130 south and after 5.5 miles take the exit onto the A132 signposted Wickford. At the roundabout take the first exit and then at the next roundabout take the fourth exit onto the A132 towards South Woodham Ferrers. Stay on this road for 2.5 miles then at the roundabout take the 3rd exit onto Ferrers Road, follow it for just over a mile, passing over a mini roundabout and at the next roundabout take the third exit onto Inchbonnie Road. After half a mile turn left onto Marsh Farm Road and drive all the way to the end and park in the car park on the right. If the car park is closed there are a few spaces on the verge on the left by the sailing club.

Lat/Long:	51.63132, 0.6129
what3words:	///gentle.toolbar.barbarian
Grid Ref:	TQ 809 957
Postcode:	SS5 6PJ

Nearest Tide Station
Hullbridge

Accessibility ♿
There is wheelchair access to the slipway and the path along the sea wall. Although a little uneven, it's largely flat and firm.

Best time of year/day
Early mornings are the best time of day here. From spring to early autumn the sun will be rising along the river to the east and there will also be more boats here at this time of year. Later in the year the sun can be seen setting along the river to the west and the end of the day can often be a good time for last light on the boats. It's the chance of a veil of mist across the river that make mornings more attractive however. Look for calm days when there is a better chance of reflections.

Boats and swans in the mist. Canon 5D IV, 70–200mm at 120mm, ISO 400, 1/1600s at f/8. Sep.

3 NORTH FAMBRIDGE

North Fambridge, as the name suggests, was once linked by a bridge to its opposite number, South Fambridge, across the river. There were in fact two bridges that met on an island in the middle of the river. Both bridge and island were washed away hundreds of years ago and replaced by a ferry and although today there is a Ferry Road and a Ferry Boat Inn, the ferry itself has long gone.

The main draw to this quiet riverside spot for photographers is Port Moor Cottage, little more than a wooden shack on a remote island way out on the edge of the saltmarsh. The tiny island on which the cottage rather precariously sits is actually the remains of the original sea wall, breached by flooding in 1897, and the saltmarsh was once farmland.

What to shoot and viewpoints

Continue on foot down Ferry Road and after passing a pretty row of traditional shiplapped cottages, Port Moor cottage will soon come into view across the marsh on the right. Stop on the way to shoot from the roadside (or for a slightly higher view, from the sea wall behind). This is a particularly good angle at high tide when the foreground marsh will be a sea of small islands. For the classic view head to the end of Ferry Road and turn right onto what's left of the old sea wall. Where the wall rather abruptly ends, there's a clear view of the cottage reflected (if it's calm enough) in the water flooding around the sliver of an island. Looking back in the other direction there are also good views of the yacht club berths stretching out into the river. The curve of the sea wall makes a great lead-in line and the grasses provide foreground interest for shots in either direction.

For a more distant view of the cottage, head up the wonky concrete steps to the small quay on the other side of Ferry Road. There is more to attract photographers here than the cottage though: moored at the small yacht club (there is a larger one tucked down the creek to the west) is usually an interesting mix of boats, including a Thames barge or two.

A long exposure of Port Moor cottage at high tide.
Canon 5D IV, 24–70mm at 33mm, ISO 100, 1/10s at f/11, LEE Big topper & 0.6 med ND grad, tripod. Dec

Previous spread: *Port Moor cottage at a dawn high tide.*
Canon 5D IV, 24–70mm at 33mm, ISO 100, 1/10s at f/11, LEE 0.6 med ND grad, tripod. May.

Past the yacht club along the sea wall to the east you'll find views along the Crouch and across the Blue House Farm Nature Reserve (see page 408) to the low hills that flank the river. In fact, for nature lovers the riverside walk around the nature reserve or indeed the 600-acre nature reserve itself is well worth a visit.

How to get here

North Fambridge is a village on the River Crouch, 12 miles south east of Chelmsford.

From the A12 Chelmsford bypass take the A130 south and after 5.5 miles take the exit onto the A132, signposted Wickford. At the roundabout take the first exit and then at the next roundabout take the fourth exit onto the A132 towards South Woodham Ferrers. Stay on this road for 4 miles passing three roundabouts around South Woodham Ferrers, then at the next roundabout take the 1st exit onto Woodham Road. After nearly 3 miles turn right onto Fambridge Road, continue for a mile onto Ferry Road and park in the small dirt lay-by on the right, just before the cottages opposite the entrance to the boatyard or in the pub car park. At high tide Ferry Road can flood so don't be tempted to park further down.

- Lat/Long: 51.63933, 0.67604
- what3words: ///polices.cabinet.copes
- Grid Ref: TQ 852 967
- Postcode: CM3 6LR

Nearest Tide Station

North Fambridge

Accessibility

It's an easy 250m walk along the road or along the sea wall beside it to the river, both are suitable for wheelchairs and it's possible to photograph the cottage from either. The path along the old sea wall can be rough and muddy and the road and the marsh can flood at high tides so wellies are recommended. Pay close attention to tide times and heights.

Best time of year/day

Either end of the day works well here throughout the year: sunset for colourful skies looking west towards the cottages; sunrise for views down the river or first light on the cottage. Even winter afternoon side light can be impressive. In fact, the tide is probably the most important consideration here: high tide is far more desirable for water around the cottage.

3 NORTH FAMBRIDGE

A view over the River Crouch. Canon 5D IV, 24–70mm at 55mm, ISO 100, 1/15s at f/16, tripod. May.

Top: Mirror-like reflections on the Crouch. Canon 5D IV, 24–70mm at 35mm, ISO 100, 1/20s at f/16, LEE polariser, tripod. May
Middle: Looking along the sea wall to the cottage. Canon 5D IV, 24–105mm at 40mm, ISO 100, 1/13s at f/16, LEE 0.6 med ND grad, tripod. Jan. *Bottom*: The marina in winter afternoon light. Canon 5D IV, 24–70mm at 26mm, ISO 100, 1/40s at f/11, tripod. Dec.

4 BURNHAM-ON-CROUCH

Known as the 'Cowes of the East Coast', Burnham-on-Crouch is a quiet, unspoilt town on the banks of the River Crouch and one of Britain's leading places for sailing.

It holds attractions for photographers too – amongst the sailing clubs, boatyards and weatherboard cottages that line the historic quayside are plenty of old jetties, boats and quirky details to point a camera at, as well as places to sit and people watch.

What to shoot and viewpoints

A paved promenade runs conveniently along the river from one end of the town to the other, so while there are one or two particular points of interest to mention along the way, this is really a place to wander and see what takes your fancy amongst the boats and buildings lining the busy riverfront.

From the parking on the High Street it's a short walk south down Shore Road to the river. You'll emerge alongside the Anchor pub, in front of which is the ferry landing jetty, one of only a couple of the jetties along the river that aren't private. As well as making an interesting subject, it has views down the river in both directions, making it an excellent vantage point from which to photograph boats on the river or the view looking back towards the buildings along the quayside.

Turn left and head east for 500m along the waterfront, passing behind the Royal Corinthian Yacht Club and there is a similar jetty. Being at the eastern end of town, this one is better at sunrise.

Head in the opposite direction from the Anchor pub past a jumble of houseboats and boatyards and 500m along the river are a couple of dilapidated old jetties just before the Burnham Sailing Club. These make particularly interesting subjects for long exposures. Keep an eye on the position of any boats in the river though; these are likely to blur as they move during the long exposure so try and position them so they will be easier to clone out afterwards.

The end of the promenade is at the entrance to the marina a further 500m past the sailing club. You'll pass further, perhaps more photogenic, houseboats and an old slipway along the way.

If you'd like to explore further, the path does continue around the marina and along the river to Creeksea and beyond.

Opposite: A storm brewing over the Crouch. Canon 5D IV, 24–70mm at 24mm, ISO 50, 1/15s at f/16, tripod. May.

How to get here

Burnham-on-Crouch is a village on the River Crouch, 12 miles south east of Maldon.

Take the B1010 Fambridge Road south from Maldon and after 4.5 miles at the double mini roundabout go right and then left to continue on the B1010. After 1 mile turn left at the T-junction and follow the B1010 for 6.5 miles to Burnham. Turn right at the junction and after almost a mile park in one of the spaces in front of the One Stop shop on the left hand side of the High Street.

- **Lat/Long:** 51.62537, 0.81918
- **what3words:** ///occurs.form.cork
- **Grid Ref:** TQ 952 956
- **Postcode:** CM0 8AA

Nearest Tide Station

Burnham-on-Crouch

Accessibility

The river and nearest views are 100m from the High Street parking and the total walk along the riverside is around 1.5km on a flat paved promenade. The slope down to the ferry jetty is a little steep and it's a pontoon so moves with the tide.

Best time of year/day

Burnham looks south and slightly west over the river so winter is the best time of year to catch the sun rising or setting across the Crouch but through most of the year the river will be bathed in the last warm side light of the day. High tide is more photogenic than the muddy expanse of shoreline revealed at low tide and is the better time for long exposures of the various jetties.

4 BURNHAM-ON-CROUCH

Top: Burnham marina from above. DJI Mavic 2 Pro, 28mm, ISO 100, 1/30s at f/6.3. July.

Above: Traditional clapboard cottages. Canon R5, 24–105mm at 94mm, ISO 100, 4s at f/11, tripod. July.

Burnham riverfront at last light. Canon 5D IV, 24–70mm at 50mm, ISO 100, 1/40s at f/8, LEE polariser, tripod. May.

Top: A wreck along the river front. Canon 5D IV, 16–35mm at 19mm, ISO 200, 30s at f/11, LEE Big Stopper, tripod. Jan.

Above: One of the old jetties along the river. Canon 5D IV, 24–70mm at 35mm, ISO 50, 30s at f/16, LEE Big Stopper, tripod. May.

Top: Boats on a calm River Crouch at last light. Canon 5D IV, 70–200mm at 100mm, ISO 100, 1/30s at f/11, LEE polariser & 0.6 med ND grad, tripod. May.

Above: Sunrise over the River Crouch from above. DJI Mavic 2 Pro, 28mm, ISO 100, 1/80s at f/6.3. July.

5. LION WHARF

Sitting at the head of Lion Creek, once part of the River Crouch estuary until cut off by the building of a sea wall, Lion Wharf would years ago have been busy with Thames barges carrying cargo. Today there is just a solitary, but very photogenic, hut on the banks of the creek, believed to be an old oyster shed left over from the 19th century when the creek was used for oyster farming.

If you notice a number of strange wooden blocks, scattered about on the saltmarsh in varying states of decay (and measuring over 2 metres across, they are hard to miss), they actually contain airtight steel drums and were originally part of the thousands of floating defence booms holding huge nets to trap submarines, that were strung across the mouth of the River Thames during WWII. How they ended up here however is a mystery.

What to shoot and viewpoints

The main attraction for photographers is the old oyster shed, its lonely shape standing out clearly above the flat marsh from every direction. A wide-angle lens is useful here for emphasising the feeling of space and the solitude of the shed in the landscape, especially if there is a dramatic sky.

The classic shot here is from the opposite bank with the shed reflected in the creek. To reach the opposite bank walk 50m back down the road from the parking spot, taking care as there is no pavement, and take the public footpath on the right. Around 100m along the path there's an opening in the bushes providing access to the saltings. The best angle will depend largely on the position of the sun; looking diagonally across the creek from slightly south of the shed works well but keep an eye on how your height and position affect any reflections. While on this side of the creek, it's worth exploring a little as there are views across Lion Creek further along.

To shoot the shed from the other side, walk east along the road around 70m where there is a path onto the marsh. Look out for creeks or pools that lead to or reflect the shed

Winter sunrise across Lion Creek. Canon R5, 24–105mm at 24mm, ISO 100, 1.6s at f/11, LEE 0.9 hard ND grad, tripod. Dec.

Previous spread: *Sunrise from the south of the shed at high tide. Canon 5D IV, 16–35mm at 18mm, ISO 100, 1/3s at f/22, LEE 0.9 hard ND grad, tripod. May.*

Opposite: *The classic view. Canon 5D IV, 24–70mm at 25mm, ISO 100, 1s at f/22, LEE 0.9 hard ND grad, tripod. May.*

– there is a particularly good, curvy channel just to the south of it. As always, pay attention when walking on the marsh as there may be holes or channels partially hidden by the vegetation.

If you are looking for different angles of the shed, there are distant views from the footpaths that run around Lion Creek or try shooting across the saltmarsh from the roadside to the east.

5 LION WHARF

How to get here

Lion Creek is a tributary of the River Crouch, 8 miles north of Southend-on-Sea.

Take the A127 (Victoria Avenue) north west from the centre of Southend and at the roundabout take the 2nd exit onto A1159. At the next roundabout take the 4th exit and follow the road for around 1 mile into Rochford. Take the 2nd exit at the mini roundabout, signposted town centre, and continue straight on for half a mile then turn right towards Stambridge. Follow Stambridge Road for around 2.5 miles then at the T-junction turn right and follow the road for just over 1 mile When you see the boathouse straight ahead, park in the small lay-by on the left at the bend in the road. If there is no space, there's another lay-by on the right at the next bend.

- **Lat/Long:** 51.61836, 0.77759
- **what3words:** ///nobody.newsreel.without
- **Grid Ref:** TQ 923 947
- **Postcode:** SS4 2EY

Nearest Tide Station
Burnham-on-Crouch

Accessibility
Although there isn't much walking involved, there is no wheelchair access to the path or marsh, there are also no facilities here. Wellies are recommended.

Best time of year/day
It's possible to photograph the oyster shed from several directions so it is a good location at any time of day. My preference is sunrise when you can include the rising sun in the image or the first light shining on the boathouse throughout the year. The tide is the main consideration – the water drains completely at low tide revealing a lot of mud so high tide or somewhere near is the best time if you want reflections. Be aware that at the highest spring tides the road here will flood in places.

Above: Low tide at Lion Wharf. Canon 5D IV, 16–35mm at 24mm, ISO 100, 5s at f/16, LEE 0.9 med ND grad, tripod. Aug.

Opposite: Using mud patterns as foreground interest. Canon 5D IV, 16–35mm at 33mm, ISO 100, 1.3s at f/16, tripod. Aug.

6 PAGLESHAM

Split into two hamlets, East End and Church End, Paglesham is one of Essex's oldest fishing villages but in years gone by it was also renowned for a somewhat shadier trade …

Its location on the banks of the River Roach, hidden amongst a maze of islands and marshes close to the coast, made it perfect smuggling country and at night, fishing boats loaded with illicit cargos of tea, gin and tobacco would ghost through the shallow muddy creeks to the village.

HMS Beagle, the famous ship in which Charles Darwin circumnavigated the world, ended its days at Paglesham as a static ship guarding against smugglers and the remains of the vessel are believed to lie under the mud somewhere here alongside the many other wrecks.

We may not be able to see the Beagle, but other wrecks are visible and it is these that are the main attraction for photographers here.

What to shoot and viewpoints

The river is a walk of around 650m down Waterside Road next to the pub and through the boatyard at the end.

There is interest for photographers along the sea wall in either direction. In the first 100m or so to the right the wooden jetty and clusters of old posts on the marsh provide an abundance of foreground interest for river views or as subjects in their own right.

The main attraction though is around 500m along the sea wall to the left in the unusually blocky shape of a rusty metal wreck. This works especially well as a long exposure at high tide when the unusual boat is isolated and the surrounding mud and marsh submerged. Try using a low angle from down on the marsh to outline the shape against the sky.

There is far more to Paglesham though: the walk to the wreck takes you past a stretch of marsh dotted with photographic inspiration – old houseboats, wooden walkways, wrecks and many signs of the once thriving oyster industry. Continue along the sea wall past the wreck and the stretch of marsh just beyond the concrete pill box is also scarred by the shapes of more oyster beds (there would have been around 200 at one time) that look fantastic with a big sky looming over the flat landscape.

Bring a long lens with you as it's a good place to hunt for frame-filling detail shots.

The wreck at high tide. Canon 5D IV, 16–35mm at 27mm, ISO 100, 30s at f/11, LEE Little Stopper & 0.6 hard ND grad, tripod. July.

Previous spread: *Sea lavender on the marsh at sunrise. Canon 5D IV, 16–35mm at 17mm, ISO 100, 1/15s at f/22, LEE 0.9 hard ND grad, tripod. July.*

How to get here

Paglesham East End is village on the River Roach, 8 miles north east of Southend-on-Sea.

Take the A127 north from the centre of Southend for 1 mile, take the second exit at the roundabout onto the A1159 and at the next roundabout take the 4th exit onto Southend Road. After just over a mile at Rochford take the second exit at the mini roundabout onto South Street and continue onto North Street. As the road splits, bear right onto Weir Pond Road then continue onto Stambridge Road and follow that for 2.5 miles. At the T-junction turn right and then take the next right at the Shepherd and Dog pub onto Paglesham Road and follow it for two miles to the Plough and Sail pub. Park in the pub car park. If arriving early, do so quietly, if visiting when the pub is open, pop in for a drink or meal.

- **Lat/Long**: 51.59609, 0.80523
- **what3words**: ///cling.centrally.packet
- **Grid Ref**: TQ 943 923
- **Postcode**: SS4 2EN

Nearest Tide Station

Burnham-on-Crouch

Accessibility

It's an easy walk along the lane to the river and then a short walk further along the sea wall to the viewpoints but there is no access for wheelchairs. Wellies are recommended as it is muddy and wet.

Best time of year/day

Early mornings are my favourite time to visit, not just because the sun rises over the river for most of the year but on calm mornings, the atmosphere with mist over the marshes is magical. In summer the sun rises a little too far north to be in shot but you will benefit from early morning side light and a sprinkling of wildflowers. Winter afternoons are another good time for side light.

6 PAGLESHAM

Top: Sunrise at the wreck. Canon 5D IV, 16–35mm at 18mm, ISO 100, 1/20s at f/11, LEE 0.9 hard ND grad, tripod. Mar.

Above: Detail of the old sheds by the river. Canon R5, 24–105mm at 65mm, ISO 160, 1/30s at f/11. Dec.

First light at the pill box. Canon 5D IV, 16–35mm at 24mm, ISO 100, 1/20s at f/11, LEE 0.6 med ND grad, tripod. Mar.

Top: The marshes have many old boats and creeks. Canon 5D IV, 16–35mm at 16mm, ISO 100, 1/20s at f/11, LEE 0.6 hard ND grad, tripod. Mar.

Above: Sunrise on a calm morning. Canon 5D IV, 100–400mm at 250mm, ISO 100, 1/20s at f/11, tripod. Mar.

Top: The tide flooding in around the wreck. Canon 5D IV, 16–35mm at 35mm, ISO 100, 1/8s at f/16, LEE 0.6 med ND grad, tripod. July.

Above: Boats and old sheds at first light. Canon 5D IV, 70–200mm at 130mm, ISO 100, 1/15s at f/8, tripod. July.

7. BARLINGHALL CREEK

Standing on the sea wall overlooking Barlinghall Creek, beside the ancient village of Barling, it's hard to believe that this peaceful river is only a stone's throw from the advancing sprawl of Southend-on-Sea. A tributary of the nearby River Roach, the creek is one of several that twist and weave through the marshes around the group of islands that make up this forgotten tip of Essex.

The landscape here is rather flat and featureless, miles of saltmarsh and farmland, but photographers will be drawn to the boats, both the floating kind that line the creek and those on the marsh that have bags of texture and detail but look a little less seaworthy.

What to shoot and viewpoints

To reach the creek, head down the lane beside the church (a private road but public footpath). Just after a house on the left the lane splits, keep right going around the gate and follow the lane to the sea wall around 200m ahead.

The first thing you'll notice is the rather unusual quay in the form of a concrete barge, possibly one of those used to create artificial harbours in Normandy for the D-Day landings. The barge is useful as a vantage point for views along the river in either direction, while the cluster of small craft pulled up on the small beach beside it serve as foreground interest for those same views.

There are boat wrecks on the marshes in either direction along the seawall – indeed, there are miles of footpath to explore, but the better area is around 250m along the sea wall to the right where several fishing boats and dinghies, old and new are scattered over the saltmarsh.

Getting close up to the boats involves walking out onto the marsh. There is a path down in the corner of the sea wall, beyond which it's a bit of a maze of creeks and pools, some small and overgrown so watch your footing. The aforementioned creeks work well as leading lines and there are abundant posts and ropes for foreground interest.

Opposite: Sunrise at the creek. Canon 5D IV, 16–35mm at 19mm, ISO 50, 13s at f/16, LEE 0.9 hard ND grad, tripod. Feb.

A calm morning at high tide. Canon 5D IV, 16–35mm at 16mm, ISO 100, 1.3s at f/22, LEE 0.9 hard ND grad, tripod. Apr.

7 BARLINGHALL CREEK

Creeks make useful leading lines. Canon 5D IV, 16–35mm at 30mm, ISO 50, 2s at f/16, LEE 0.6 med ND grad, tripod. Aug.

Boat details. Canon 5D IV, 16–35mm at 25mm, ISO 100, 2s at f/11, LEE 0.6 med ND grad, tripod. Aug.

Opposite top: A calm morning at high tide. Canon 5D IV, 16–35mm at 35mm, ISO 100, 1.6s at f/11, LEE 0.9 hard ND grad, tripod. Aug.
Bottom: Evening at the creek. Canon 5D IV, 24–70mm at 50mm, ISO 50, 0.4s at f/16, LEE 0.9 med ND grad, tripod. Auf.

How to get here

Barlinghall Creek is a tributary of the River Roach, 5 miles north east of Southend-on-Sea.

Take the A13 east from the centre of Southend for 2 miles, take the second exit at the Bourne Green roundabout and then bear left as the road splits, following the sign to Barling. After half a mile take the first exit at the mini roundabout onto Barling Road and follow it for almost 2.5 miles. Turn left onto Church Lane and park in the lane beside the church.

- Lat/Long: 51.57337, 0.78625
- what3words: ///ally.spider.loaded
- Grid Ref: TQ 931 897
- Postcode: SS3 0LS

Nearest Tide Station

Burnham-on-Crouch

Accessibility

The walk to the river is around 500m along a flat track but access up on to the sea wall and along to the marsh would be difficult for wheelchairs. As always where saltmarsh and mud is involves, wellies are recommended and pay close attention to tide times and heights.

Best time of year/day

With wildflowers adding colour to the marshes in summer and frost adding atmosphere in the winter, Barlinghall Creek is a great location all year. Most views are roughly easterly so sunrise is the better time of day both for the colourful skies and the chance of calmer misty conditions but last light is also good for side light on the boats.

8 THE BROOMWAY

Geographically, Essex is devoid of the sort of extremes of height, terrain or remoteness that might make a hike dangerous or even particularly taxing so it is somewhat surprising that the county harbours a notorious route known as 'Britain's deadliest path'.

The Broomway, so called because it was marked by a line of stakes resembling brooms driven into the mud, is an ancient track that covers the 6 miles across the Maplin Sands from Wakering Stairs on the mainland to Foulness Island. Until a bridge was built in the 1920s, it was the only way onto the island other than by boat and over the centuries many people have died attempting the route. Some mistimed the walk and got caught out by the incoming tide, which floods across the flat sands faster than a man can run. Others met their fate by getting stuck in one of the pockets of quicksand that line the route, and some by becoming lost in the fog, which often rolls in out of nowhere.

These days it is easier than ever to get lost out in that bleak emptiness because the route, marked (in large pink letters) on the OS map with the words 'WARNING Public Rights of Way across Maplin Sands can be dangerous' is no longer physically marked by brooms or indeed anything at all.

The path runs about 400m off shore across the relatively firm ground of the Maplin Sands firing range and is flanked to the landward side by the dangerously soft mud known rather ominously as the Black Grounds and on the seaward side by the perils of water-filled craters or even unexploded bombs and, of course, the sea.

The dangers are very real: even in good conditions it is very easy to become disorientated and under no circumstances should anyone attempt it without the help of an experienced guide. On a lighter note, many people walk the Broomway every year on guided walks and it is an amazing opportunity for photography – perhaps the ultimate place for big skies.

Sunset on the Broomway. Canon 5D IV, 16–35mm at 16mm, ISO 200, 6s at f/16, LEE 0.9 hard ND grad, tripod. Aug.

8 THE BROOMWAY

How to get here

The start of the Broomway is at Wakering Stairs, 5.5 miles east of Southend.

Follow the A13 east from the centre of Southend then after 3 miles take the 2nd exit at the roundabout onto the B1017 to Great Wakering. After half a mile, just after the national speed limit sign, turn right on the bend and follow the road for 1.5 miles. Just before the church, turn right onto New Road, signposted Foulness and follow it to the gates of the Ministry of Defence Shoeburyness. Go through the gates, take the second exit at the roundabout and follow the lane all the way to the end where there is a small car park just behind the sea wall. This lane is only open when the firing range is inactive.

- **Lat/Long:** 51.54844, 0.83905
- **what3words:** ///squares.rehearsed.fenced
- **Grid Ref:** TQ 969 871
- **Postcode:** SS3 9XE

Nearest Tide Station

Southend-on-Sea

Accessibility

Wakering Stairs is only accessible when the MOD is not firing on Maplin Sands. Despite being flat, the route is boggy, wet and slippery. This and the distance makes it unsuitable for anyone with mobility issues. For the same reasons, wellies are essential.

Best Time of Year/Day

Calm weather is an ideal time to visit when the big skies are reflected in the wet sands and the tides often coincide with sunrise or sunset, which are magical out on Maplin Sands, but all planning should be left to your guide.

Further information

Information about walking routes: *www.qinetiq.com/en/shoeburyness/public-access/public-right-of-way-routes*

Guided walks led by Tom Bennett:- *www.thebroomway.co.uk*

THE BROOMWAY IS DANGEROUS AND SHOULD ONLY BE UNDERTAKEN WITH AN EXPERIENCED GUIDE.

Top: Clouds blowing over the Broomway. Canon 5D IV, 24–70mm at 24mm, ISO 100, 30s at f/13, LEE Big Stopper, tripod. Aug.

Middle: Clouds blowing over the Broomway. Canon 5D IV, 24–70mm at 24mm, ISO 100, 30s at f/16, LEE Big Stopper, tripod. Aug.

Bottom: The wreck of Pisces. Canon 5D IV, 16–35mm at 20mm, ISO 200, 25s at f/11, LEE Big Stopper & 0.6 hard ND grad, tripod. Apr.

Opposite top: Cool dusk tones on the Broomway. Canon 5D IV, 16–35mm at 16mm, ISO 100, 3.2s at f/16, tripod. Aug.
Bottom: Sunrise at the Havengore maypole. Canon R5, 14–35mm at 14mm, ISO 100, 1/4s at f/16, LEE 0.9 hard ND grad, tripod. Feb.

8 THE BROOMWAY

Figures give a sense of scale. Canon R5, 14–35mm at 17mm, ISO 100, 1/20s at f/11, LEE 0.6 med ND grad, tripod. Feb.

What to shoot and viewpoints

The Broomway starts at the end of Stairs Road just beyond the car park. Walk up onto the sea wall and at low tide the first 100m or so of the path, made from crumbling concrete, is clearly visible sloping away onto the sands below. In fact this first stretch, which ends with a large green marker post, is a good spot to photograph the sunrise if you wanted to visit without a guide. Beyond that, the path disappears into the seemingly endless expanse of Maplin Sands and from this vantage point you could be forgiven for wondering exactly what there is to photograph out in that featureless landscape.

Out on the sands though there are endless possibilities in the pools and streams of standing water and shapes and patterns in the mud and sand. If the weather is calm, these pools fill with reflections of big skies while on windy days (and it can be very windy out there) experimenting with ND filters to slow the shutter speed down can create interesting patterns by smoothing the ruffled surface of the water.

The incredible sense of space you feel out on the sands can be difficult to capture. A wide-angle lens works well (or the wide end of a standard zoom lens, 24–70mm on a full frame camera for example) and try using something

in the foreground – a pattern in the sand or a post for example to add a sense of depth. Streams of water receding away to a vanishing point are also effective for adding depth and distance and the contrast between the sand and reflective water adds interest. Including other people on the guided walk in the shot will also lend a much needed sense of scale to the vast landscape, especially when their shapes are silhouetted against the sky.

There are some features along the Broomway to add a point of interest, notably the marker posts which guide boats into Havengore Creek and there are one or two stumps of the original brooms remaining. Perhaps the highlight though is the wreck of a ship that ran aground while trying to beat a receding tide.

The Broomway is wet and muddy and even a short walk is going to cover several km so it is best to keep gear to a minimum. I would recommend lenses covering 16–35mm and 24–70mm lenses, ND and graduated ND filters, shutter release cable, spare batteries, tripod, water, energy bars and waterproofs.

9 RED SANDS FORT

Standing alone miles offshore, the rusting hulks of Red Sands Fort look like something from a sci-fi movie – Star Wars or perhaps War of the Worlds springs to mind.

Known as Maunsell Forts after their designer, Guy Maunsell, Red Sands is one of three anti-aircraft forts built in the mouth of the Thames Estuary during the Second World War. Each fort consists of seven towers – five gun towers arranged around a central command tower with a searchlight tower off to one side.

Aside from the occasional occupation by pirate radio, the forts have long been abandoned, the rust and decay only adding to their attraction for photographers.

What to shoot and viewpoints

Remote it may be but the fort is easily accessible on one of the regular boat trips run from Southend Pier. At the time of writing Jetstream Tours are the only operators running trips from this side of the Thames and this guide has been written based on one of their trips on the Jacob Marley.

Southend Pier is a 600m walk along the promenade from the car park. A train runs to where the boat departs at the end of the pier or it's a pleasant 2km walk if you want to take photos along the way.

It takes the boat over an hour to reach the towers 9 miles away and while it's tempting to sit on the front deck to be ready for the best views, there can be quite a bit of spray out there. It's more comfortable to sit on the back deck or inside for what is a fairly uneventful journey and go out when closer to the towers.

Approaching the fort is a good opportunity for 'big sky' shots to show how isolated they are and Shivering Sands Fort should also be visible on the horizon in the distance.

The classic shot is of the group of towers looming out of the sea. For the most impact this is best taken when the boat passes close by. It will require the wide end of a wide-angle lens (16–35mm on full frame for example) to fit it all in and the low angle of the boat will result in some converging verticals making the towers appear to lean in; that only adds to the effect. As the boat circles, keep an eye on the spacing between towers to try and avoid jumble compositions. In addition to the wide-angle lens, a telephoto lens is useful to pick out details amongst the rust-streaked metal. Keep an eye on the shutter speed and framing with the longer lens on a moving boat though.

While the boat isn't cramped, space is a little tight so it's best to keep gear to a minimum. A shoulder bag or small backpack with a couple of lenses (on separate bodies if you have them to avoid changing lenses) or a single superzoom lens, spare batteries, cleaning cloth and perhaps a circular polariser filter should suffice. It can be chillier out on the water so an extra layer is also a good idea.

How to get here

Southend is a seaside town 20 miles south east of Chelmsford.

From the A12 Chelmsford bypass take the A130 south for 14 miles then at the roundabout turn left onto the A1245. At the next roundabout take the third exit onto the A127. Follow the A127 for 6 miles and then take the second exit at the roundabout onto the A1159 towards Shoeburyness and follow it all the way to the sea front at Thorpe Esplanade. Turn left at the roundabout and park in the row of pay and display spaces.

	Lat/Long:	51.5319, 0.72521
	what3words:	///plant.scrap.shave
	Grid Ref:	TQ 891 849
	Postcode:	SS1 2ER

Accessibility

There are trains to the end of the pier and it is a short walk to the boat. Access is via a sloping ramp. There is no wheelchair access to the boat at Southend Pier but there is from some departure points in Kent. The boat has indoor and outdoor seating, toilet facilities and refreshments.

Best time of year/day

Unless you charter a boat, there isn't really a choice of time of day or weather here. Boat trips only run at certain times of day during the summer months when the weather should be calmer. They are popular so you have to book in advance and hope for the best, though the trip won't run if bad weather is forecast.

Further information

Boat trips: www.jetstreamtours.com

Views of the forts near and far. **Above**: Canon 5D IV, 16–35mm at 59mm, ISO 200, 1/1600s at f/8. July. **Top left**: Canon 5D IV, 24–70mm at 59mm, ISO 200, 1/640s at f/8. July. **Left**: Canon 5D IV, 24–70mm at 70mm, ISO 200, 1/320s at f/8. July. **Below**: Canon 5D IV, 16–35mm at 16mm, ISO 200, 1/500s at f/8. July.

Sunrise at the anti-submarine boom at low tide (VP1). Canon 5D IV, 16–35mm at 16mm, ISO 100, 1/13s at f/22, LEE 0.9 hard ND grad, tripod. Mar.

[10] SHOEBURYNESS

Since the mid 19th century Shoeburyness has been used by the army both for testing artillery and, during wartime, for defence. Back then the town was home to a large garrison and although the land has now been sold and inevitably turned into houses there are still plenty of signs of a military past dotted along the coast here and it is these which are the main attractions for photographers.

The firing ranges today are slightly further north along the coast at Pigs Bay but it's worth noting that the beaches at Shoeburyness are former live weapons testing areas still owned by the Ministry of Defence (MOD) so for your own safety, take heed of all notices. For up-to-date information visit *qinetiq.com/en/shoeburyness/public-access*

What to shoot and viewpoints

Viewpoint 1 – East Beach

East Beach is the only beach with public access east of Shoebury Common Beach but it is (very) occasionally closed so keep an eye on the signs or check the website above before visiting.

The main interest here is the anti-submarine boom – a line of concrete posts stretching out for 2km across the estuary. It was built in the early 1950s as a Cold War defence against submarines and was obsolete almost as soon as it was finished. It is now a scheduled monument and a rather good focal point in the vast coastal landscape here.

The boom works well at any tide – at high tide it makes a great subject for a minimal long exposure with the line of posts surrounded by water vanishing into the distance. There is an outflow pipe to one side, which can make an interesting addition to a long exposure, but if you don't wish to include it, it is usually submerged for around 30 minutes at high tide. Low tide reveals sand ripples, pools, channels of water and a huge beach. It is possible to walk out onto the flat sands, opening up further options (there is a line of yellow buoys marking the limit of public access when the range is active). Get closer to the boom for a dramatic angle looking out along it or perhaps look straight at it using the streams running across the sand as lead-in lines. It's not just about the boom here though; there is an incredible feeling of space on these sands and with a seemingly endless horizon it's a great place for days with dramatic cloudscapes filling the big skies. »

Dawn at high tide (VP1). Canon 5D IV, 24–70mm at 50mm, ISO 100, 30s at f/16, LEE Little Stopper & 0.6 hard ND grad, tripod. Jan.

Opposite: *A minimal mono (VP1). Canon 5D IV, 24–70mm at 44mm, ISO 30s at f/13, LEE Big Stopper, tripod. Apr.*

How to get here

Shoeburyness is a small town 4 miles east of Southend-on-Sea.

Take the A13 east from the centre of Southend and follow it for 4 miles then at the roundabout take the first exit onto Elm Road. Stay on Elm Road for almost a mile then at the crossroads, go straight across onto Blackgate Road. Park at the end of the road in the small parking area on the right or along the road.

Viewpoint 1 – East Beach

- **Lat/Long:** 51.53371, 0.80371
- **what3words:** ///towels.egging.funded
- **Grid Ref:** TQ 945 853
- **Postcode:** SS3 9SR

Viewpoint 2 – Gog's Berth

- **Lat/Long:** 51.52485, 0.78556
- **what3words:** ///leaps.basin.worked
- **Grid Ref:** TQ 933 843
- **Postcode:** SS3 9FD

This car park opens at 7.30am and the closing time is posted at the entrance but it may be closed after a sunset shoot. Outside these hours, park in one of the blocked off turnings along New Barge Pier Road. There is one on the left just before the bend on the way to the car park and two on the same side just past the car park.

Nearest Tide Station

Southend-on-Sea

Accessibility

It's a short distance along paved paths to the seafront but access to the beach involves climbing over a low wall and down an embankment so a reasonable level of agility is required. There are however views from the promenade.

Best time of year/day

Late autumn to early spring is a good time of year to visit Shoeburyness when the coast is quieter and the sun rises and sets over the Thames Estuary. East Beach is best at sunrise when the sun can be seen rising through the posts of the boom throughout the year. Gunners Park is good at either end of the day but both viewpoints work very well at any time of day in dramatic cloudy conditions. Tides are as important as the weather so be sure to check these when planning your visit.

10 SHOEBURYNESS

A note on safety: the sand is generally firm but there may be pockets of softer sand so proceed with caution particularly around streams and with the history of this area in mind, don't touch anything found in the sand!

Viewpoint 2 – Gog's Berth

A structure as unusual as its name, Gog's Berth and neighbouring Barge Pier are old and unusual docking points for the garrison. A footpath runs the 1.5km here from East Beach passing several more relics – a recommended walk for those interested in the history.

The structures that make up Gog's Berth make a great subject for long exposure, be it parts of them or the whole thing, particularly at high tide when the water isolates them against the background. Or even when there is just enough water to cover the rather messy beach. There are plenty of compositional options here for Gog's Berth or Barge Pier individually but the two also work well together, angling into the composition from opposite sides. Whichever composition you come up with, please remember that this is MOD property so for your own safety take heed of all notices.

High tide at Gog's Berth (VP2). Canon 5D IV, 24–70mm at 35mm, ISO 200, 30s at f/11, LEE Big Stopper, tripod. Jan.

Gog's Berth at dusk (VP2). Canon 5D IV, 16–35mm at 16mm, ISO 1600, 0.8s at f/4, tripod. Mar.

Opposite left: A damaged section of the boom (VP1). Canon 5D IV, 16–35mm at 30mm, ISO 100, 3.2s at f/16, tripod. Aug.
Right: Barge Pier at sunset (VP2). Canon 5D IV, 16–35mm at 16mm, ISO 100, 0.8s at f/22, LEE 0.9 med ND grad, tripod. Mar.

11 SOUTHEND-ON-SEA

Originally little more than a fishing village (the name Southend refers to the southern end of nearby Prittiwell) Southend grew in the 18th & 19th centuries to be the largest resort in Essex.

Famous for its pier (which at a little over a mile and a quarter is the longest pleasure pier in the world) and home to the world's first amusement park, the town may seem a bit of an unlikely place for landscape photography. While it's fair to say that the never ending pier isn't especially photogenic, there is a lot of potential along this stretch of seafront, particularly to the east of the pier, which is where we are going to turn our attention.

There are plenty of boats to choose from spread across a couple of kilometres of beach so it is worth spending a moment using the elevated position of the promenade, just across the road from the parking, to assess potential subjects before heading down onto the sand. Indeed the promenade is a good spot from which to photograph the streams of water meandering across the beach using a telephoto lens to pick out small groups of boats.

Down on the beach, try and keep it simple by isolating an interesting boat or group of boats. Sand ripples, streams,

Beach huts at Thorpe Bay (VP1). Canon 5D IV, 24–70mm at 30mm, ISO 100, 1/20s at f/11, tripod. Dec.

What to shoot and viewpoints

Viewpoint 1 – Thorpe Bay
Far enough to the east of Southend seafront to be just out of earshot of the bustle and amusements, Thorpe Bay is a long stretch of sand lined with beach huts. As the tide goes out here it leaves scores of boats scattered across a vast flat beach that appears to reach the horizon. It is these boats that are the main attraction for photographers.

Streams across the mudflats at sunrise (VP1). Canon R5, 24–105mm at 70mm, ISO 100, 1/40s at f/11, LEE 0.9 hard ND grad, tripod. Dec.

How to get here

Southend is a seaside town 20 miles south east of Chelmsford.

From the A12 Chelmsford bypass take the A130 south for 14 miles then at the roundabout turn left onto the A1245. At the next roundabout take the third exit onto the A127. Follow the A127 for 6 miles and then take the second exit at the roundabout onto the A1159 towards Shoeburyness and follow it all the way to the seafront at Thorpe Esplanade. Turn left at the roundabout and park in the row of pay and display spaces.

Viewpoint 1 – Thorpe Bay

- Lat/Long: 51.52799, 0.76033
- what3words: ///much.zooms.petal
- Grid Ref: TQ 915 846
- Postcode: SS1 3NP

Viewpoint 2 – Southend beach

- Lat/Long: 51.5319, 0.72521
- what3words: ///plant.scrap.shave
- Grid Ref: TQ 891 849
- Postcode: SS1 2ER

Nearest Tide Station

Southend-on-Sea

Accessibility

While the sands at Thorpe Bay aren't accessible for wheelchair users, a paved promenade runs for miles along the beach with plenty of beach access and options for photography. Wellies are essential on the beach at Thorpe Bay.

Best time of year/day

As always, early mornings and evenings are the times of day to catch the best light and avoid the crowds. Out amongst the boats at Thorpe Bay there are so many different angles you could get a shot here at any time of year but if you want to photograph the sun rising or setting over this south-facing beach, visit during the winter months.

Previous spread: Low tide at Thorpe Bay on a winter dawn (VP1). Canon 5D IV, 16–35mm at 16mm, ISO 100, 1.3s at f/26, LEE 0.9 med ND grad, tripod. Dec.

Above: Reflections and boats on the mudflats at low tide (VP1). Canon 5D IV, 16–35mm at 19mm, ISO 100, 1/10s at f/22, LEE 0.9 hard ND grad, tripod. Dec.

11 SOUTHEND-ON-SEA

Beached boats in the sunlight (VP1). Canon 5D IV, 70–200mm at 184mm, ISO 100, 1/800s at f/11, tripod. Apr.

pools, chains, anchors and buoys all work well as foreground interest or lead-in lines and getting down low and close with a wide-angle lens works well for a dramatic look. Whatever you do, don't forget your wellies and tread carefully – the sand and mud can be soft in places.

If you notice what appears to be a couple of big blocks out in the distance, it's a World War II caisson, a damaged and discarded section of the Mulberry Harbour used in the D-Day landings.

Viewpoint 2 – Southend seafront

Dotted along this stretch of seafront is a variety of jetties and slipways that photographers love. It's a 3km walk west along the promenade to Southend Pier from the Thorpe Bay parking so if you haven't the time or inclination for the walk then use the Southend beach parking information.

From the car park head towards the pier where, in front of Adventure Island amusement park, there is a simple worn wooden jetty that makes a great subject for a minimal long exposure. At low tide this is also one of the better angles from which to photograph the pier. Wander out onto the sand where there are pools and boats to use as foreground interest.

Walk along the promenade in the other direction and around 600m east of the car park is another, longer jetty followed by another 200m further on. Occasionally lined with boats and with wooden steps leading down from either side adding interest, this last one is probably the best for both long exposures and more traditional coastal images. As with all of them, high tide is the best time to visit.

Opposite top left: Wooden jetty in mono (VP2). Canon 5D II, 17–40mm at 27mm, ISO 50, 175s at f/8, LEE Big Stopper & 0.9 ND, tripod. Jan. Right: Reflections in the mudflats (VP1). Canon R5, 24–105mm at 100mm, ISO 100, 1/10s at f/11, tripod. Dec. Middle: Long exposure of a wooden jetty new Southend pier (VP2). Canon 5D II, 17–40mm at 35mm, ISO 50, 166s at f/11, LEE Big Stopper & 0.9 ND, tripod. Jan. Bottom: Changeable weather at Southend (VP2). Canon 5D IV, 16–35mm at 16mm, ISO 100, 1.3s at f/16, LEE Big Stopper & 0.9 med ND grad, tripod. Apr.

12 LEIGH-ON-SEA

There has been a fishing industry at Leigh-on-Sea for 1000 years. By Medieval times, the village had grown over the centuries to become the largest port this side of Harwich.

Leigh Creek has silted up over the years and now only the smallest craft can reach the harbour but the fishing industry, particularly shellfish for which it is known, still thrives here. In recent years Leigh-on-Sea has grown to merge with the sprawl of Southend but Old Leigh – the jumble of boats and old buildings squeezed between the railway line and the river – has retained the quaint atmosphere of an old fishing village and this is the area that holds the most interest for photographers

What to shoot and viewpoints

Viewpoint 1 – The quay
Before heading down to the quayside, which is usually lined with colourful fishing boats, there are views worth exploring from the bridge itself. Grab a 70–200mm lens and from up here you can look east over the fishing boats in Leigh Creek to Southend Pier in the distance, west along the same creek towards Two Tree Island or pick out groups of boats in the river in between.

Down the hill at the quayside the same lens is useful for compressing the distance between the boats there, filling the frame with interest and making them feel closer together. Wider shots also work well here but zoom in even closer and there is also a wealth of colourful details to be photographed on these boats.

Viewpoint 2 – Boatyard
Follow the footpath under the bridge from the quay and west alongside the railway line for 150m and beyond the buildings it opens up to a small beach covered with boats of all shapes, sizes and states of repair. The elevated view from the footpath allows you to see into the boats and to the marsh and river beyond but it is possible to get down onto the beach and closer to the boats for a bolder composition: clamber down the slope either side of the outlet channel. Getting down is easy enough, though getting up requires a bit more effort. To the right of this channel the shore is muddier and whilst it's possible to walk out close to the boats, tread carefully as the mud is soft in places. >>

Dusk at the boatyard (VP2). Canon 5D IV, 24–105mm at 32mm, ISO 100, 0.6s at f/16, LEE 0.6 med ND grad, tripod. Mar.

How to get here

Leigh-on-Sea is a seaside town 18 miles south east of Chelmsford.

From the A12 Chelmsford bypass take the A130 south for 14 miles then at the roundabout turn left onto the A1245. At the next roundabout take the third exit onto the A127. Follow the A127 for 1 mile and then take the next exit, signposted A129 Rayleigh. Take the third exit at the roundabout onto the A129 and follow it for 1.5 miles. At the roundabout take the first exit onto the A13 and after 1.5 miles turn right at the traffic lights onto Thames Drive. At the next junction continue onto Belton Way West and then at the roundabout just past the railway station, turn right onto Belton Gardens then take the next right onto Belton Bridge. Park in one of the pay and display spaces along the roadside. If they're all full continue to the bottom of the hill and turn left where there is a small car park.

	Lat/Long:	51.54091, 0.64666
	what3words:	///union.views.stir
	Grid Ref:	TQ 836 857
	Postcode:	SS1 2ER

Nearest Tide Station

Southend-on-Sea

Accessibility

Aside from going down onto the beach, all of the areas here have good accessibility and walking is on flat paved paths.

Best time of year/day

The winter months are one of the best times to visit, when there are fewer people (Leigh gets busy during the summer months) and the sun can be seen rising and setting over the river. But spring and autumn when low side light shines across the views here at first and last light are just as good.

Above left: The boatyard in the mist (VP2). Canon 5D IV, 24–70mm at 35mm, ISO 100, 30s at f/8, tripod. Dec. **Right**: One of many interesting boats in the boatyard (VP2). Canon 5D IV, 16–35mm at 24mm, ISO 100, 0.4s at f/11, LEE 0.6 med ND grad, tripod. Mar.

SOUTH ESSEX – LEIGH-ON-SEA   287

12 LEIGH-ON-SEA

For a different view, wander down the lane between the buildings to the left and head down to the shore. Looking in a westerly direction, this is a good angle at sunset especially at high tide. There are a lot of boats and buildings here so wherever you choose to stand, pay close attention to your composition, particularly the edges of the frame to avoid including unwanted distracting elements.

Viewpoint 3 – Footbridge ♿

Walk in the opposite direction from the quay, heading east along the narrow High Street crowded with white shiplapped and yellow brick cottages. This is a wonderful area to explore for details, views down narrow alleys to the river, blue hour shots with the streetlights on or maybe just to stop and refuel at one of the pubs. The High Street ends after 350m at a small beach but continue along the path for a further 500m past the Essex Yacht Club with its unusual clubhouse and you'll find an interesting footbridge which crosses the railway and spirals down to the path. You can easily lose an hour or so here looking up or down and finding unusual angles and curves with a wide-angle lens.

Top: Looking up at the footbridge (VP3). Canon 5D IV, 16–35mm at 16mm, ISO 100, 1/60s at f/22, tripod. May.

Middle: A misty start at Old Leigh (VP1). Canon 5D IV, 24–70mm at 55mm, ISO 200, 1/2s at f/8, tripod. Dec.

Bottom: Fishing boats at the quay (VP1). Canon 5D IV, 24–105mm at 90mm, ISO 100, 0.6s at f/16, LEE Little Stopper, tripod. Jan.

Opposite top: A distant view of Southend pier (VP1). Canon 5D IV, 100–400mm at 260mm, ISO 100, 1/30s at f/16, tripod. May.
Bottom: Dramatic skies at Old Leigh (VP1). Canon 5D IV, 24–105mm at 55mm, ISO 100, 0.4s at f/16, LEE 0.6 med ND grad, tripod. Jan.

13 TWO TREE ISLAND

How to get here

Two Tree Island is near Leigh-on-Sea, 18 miles south east of Chelmsford.

From the A12 Chelmsford bypass take the A130 south for 14 miles then at the roundabout turn left onto the A1245 and at the next roundabout take the third exit onto the A127. Follow the A127 for 1 mile and then take the next exit, signposted A129 Rayleigh. Take the third exit at the roundabout onto the A129 and follow it for 1.5 miles. At the roundabout take the first exit onto the A13 and after 1.5 miles turn right at the traffic lights onto Thames Drive. At the next junction continue onto Belton Way West and then turn right at the railway station, follow the road over the bridge onto Two Tree Island and all the way across the island to the car park at the end.

- **Lat/Long:** 51.53285, 0.62669
- **what3words:** ///comet.feels.vouch
- **Grid Ref:** TQ 822 848
- **Postcode:** SS9 2GB

Nearest Tide Station

Southend-on-Sea

Unsurprisingly, Two Tree Island was named after a pair of trees. Visitors to the island today could be forgiven for wondering at the origin of the name though because the trees in question – a pair of elms that were once prominent landmarks on the island – blew down in 1965.

Reclaimed in the 17th century the island has always been split into two parts: the western end, once known as Haughness and the eastern, Oxfleet. Today it is no different. A road bisects the island and the eastern end is a nature reserve managed by Essex Wildlife Trust, while the western end is part of Hadleigh Castle Country Park (unlike the castle itself which isn't actually in the park!). It is now considerably higher than the surrounding low-lying marsh – up to 5 metres in places, because for 30 years it was used as a refuse tip before being capped with earth and left to be reclaimed by nature.

What to shoot and viewpoints

Viewpoint 1 – The slipway

At the end of the car park, a long concrete slipway descends into Hadleigh Ray, the channel between Two Tree Island and Canvey Island to the south. At mid to high tide it makes a great subject for long exposures, especially on days when big billowy clouds are scudding overhead, while at low tide it serves as a useful vantage point for shooting the boats along the creek. Obviously, its intended purpose is launching boats and so summer days are best avoided when it will be busy with paddleboards and kayaks. Instead, visit in winter to see the sun setting over the river.

Viewpoint 2 – Causeway

Take the path along the sea wall, west from the slipway and follow it round for 1km to the north west corner of the island, where an old (but still used) causeway crosses the narrow creek at low tide. The path plunging down into the stream makes a great lead-in line towards Hadleigh Castle, visible up on the ridge to the north and, in summer, the setting sun.

Old boats on the marsh (VP3). Canon 5D IV, 24–105mm at 50mm, ISO 100, 1/3s at f/16, LEE polariser, tripod. Aug.

Accessibility

The slipway has easy access from the car park but footpaths to the other viewpoints, while flat are uneven and often muddy so aren't ideal for wheelchairs. Wellies are advisable for viewpoint 3 as is a check of the tide table as the marsh completely floods at very high tides.

Best time of year/day

With views in several different directions there is something of interest here all year but winter is probably the best time, especially for views looking south. The busy summer months are best avoided unless visiting early in the morning or late in the evening.

13 TWO TREE ISLAND

Viewpoint 3 – Wreck

There are several boats old and new dotted across the marsh on either side of Leigh Creek. One in particular on the mainland side of the creek is worthy of mention. Head back across the bridge and take the footpath behind the boatyard on the right, which runs east along the sea wall. It's a 750m walk from the car park or, if you want to park closer, there are several parking spaces just across the road from the boat yard. Follow the path for 300m then take the path down to the old boat sitting alone on the marsh. The boat is called the Souvenir but there is more to it than meets the eye. It is actually an art installation entitled The Graveyard of Lost Species and the names of various things lost from the estuary (flora, fauna, occupations, words) have been carved onto the boat's exterior rails, hull and upper deck.

For photographers it makes a wonderfully isolated subject amongst the marsh, particularly when bathed in warm, winter afternoon light or with the sun rising behind it. At any time of year it is best shot at high tide when the rising water adds reflections and masks the countless footprints and debris in the surrounding mud.

Viewpoint 4 – Booth's Jetty

Across the road from the path to viewpoint 3, almost 2km along the sea wall in the opposite direction, are the remains of General Booth's Jetty. In the 19th century this was a large jetty used to transport bricks from the brickworks in the Salvation Army colony on the hill above. Several lines of thick posts are all that is left but at high tide they make an interesting foreground for sunset views over the river or a focal point for minimal long exposure images. It's a pleasant walk and a peaceful spot to watch the sun go down.

Top: Winter at the slipway (VP1). Canon 5D IV, 16–35mm at 16mm, ISO 100, 30s at f/16, LEE 0.6 med ND grad, tripod. Feb.

Middle: Sunset at the slipway (VP1). Canon 5D IV, 24–70mm at 33mm, ISO 100, 1/25s at f/22, LEE 0.9 hard ND grad, tripod. July.

Bottom: Booth's Jetty at sunset on a spring tide (VP4). Canon 5D IV, 24–70mm at 28mm, ISO 50, 30s at f/16, LEE Little Stopper & 0.9 hard ND grad, tripod. Nov.

Opposite top: The Graveyard of Lost Species (VP3). Canon 5D IV, 16–35mm at 50mm, ISO 100, 1/4s at f/16, LEE 0.6 med ND grad & polariser, tripod. Aug. *Bottom*: Sunset at the Causeway (VP2). Canon 5D IV, 24–70mm at 35mm, ISO 100, 1/10s at f/16, LEE 0.9 hard ND grad, tripod. Aug.

14 HADLEIGH CASTLE

Sunrise paorama at Hadleigh Castle (VP1). Canon 5D IV, 24–70mm at 59mm, ISO 100, 1s at f/16, 2 shot HDR, tripod. Nov.

The ruins of Hadleigh Castle sit atop the Benfleet (or Hadleigh) Downs, an escarpment running from Benfleet to Leigh-on-Sea, overlooking the Hadleigh marshes and Thames Estuary. Built in the 13th century, much of the castle was dismantled for its stone some 300 years later with subsidence and erosion further reducing it in the ensuing years. The ruins were immortalised by John Constable's painting early in the 19th century and although the landscape is rather more industrial today, it is still a commanding view.

There are similarly sweeping views over the Thames Estuary from Hadleigh Country Park, immediately to the west of the castle. The park was the mountain biking venue during the London 2012 Olympics and the track is still in use.

What to shoot and viewpoints

Viewpoint 1 – Hadleigh Castle
The castle is a short walk from the parking: go through the metal gate at the end of the lane and up the track – the castle entrance is through the gate in the metal railings on the left around 200m up. Follow the path up into the ruins, where there are countless different angles to explore. The main surviving tower in the south east corner is the obvious (but not only) subject and the various ruined walls provide enough vantage points, foreground interest and leading lines to keep a photographer quiet for hours.

Viewpoint 2 – From the east

There are excellent views looking up at the castle from along the footpath that goes east from the northern side of the castle towards Leigh-on-Sea. This angle is best at first light, particularly in winter when the sun hits the castle from the side. You don't need to walk far, perhaps 100m or so but if you carry on all the way to the bottom, turn left then go through the gap in the hedge to the next field and follow the fence uphill, there is another view. The walk is around 1km but don't leave your telephoto lens behind to lighten the load – you'll need it for this more distant shot.

Previous spread: A colourful sunrise at Hadleigh Castle (VP1). Canon 5D IV, 24–70mm at 24mm, ISO 100, 1/4s at f/16, 2 shot HDR, tripod. Nov.

Evening light on the castle (VP1). Canon 5D IV, 24–105mm at 24mm, ISO 100, 0.8s at f/16, LEE polariser, tripod. Oct.

14 HADLEIGH CASTLE

Viewpoint 3 – Hadleigh Country Park ♿
This is very much an area to explore in search of different views. Over the hill to the east is Hadleigh Castle while to the west woodland and meadows stretch off over the slopes towards Benfleet. Some of the best views are fairly close to the car park, which is a good starting point.

From the car park, walk around the buildings to the lane and head south until you reach a cattle grid. Go through the gate and keep going straight, leaving the track and heading across the grass to the top of Sandpit Hill – the highest point on the downs with views out across the valley and across the Thames to Kent. Just down the slope from here, through the gap in the hedge on the opposite side of the track, is a good spot from which to photograph Hadleigh Castle on the hilltop opposite. For more views of the castle from this side, carry on down the track you just crossed, turn right and head straight down the path until it meets a gravel path at the bottom. Turn left and it's an 800m walk along and up to Hadleigh Castle with good views of the castle perched on the hilltop along the way.

Hadleigh castle from the east at first light (VP2). Canon 5D IV, 24–70mm at 47mm, ISO 100, 1/4s at f/14, tripod. Nov.

How to get here
Hadleigh Castle is 5 miles west of Southend-on-Sea.

Take the A13 west from Southend and after 4.5 miles, turn left opposite the church onto Castle Lane and follow it all the way to the end. Parking for the castle is on the roadside.

The Country Park car park is closed overnight so for sunrise or sunset it is best to either park on the approach road where legal to do so or use the castle parking. Walk back up the road and turn left onto Seaview Terrace where a footpath leads to the country park (approx. 500m).

Viewpoint 1 & 2 – Hadleigh Castle
- **Lat/Long**: 51.5471, 0.60688
- **what3words**: ///body.incomes.drift
- **Grid Ref**: TQ 808 863
- **Postcode**: SS7 2AP

Viewpoint 3 – Hadleigh Country Park
- **Lat/Long**: 51.5519, 0.59558
- **what3words**: ///fallen.influencing.lanes
- **Grid Ref**: TQ 800 868
- **Postcode**: SS7 2QH

Accessibility ♿
Hadleigh Castle is a short distance from the parking up a gentle slope but access is through an anti-motorbike gate, which may be too narrow for some wheelchairs. Also, the path is uneven and can be muddy. Hadleigh Country Park however has many paths that are accessible for all. The trails around the country park are mountain biking tracks so keep your eyes peeled for bikes.

Best time of year/day
Both locations are at their best and quietest at either end of the day. I prefer evenings for side light on the castle and sunrise for colour in the sky and the chance of mist over the estuary. There are options all year round and the landscape in the park especially changes with the seasons but the light is better mid autumn to spring when the sun will be further south.

It is a popular area so if visiting during the day, avoid weekends and holidays to dodge the crowds and the mountain bikes.

Opposite top left: Cattle grazing the country park (VP3). Canon 5D IV, 7–200mm at 70mm, ISO 100, 1/100s at f/5.6, LEE 0.9 med ND grad, tripod. May. **Middle**: Kite flying at the castle (VP1). Canon 5D IV, 100–400mm at 130mm, ISO 100, 1/800s at f/8.6. Oct. *Right*: The castle framed in the ruins (VP1). Canon 5D IV, 24–105mm at 50mm, ISO 100, 1/8s at f/16, tripod. Jan. *Bottom*: A distant view of the castle on a misty morning (VP3). Canon 5D IV, 24–70mm at 70mm, ISO 100, 1/50s at f/16, LEE 0.6 med ND grad & polariser, tripod. May.

SOUTH ESSEX – HADLEIGH CASTLE   **299**

15 COALHOUSE POINT

There have been defences on this site to protect the lower reaches of the Thames and London from seaborne attack since the 14th century. The current fort, built in 1860 and expanded during the first and second world wars is a scheduled monument and considered one of the finest examples of an armoured casemate fort in England.

Although the Thames is clearly a very busy river and the London Gateway container port is visible to the north, tucked away amongst miles of marshland, this is a surprisingly peaceful spot, especially early in the morning when you have the place to yourself.

What to shoot and viewpoints

Viewpoint 1 – Radar tower
This large hexagonal tower on the shore of the Thames had a very specific purpose during the Second World War. Built in 1941 this strange-looking structure was used to detect and plot enemy ships so that underwater mines could be detonated when they passed overhead. It's a short walk from the car park: leave the car park at the far end, cut across the grass to the main path and head south. After 350m or so the radar tower will be straight ahead. Take the path down to the river where, from either direction, the shoreline creates a lead-in line to the tower. It is also possible to photograph it from the path, especially from a little further west where there are views back along the shore and the main path itself serves as a lead-in line.

High tide is the best time to visit when, depending on the height of the tide, the tower will be surrounded by water. The rest of the time the foreground will be a mess of rather unattractive mud but lower water does reveal the remains of a jetty just west of the tower and this works well as foreground interest.

Viewpoint 2 – Coalhouse Fort
Instead of going back the way you came, return along the sea wall path, a pleasant 350m walk that takes you past an old gun emplacement before arriving across the moat from the fort. After photographing the tower at sunrise, this view of the fort nestled in the trees and reflected in the (hopefully) calm waters of the moat should be lit by early morning sunlight and is a great angle for a wider shot. It's also worth exploring closer though for frame-filling shots of the fort's details.

How to get here

East Tilbury is a village 9 miles south of Basildon.

Take the A13 south west from Basildon for 4.5 miles then turn onto the A1014 signposted Stanford-le-Hope. At the roundabout take the 2nd exit, follow the A1013 for one mile and at the traffic lights turn left onto Buckingham Hill Road. Keep heading straight on for just over 3.5 miles all the way to the car park at Coalhouse Fort Park.

	Lat/Long:	51.46538, 0.4308
	what3words:	///bunny.gent.jelly
	Grid Ref:	TQ 689 768
	Postcode:	RM18 8QD

Nearest Tide Station
Tilbury

Accessibility
There are well-maintained flat paths with plenty of opportunities for photography around the fort, park and along to the radar tower but there is no wheelchair access to the shore there.

Best time of year/day
This is a popular place and if the weather is good it will be very busy so early mornings are the ideal time to visit and not just for dodging the crowds – the sun can be seen rising behind the tower or first light illuminating it throughout the year.

Left: World London port at sunrise. Canon 5D IV, 70–200mm at 200mm, ISO 100, 1/80s at f/8, tripod. May. **Opposite**: The radar tower at sunrise (VP1). Canon 5D IV, 16–35mm at 16mm, ISO 100, 30s at f/16, LEE Little Stopper & 0.9 hard ND grad, tripod. Jan.

COALHOUSE POINT

The radar tower at sunrise (VP1). Canon 5D IV, 16–35mm at 16mm, ISO 100, 1/4s at f/11, LEE 0.9 hard ND grad, tripod. May.

Top: *The river at blue hour (VP1). Canon 5D IV, 24–70mm at 53mm, ISO 100, 30s at f/11, LEE Little Stopper, tripod. May.*

Middle: *Coalhouse fort (VP2). Canon 5D IV, 24–70mm at 45mm, ISO 100, 1/30s at f/8, tripod. May.*

Bottom: *Detail of the fort (VP2). Canon 5D IV, 24–70mm at 67mm, ISO 100, 1/8s at f/8, tripod. May.*

WESTERN ESSEX

WESTERN ESSEX – INTRODUCTION

While the first three sections of this book are largely dedicated to the eastern half of the county and its ragged encounter with the sea, this final section covers the entire western half. Everything (with a few exceptions) between the A12, which trundles north east following the old coach route from London to Colchester and beyond into Suffolk, and the Rivers Lee and Stort, which form much of the western boundary.

Although the southern edge of western Essex, where the county meets London, is undoubtedly busier than most parts it is perhaps not as busy as one might expect and gems like Epping Forest and Warley Place are to be found like oases of calm just a stone's throw from the M25.

Moving north, the capital blends quickly into the countryside and before even escaping the perimeter of the M25 there are signs of the rural side of Essex. An endless patchwork quilt of gold and green fields that billows out through the heart of the county, interrupted only by tiny villages and hamlets with curious names like Clatterford End or Good Easter. Essex's history is on full display here too – not just in the many villages and churches (see *Towns & Villages* page 382 and *Churches* page 390) or the windmills at Bocking and Mountnessing – but in the ancient meadows at Hudson Mead and the timeless Hatfield Forest.

Perhaps the character of this side of Essex is best captured in the very north west of the region though, where clusters of timber-framed buildings, thatched cottages and grand medieval churches in some of the county's most picturesque villages, Thaxted, Finchingfield and Saffron Walden are found, nestled in the gently rolling farmland.

Cottages at Clavering. Canon 5D IV, 24–70mm at 24mm, ISO 200, 1/400s at f/8, LEE polariser. June.

Previous spread: *A misty morning on the River Stort. Canon 5D IV, 100–400mm at 180mm, ISO 100, 1/1250 at f/5.6, tripod. June.*

Maps

- OS Explorer Map 174 (1:25 000) Epping Forest & Lee Valley
- OS Explorer Map 175 (1:25 000) Southend-on-Sea & Basildon
- OS Explorer Map 195 (1:25 000) Braintree & Saffron Walden

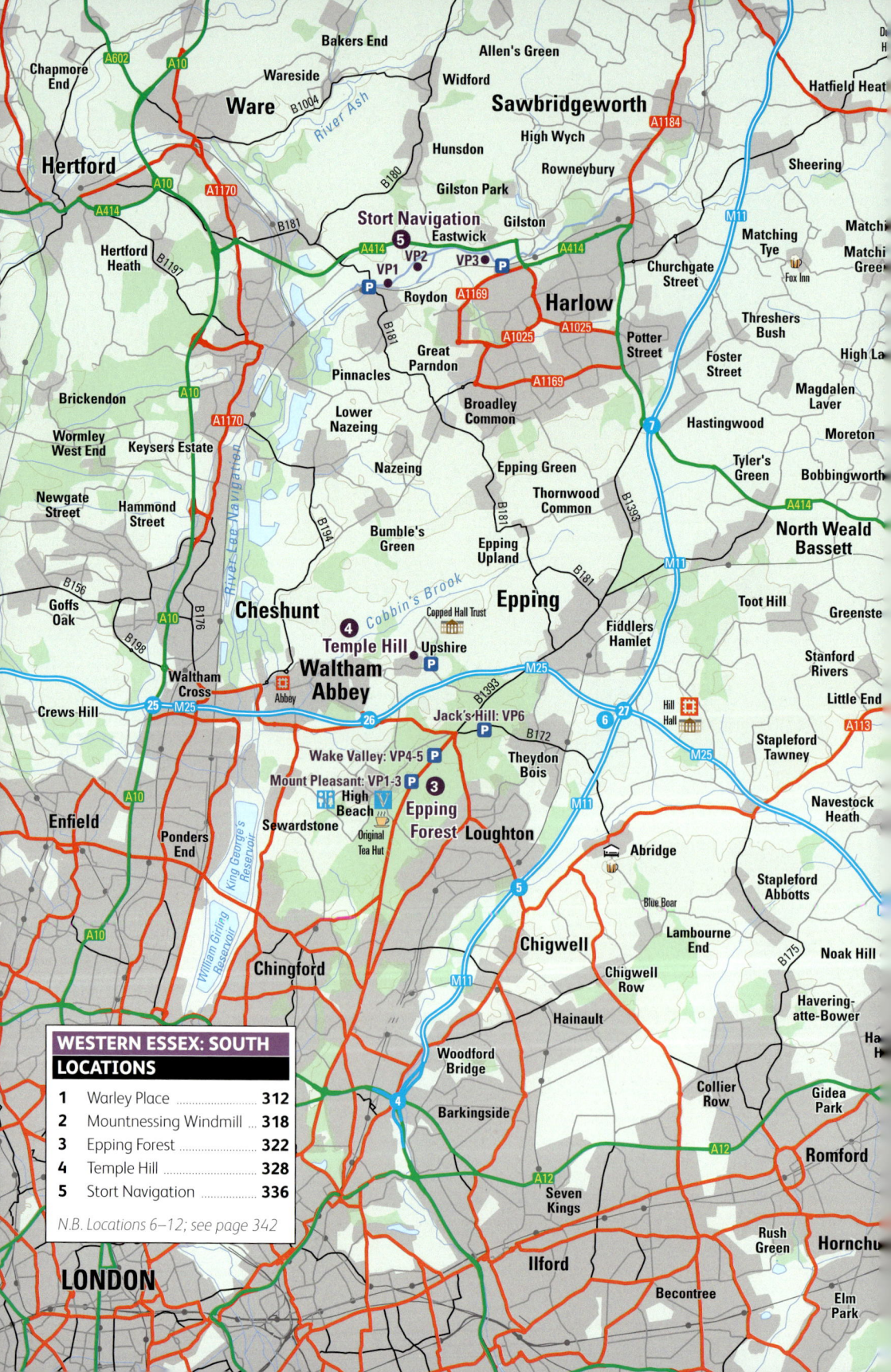

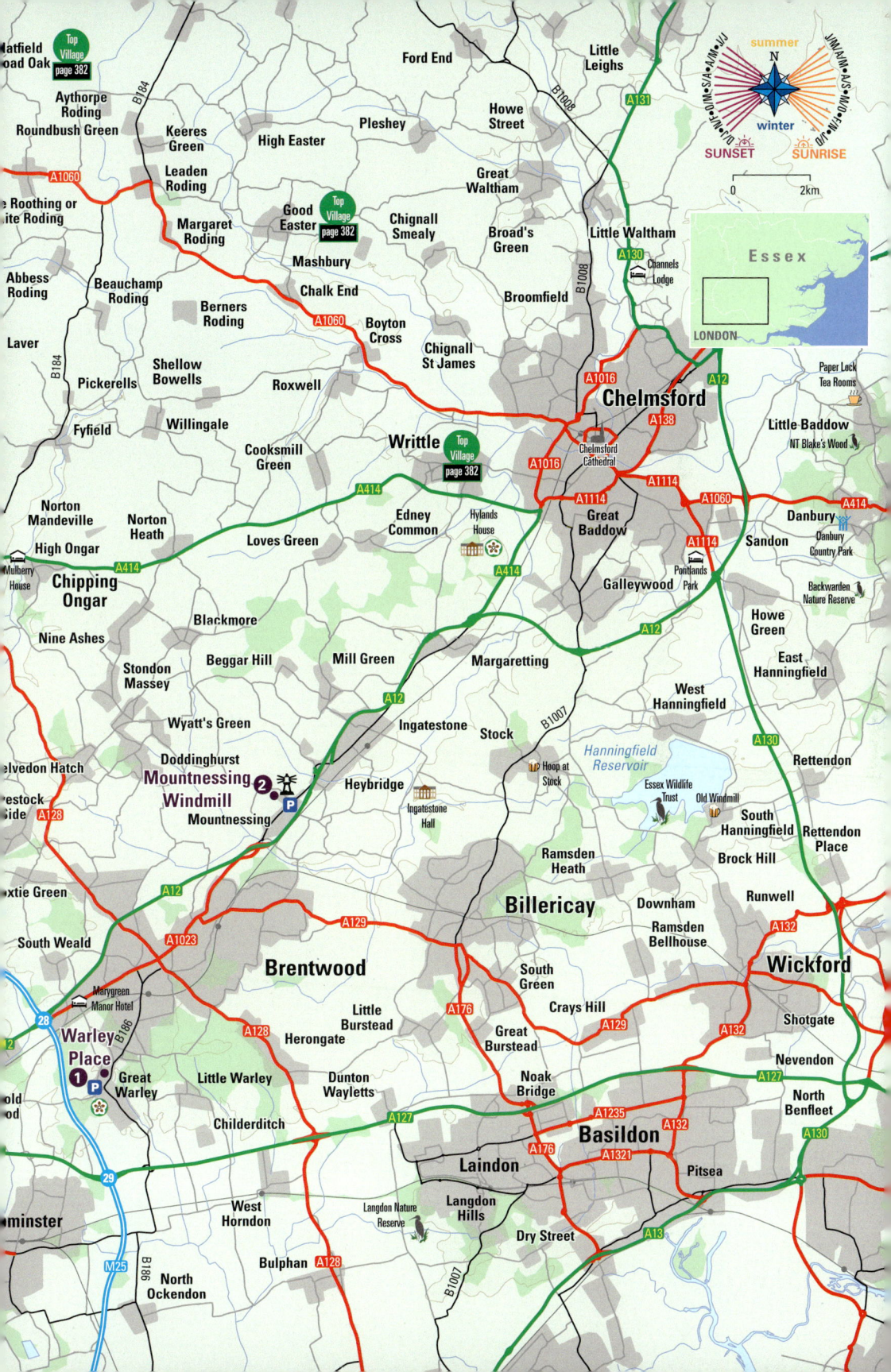

Fields of Echium near Thaxted. Canon 5D IV, 24–70mm at 70mm, ISO 100, 1/10s at f/16, LEE 0.6 med ND grad, tripod. July.

1 WARLEY PLACE

During the late 19th century Ellen Willmott began transforming the grounds at Warley Place into extensive gardens, which became famous for plants from around the world. After her death in 1934 the house was sold and eventually demolished with many of the plants plundered.

Since the late 1970s, the Essex Wildlife Trust has managed the site as a nature reserve and today Warley Place is a fascinating mix of the ruins and remains of these once spectacular gardens and the nature that has slowly taken over. It's somewhere that will appeal to anybody with an interest in any aspect of outdoor photography.

What to shoot and viewpoints

Warley Place is a relatively compact site that is easy to navigate, thanks to a marked route with information signs explaining the history of the place and pointing out hidden clues to the past. Different things here will appeal to photographers so what follows is just a guide to some of the highlights along the route.

The banks lining the main path up the slope from the car park are thick with snowdrops in late winter and foxgloves in summer along with some rather impressive trees to shoot, in particular a huge oak on the right near the gate.

After 150m at the top of the slope, a path branches off to the left. This is a short cut to the conservatory and beyond. It is also where the house originally stood and the turning circle, which was in front of the house, is still visible.

Follow the path through the rockery and eventually it passes through the remains of the cold frames, old green

Top: The conservatory through the trees. Canon 5D IV, 24–105mm at 55mm, ISO 100, 1/2s at f/16, LEE polariser, tripod. May.

Above: A row of sweet chestnuts. Canon 5D IV, 24–70mm at 30mm, ISO 100, 1/30s at f/5.6, LEE polariser, tripod. June.

Opposite top: Foxgloves by the main path. Canon 5D IV, 24–70mm at 33mm, ISO 100, 1/8s at f/11, LEE polariser, tripod. June.
Bottom: The overgrown boating lake. Canon 5D IV, 24–70mm at 35mm, ISO 100, 1/10s at f/5.6, LEE polariser, tripod. June.

Overleaf: Swathes of foxgloves in summer. Canon 5D IV, 24–70mm at 63mm, ISO 100, 1/6s at f/16, LEE polariser, tripod. June.

How to get here

Warley Place is a nature reserve 2 miles south west of Brentwood.

Take the A128 south from Brentwood High Street then at the roundabout take the second exit onto the B186. Follow the B186 for two miles – the entrance to Warley Place is on the right immediately before the Thatchers Arms pub. Go through the gate and park in the small car park. If the gate is locked, there should be parking spaces on the opposite side of the green or at the cricket club 250m west along Warley Road.

Lat/Long:	51.59379, 0.2841
what3words:	///steep.harp.cute
Grid Ref:	TQ 583 907
Postcode:	CM13 3HU

Accessibility

The site is reasonably compact but paths are often narrow and uneven and, apart from the main drive, unsuitable for wheelchairs. There are no facilities on site and no dogs (apart from guide dogs) allowed on the nature reserve.

Visitors are asked to keep to the footpaths both for the benefit of the wildlife and because some areas are dangerous with hazards such as decaying walls, deep ponds and hidden cellars.

Best time of year/day

There is something of interest year round here but the highlight is in the spring when thousands of bulbs beginning with snowdrops followed by daffodils, crocuses and then bluebells come into bloom.

1 WARLEY PLACE

houses and irrigation ponds all in various states of ruin, and overgrown with wildflowers, ivy, ferns and even trees. This is a great area for capturing details of the decay and another spot that is good for snowdrops, though it is shady so a tripod will be useful. The same is true of the walled garden, which is equally overgrown but in better condition with clear signs of the original plants still flourishing amongst the native flora.

Leaving the walled garden (this is where we meet up with the shortcut mentioned earlier), the conservatory – once part of the house and still standing – is on the left. Beyond it are the overgrown cellars – all that's now left of the main building. Although the conservatory was made structurally safe in 2006, at the time of writing it is fenced off, rather reducing photographic opportunities. The conservatory works well as part of the wooded landscape so the best option is to take the path south west to the pergola, from where vegetation hides much of the fence. The rest is easily removed in post processing.

Back on the main path, head west along the outside of the walled garden then turn right past the terrace to the daffodil bank (this part of the route involves slopes but it is possible to avoid them by turning left instead of right). As you might expect from the name, this is one of the best areas for wild daffodils in early spring. The footpath snaking through the trees works well as a leading line either up or down hill and a large turkey oak at the top of the bank makes an excellent focal point here.

From here the path loops around past a now empty boating lake before heading back uphill towards the point where the less strenuous route joins. To the right are glimpses of the West Meadow, another fantastic area for daffodils. The best views over this meadow are from the top of the hill at a line of sweet chestnuts, believed to have been planted in the 17th century. On a clear day the London skyline is clearly visible here beyond the meadow.

The path follows the edge of the meadow before crossing a bridge past the south pond (there is a bird hide down a short side path) and heading down to rejoin the main path near the entrance gate.

Sunrise on the daffodil bank. Canon 5D IV, 24–70mm at 53mm, ISO 100, 1/5s at f/22, 2 shot HDR, tripod. Mar.

Opposite left: *Trees growing in the ruins. Canon 5D IV, 24–70mm at 38mm, ISO 100, 0.6s at f/11, LEE polariser, tripod. June.*
Right: *The turkey oak. Canon 5D IV, 24–70mm at 35mm, ISO 100, 1/8s at f/11, LEE polariser, tripod. Mar.*

2. MOUNTNESSING WINDMILL

Mountnessing Windmill is a well maintained and rather fetching black wood and red brick post mill. There has been a windmill on this site since 1477 but the current incarnation, which has been restored to full working order, was built in 1807.

Fortunately for photographers, it is in a photogenic location on the edge of the village playing field, something that has spared it from being surrounded by encroaching housing – the fate of many village windmills.

What to shoot and viewpoints

Viewpoint 1 – From the playing field ♿
The most dramatic view of the windmill, looking up at it from the fence, is virtually in the car park. Being close up, it's an angle that needs a wide-angle lens but it also has the virtue of hiding the slightly obtrusive hedge that almost totally surrounds the base of the mill. It won't necessarily be the best angle however – the windmill can be turned to face the wind by pushing its tail pole, something which is often done on school trips and open days, so the best angle will depend largely on which direction it happens to be facing when you visit. Fortunately, it's possible to photograph it from any direction.

Moving further away, trees along the end of the field to the north or south west provide interest with which to frame longer views of the windmill.

Viewpoint 2 – From the farmland
For a different composition, head around the tennis court behind the windmill – a public footpath goes through the trees and across the field beyond. About 150m down the hill a path branches off to the right, along which are views back up the hill to the windmill rising up between the trees with lines through the crops acting as leading lines across the field.

The windmill framed by trees (VP1). Canon 5D IV, 16–35mm at 31mm, ISO 100, 1/2s at f/11, tripod. Apr.

A distant view of the windmill across the fields (VP2). Canon 5D IV, 24–105mm at 28mm, ISO 100, 1/8s at f/11, tripod. July.

How to get here

Mountnessing is a village 8 miles southwest of Chelmsford.

Take the A414 south from Chelmsford all the way to the A12 then join the A12 heading south towards London. Follow the A12 for 3 miles and leave at Junction 13, signposted Ingatestone. At the T-junction at the end of the slip road, turn right onto B1002 and after 1 mile turn right into the Mountnessing village hall/tennis club where there is a free car park. Take care: the entrance to the car park is very narrow.

- **Lat/Long**: 51.65646, 0.35663
- **what3words**: ///tolls.frog.sunset
- **Grid Ref**: TQ 631 979
- **Postcode**: CM15 0UG

Accessibility

There are views of the windmill just a few steps from the car park and those from the playing field are only a short distance across a flat field and easily accessible. The footpath across the farmland to the rear is less even and down a gentle slope.

Best time of year/day

Sunrise or sunset are the best times of day when the playing field will be quieter but as it's possible to photograph the mill from many different angles, it works well throughout the year. Longer views from the farmland are best when there is a crop in the field, usually in spring or summer depending on the crop in question.

Above: A long exposure of the windmill (VP1). Canon 5D IV, 16–35mm at 20mm, ISO 50, 60s at f/16, LEE Big Stopper, tripod. July.

3. EPPING FOREST

Covering 6000 acres, Epping Forest is one of the last remaining areas of the Forest of Essex, an ancient woodland that would originally have covered 60,000 acres of the county. Thankfully, what is left of the forest is protected and according to the Epping Forest Act of 1878, "shall at all times be kept unenclosed and unbuilt on as an open space for the recreation and enjoyment of the people."

The forest has a rich, if rather grisly, history. Legend has it (though not evidence) that Boudica made her last stand against the Romans in one of the forest's Iron Age hill forts and 18th-century highwayman Dick Turpin is said to have hidden out in the forest and preyed on passing coaches. Stories are also told of a hidden, dark and evil pond known as the suicide pool and over the years, the forest has earned a notorious reputation as a convenient place to dispose of inconvenient bodies.

For those of us looking to do nothing more sinister than take photographs, Epping Forest has much to offer: an abundance of wonderful beech trees (other predominant species are hornbeam, silver birch and oak), a smattering of ponds and the tendency to harbour pockets of mist and fog when conditions are favourable.

What to shoot and viewpoints

There are many interesting areas waiting to be discovered. Below are some good starting points.

Viewpoint 1 – Loughton Camp

Loughton Camp is the site of an Iron Age hill fort a short walk from Mount Pleasant car park. Take the main path on the right, After 600m, it forks and meets another path – keep going right. After 50m, just beyond the turning to the left, a wooden marker post with a yellow arrow on the right side of the path points the way to Loughton Camp. The path isn't very clear but if you head west for about 100m you'll come to a large open area of beech trees amongst raised embankments (all that is left of the 2500-year-old ramparts) and a small information board. There are endless compositions to be found in all directions here depending on the light. Take your time and wander around looking for an interesting tree or group of trees to use as a focal point in a wider view or as a subject themselves. On the topic of wider views, this is a great place for stitched panoramas.

For film fans, just down the hill on the main path from here to Loughton Brook, the small bridge crossing the stream is the Black Knight's Bridge from Monty Python's Holy Grail!

Viewpoint 2 – Blackweir Pond

Follow the directions to Loughton Camp but just before the main track to the left, take the smaller path on the left into the trees. The path goes roughly north east for around 200m to Blackweir Pond or the Lost Pond as it is known locally (rather curiously for something so easy to find). There are some fabulous trees around the small pond and surrounding area including a particularly nice stand of beech trees to the north and in the early summer, yellow flag iris grows in the margins. Early mornings are good here for mist and, being quite high, the trees on the west side get the first sunlight.

Viewpoint 3 – High Beach

Across the road from Mount Pleasant car park, paths lead to the Epping Forest Visitor Centre. Take care crossing as it's a busy road. Wheelchair users would be advised to park at the visitor centre itself where access is better. Head to the left and there are plenty of gnarled old beech trees along the undulating path. A particularly good area is around 500m along, where the path can be used as a leading lane through the overhanging trees as it disappears down the hill. If you're wondering about the spelling of High Beach as opposed to High Beech (although both are used), it refers to areas of sand and gravel found in this part of the forest rather than the tree.

Previous spread: Autumn beeches at Loughton Camp (VP1). Canon 5D IV, 70–200mm at 75mm, ISO 200, 1/3s at f/8, LEE polariser, tripod. Nov.

Opposite top: Beeches at Loughton Camp (VP1). Canon 5D IV, 24–70mm at 70mm, ISO 200, 1/3s at f/8, LEE polariser, tripod. Aug.
Bottom: Morning light through the trees (VP1). Canon 5D IV, 24–70mm at 70mm, ISO 200, 1/25s at f/8, LEE polariser, tripod. Aug.

EPPING FOREST

How to get here

Epping Forest straddles the Essex/Greater London border 8 miles south of Harlow.

Take the A414 south from Harlow and at the roundabout take the 3rd exit to join the M11 south then after 4 miles take the exit to join the M25 towards the M1. Leave the M25 at the next exit (junction 26) and at the roundabout take the first exit onto the A121 towards Loughton and follow that road for 2 miles. At the roundabout take the 4th exit onto the A104 Epping New Road and the Mount Pleasant car park is 1 mile along on the left.

Viewpoint 1-3 – Mount Pleasant

- Lat/Long: 51.66526, 0.04857
- what3words: ///cage.belly.glue
- Grid Ref: TQ 417 982
- Postcode: IG10 4AF

Viewpoint 4 & 5 – Wake Valley

- Lat/Long: 51.67054, 0.05495
- what3words: ///large.panic.caring
- Grid Ref: TQ 413 981
- Postcode: IG10 4AF

Viewpoint 6 – Jacks Hill

- Lat/Long: 51.67628, 0.07431
- what3words: ///empire.hogs.luck
- Grid Ref: TQ 435 995
- Postcode: IG10 2NY

Accessibility

There are many hard paths through the forest for wheelchair users, particularly around the visitor centre at High Beach (visit *accessibilityguides.org/content/epping-forest* for more information). The forest is hilly but while paths do undulate they are not steep. They can be very muddy at certain times of year though, particularly off the main paths so walking boots or wellies are advised. It's difficult to get too lost but an OS map or an app/GPS device that keeps track of your locations is also useful to be on the safe side and to mark good spots for future reference.

Best time of year/day

The best times of year are spring, when the forest is lush with fresh greens, and autumn when the leaves turn shades of gold and copper. At these times of year pockets of fog or mist are common if conditions are right but if you're not lucky enough to catch such atmospheric conditions, uninspiringly overcast days are perfect for woodland photography. The forest is a popular place, though big enough to never feel too busy. Early mornings are quietest.

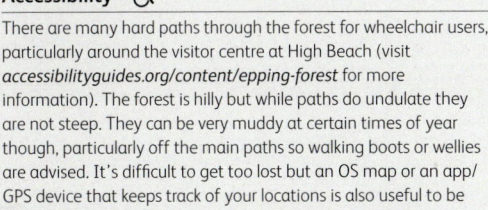

Opposite top: *Grassland north of Jacks Hill in autumn (VP6). Canon 5D IV, 24–70mm at 57mm, ISO 100, 1/20s at f/11, LEE polariser, tripod. Oct.* **Bottom**: *Autumn colour at Sunshine Plain (VP5). Canon 5D IV, 24–70mm at 70mm, ISO 100, 1/8s at f/8, LEE polariser, tripod. Oct.*

High Beach through the seasons (VP3)

3 EPPING FOREST

Viewpoint 4 – Wake Valley Pond
Wake Valley Pond is a small pond close to the road and the Wake Valley car park. Go through the small gate on the left side of the car park and the pond is just over 100m straight ahead. From this side of the pond there are good views across it through the gaps in the reeds. Head right along the shoreline and you can walk all the way round to the opposite side. It's a good idea to wear wellies as there are some boggy areas to cross. Hemmed in by trees and reeds, it is quite a 'busy' location so careful composition or tighter framing is needed to keep things simple. In the early morning with mist swirling over the calm water, it's beautiful.

Viewpoint 5 – Sunshine Plain
This area can be a little harder to find: take the large gate at the back of Wake Valley car park and then immediately turn right onto a small track and head north through the woods. After around 150m you'll enter an open area of heathland dotted with trees. Summer is a good time to visit Sunshine Plain, when the heath is splashed with pink and purple heather and often grazed by a herd of Longhorn cattle.

Viewpoint 6 – Jacks Hill
There is a small car park on each side of the road at Jacks Hill and a very different landscape in each direction; whichever way you go you could lose hours exploring. Head south and the path sweeps through an area of woodland similar to that of Loughton Camp, indeed, you can take a path west that will eventually lead you there. To the north however is an open area of boggy grassland, dead trees and small ponds interspersed with groups of oak and silver birch which is reached by taking the small path to the left of the car park and following the track for 100m or so. Also of note here is Ambresbury Banks, another Iron Age hill fort now filled with beech trees, just off the main path around 700m north of the car park.

Top: Autumn beeches by Blackweir Pond (VP2). Canon 5D IV, 24–70mm at 40mm, ISO 200, 1/13s at f/8, LEE polariser, tripod. Nov.

Autumn colour at Wake Valley Pond (VP5). Canon 5D IV, 24–105mm at 85mm, ISO 100, 1/6s at f/11, LEE polariser, tripod. Nov.

Mandarin duck at Blackweir Pond (VP2). Canon R7, 100–500mm at 500mm, ISO 1600, 1/2000s at f/7.1. Apr.

Reflections at Blackweir Pond (VP2). Canon 5D IV, 24–70mm at 33mm, ISO 200, 1/4s at f/8, LEE polariser, tripod. Nov.

4 TEMPLE HILL

A wide view of Temple Hill (VP1). Canon 5D IV, 24–70mm at 70mm, ISO 100, 1/15s at f/11, 7 shot pano, tripod. Nov.

Part of Warlies Park, 1300 acres of undulating parkland between Waltham Abbey and Epping, Temple Hill provides sweeping views towards the Lee Valley and despite being little more than a stone's throw from the M25 it is a surprisingly peaceful spot. The temple from which the hill takes its name is actually a folly built in 1737, which sits on a rise halfway down the hill and provides a splendid focal point in the landscape.

What to shoot and viewpoints

Viewpoint 1 – Top of the hill

Walk back down Fernhall Lane from your parking place and just before the T-junction, bear right onto the (often muddy) footpath that cuts through the woods. On the other side of the woods, follow the small path diagonally right then go through the gate to the top of Temple Hill. There are views of the temple from anywhere along the top of the hill but perhaps the better angle is over to the right where a small stand of trees can be included in

the foreground for additional depth. A lens in the 70–200mm range is very effective here, either used at the long end with the temple as the main subject or to create a stitched panorama with the temple a point of interest in the impressive wider views looking towards the Lee Valley.

Viewpoint 2 – Bottom of the hill

It is possible to get close to the temple and use it as a foreground for wide-angle shots but it is surrounded by (admittedly discreet) metal railings and the fenced-off area is often overgrown which can distract a bit. From lower down the slope beneath the temple on either side its shape and that of nearby twisted trees can be outlined against the sky – very effective either lit by or silhouetted against the sunrise or sunset. From the northern side of the temple, Boudica's Obelisk is visible on the hilltop to the north east.

Overleaf: First light on the temple (VP2). Canon 5D IV, 24–70mm at 24mm, ISO 100, 1/30s at f/11, LEE polariser, tripod. May.

4 TEMPLE HILL

Top: *The temple framed in the trees (VP1). Canon 5D IV, 100–400mm at 210mm, ISO 100, 0.8s at f/16, tripod. Jan.*

Above: *Sunrise silhouette (VP2). Canon 5D IV, 24–70mm at 24mm, ISO 100, 1/100s at f/22, LEE polariser, tripod. May.*

The temple in infrared (VP2). Fuji X-Pro1, 14mm, ISO 200, 1/850s at f/4. May.

How to get here

Temple Hill is in Upshire, 8 miles south of Harlow.

Take the A414 south from Harlow and at the roundabout take the 3rd exit to join the M11 south. After 4 miles take the exit to join the M25 towards the M1. Leave the M25 at the next exit (junction 26) and at the roundabout take the first exit onto the A121 towards Loughton and follow that road for 2 miles. At the roundabout take the 1st exit onto Epping Road and after around a mile turn left onto Crown Hill. Follow the road out of the forest, under the M25 then at the top of the hill, after the row of houses on the left, turn right onto Fernhall Lane and park in one of the lay-bys.

- **Lat/Long:** 51.69091, 0.05351
- **what3words:** ///yarn.crass.intervals
- **Grid Ref:** TL 420 011
- **Postcode:** EN9 3TA

Accessibility

Although a short flat walk to the views from the top of the field, it's over uneven and often muddy ground – difficult for wheelchairs. The walk to the temple and closer compositions whilst still not far, involve uphill sections.

Best time of year/day

This is an excellent location through the seasons and with views from all directions it is possible to capture both the sunrise and sunset here. The view from the top of the hill is especially good in spring and autumn when the temple is side lit by first light. These are also good times to combine it with a visit to nearby Epping Forest.

Opposite: *First light on the temple (VP2). Canon 5D IV, 24–70mm at 35mm, ISO 100, 1/40s at f/16, tripod. May.*

Morning light on the Stort Navigation (VP1). Canon 5D IV, 24–105mm at 98mm, ISO 100, 1/5s at f/16, tripod. June.

5 THE STORT NAVIGATION

The Stort Navigation is a canalised section of the River Stort running from Bishop's Stortford to its confluence with the Lee Navigation near Hoddesdon. For much of its length the river forms the border between Essex and Hertfordshire so we'll be tiptoeing along (and occasionally stepping over) the very western edge of Essex.

This is a short but interesting section of the river with a variety of subjects in a relatively small area so it serves equally well as a standalone location to photograph or as a starting point from which to explore further. The footpath runs virtually the whole length of the navigation so there is plenty of countryside to discover.

What to shoot and viewpoints

Viewpoint 1 – The river

Turn right from the station car park and take the footpath on the opposite side of the road immediately after the level crossing. This path follows the navigation to Hunsdon Mead (1km) and on to Parndon Mill (around 4km). The only place you could go wrong is about 500m along just before Roydon Lock, where the path splits: take the footbridge to cross the tributary (rather than continuing along it) then carry on alongside the lock and the river beyond.

There are points of interest to use in compositions all along the path: canal boats, overhanging trees, bends in the river and the path itself makes an excellent lead-in line, especially when overgrown with wildflowers. The most interesting stretch is probably the kilometre or so from Roydon Lock onwards, after which it straightens out and is flanked by a continuous hedge that rather hampers compositions. It is worth continuing to the end of this stretch though where, at the far end of Hunsdon Mead, there is another lock and a house by the river.

Top: A misty morning on the Stort (VP1). Canon 5D IV, 24–105mm at 70mm, ISO 100, 1/80s at f/11, LEE 0.6 med ND grad, tripod. June.

Canal boats on the Stort (VP1). Canon 5D IV, 24–70mm at 35mm, ISO 100, 0.6s at f/11, LEE 0.9 med ND grad, tripod. May.

Detail by the lock (VP1). Canon 5D IV, 24–70mm at 47mm, ISO 100, 1/13s at f/8, tripod. May.

The riverside path in spring (VP1). Canon 5D IV, 24–70mm at 59mm, ISO 100, 1/30s at f/8, tripod. May.

5 THE STORT NAVIGATION

Viewpoint 2 – Hunsdon Mead

A flood meadow beside the river, Hunsdon Mead, has been managed under the ancient Lammas system – meaning it's grazed by cattle or sheep after the hay is cut in summer – for over 600 years. As a result, it is lush with wildflowers and butterflies.

The towpath alongside the navigation provides a raised viewpoint over the meadow for wide views but if you want to get closer for tighter or even macro shots of the flowers and butterflies, there is a narrow permissive footpath running around the edge of the meadow. Hunsdon Mead is a nature reserve and Site of Special Scientific Interest so please don't wander across it between March and July as it damages the plants.

Viewpoint 3 – Parndon Mill ♿

If you don't fancy the 4km walk or you just want to visit Parndon Mill, there is parking here in a lay-by on the bend just after the railway bridge. From this parking place there is a circular walk starting at the footpath at the bend in the road. Follow it east for a few minutes then after crossing a footbridge, turn left and walk back along the opposite bank to views of the mill and canal boats moored in front of it. This is a great angle early in the morning; the mill and boats will be bathed in early morning light and reflect in the river if it's suitably calm. Continue along the path, past the lock, across the bridge and either follow the path towards Hunsdon Mead and views of the back of the mill or go through the gate on the left to go around the front of the mill. From the path in front of the mill there are great views east along the river with canal boats and the occasional sculpture (Parndon Mill is an arts centre). Follow the lane to the parking place to complete the loop but before doing so, there is another path between the buildings from the car park to the mill pond – a great spot for reflections.

Top: Summer on the River Stort (VP3). Canon 5D IV, 24–70mm at 35mm, ISO 100, 1/3s at f/16, LEE 0.6 med ND grad, tripod. June.

Middle: Reflections in the River Stort (VP3). Canon 5D IV, 100–400mm at 310mm, ISO 800, 1/500s at f/5.6. June.

Bottom: A misty morning at Parndon Mill (VP3). Canon 5D IV, 24–70mm at 70mm, ISO 200, 1/5s at f/11, LEE 0.6 med ND grad, tripod. June.

How to get here

This section of the Stort Navigation is 2 miles north west of Harlow.

Take the A1019 north from the centre of Harlow and at the roundabout take the first exit onto Elizabeth Way and follow it for just over a mile. At the roundabout take the third exit towards Roydon and at the next roundabout take the second exit to stay on Roydon Road. After just over a mile, turn right onto the High Street (signposted Station) and after half a mile, cross the level crossing and park in the station car park on the left.

Viewpoint 1 & 2 – Hunsdon Mead

- **Lat/Long**: 51.77553, 0.0351
- **what3words**: ///just.stars.words
- **Grid Ref**: TL 405 104
- **Postcode**: CM19 5EH

Viewpoint 3 – Parndon Mill

- **Lat/Long**: 51.7798, 0.08406
- **what3words**: ///learn.grin.jobs
- **Grid Ref**: TL 438 110
- **Postcode**: CM20 2JB

Accessibility

The walk to Hunsdon Mead is just over 1km along a flat and well maintained footpath but narrow kissing gates at the station end (and in a couple of places along the route) would appear to make wheelchair access difficult. There are accessible views of Parndon Mill

Best time of year/day

Spring is probably the best season to visit when the wildflower meadow is in bloom and the hedgerows are thick with blossom but there is something here all year, particularly on calm early mornings when, if conditions are right, there will usually be a veil of mist hanging over the river and meadows or a thick frost in winter.

Above: Dawn at Parndon Mill (VP3). Canon 5D IV, 24–105mm at 28mm, ISO 100, 1/4s at f/11, LEE 0.6 med ND grad, tripod. June.

5 THE STORT NAVIGATION

Top: Mist at Hunsdon Mead (VP2). Canon 5D IV, 24–70mm at 50mm, ISO 100, 1/100s at f/8. May.

Middle: Dew laden wildflowers (VP2). Canon 5D IV, 100–400mm at 170mm, ISO 200, 1/125s at f/8, tripod. June.

Bottom: Golden light over the meadows (VP2). Canon 5D IV, 100–400mm at 400mm, ISO 800, 1/8000s at f/5.6. June.

Dawn on the River Stort (VP1). Canon 5D IV, 24–70mm at 42mm, ISO 100, 0.8s at f/11, LEE 0.6 med ND grad, tripod. May.

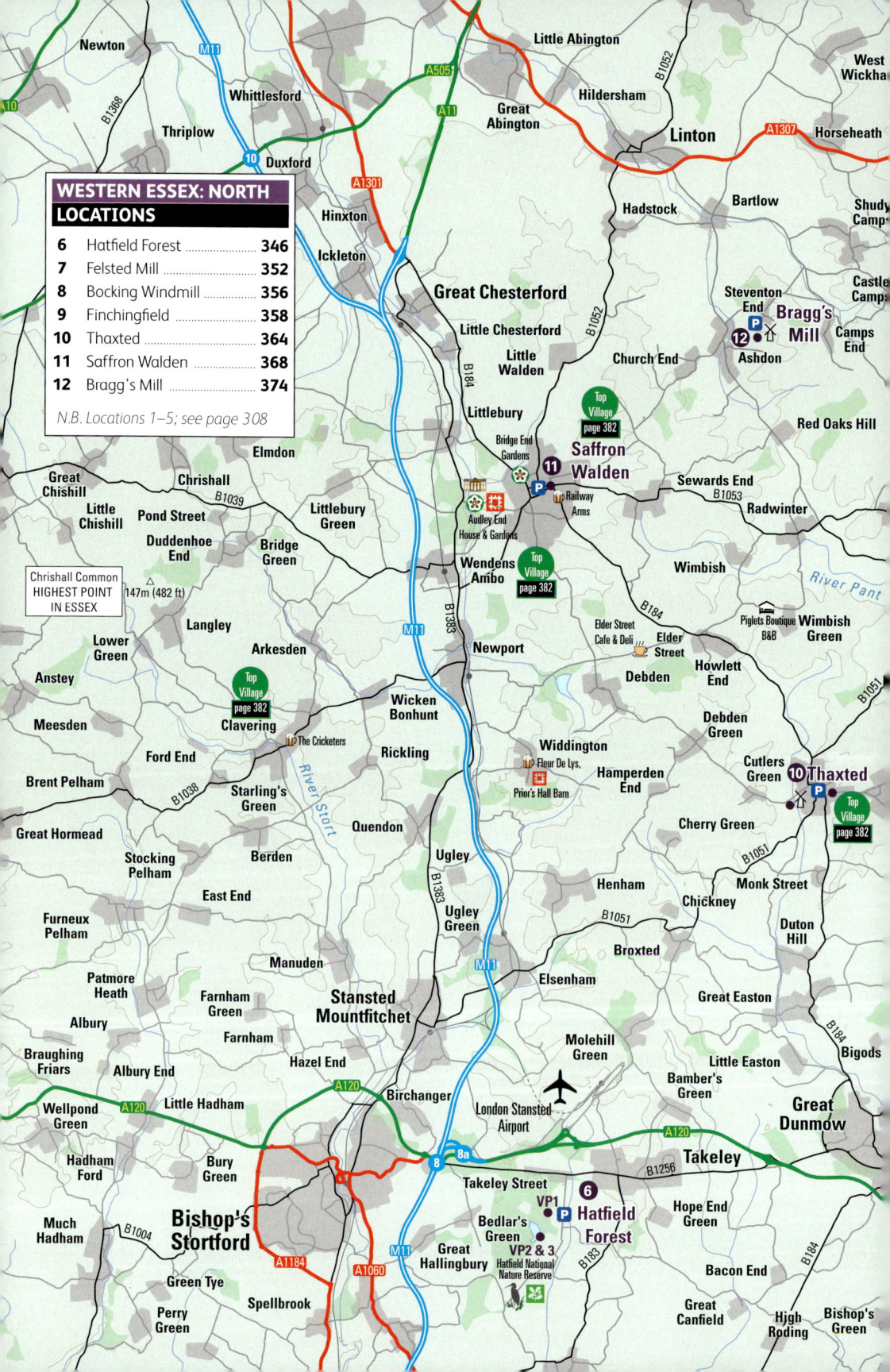

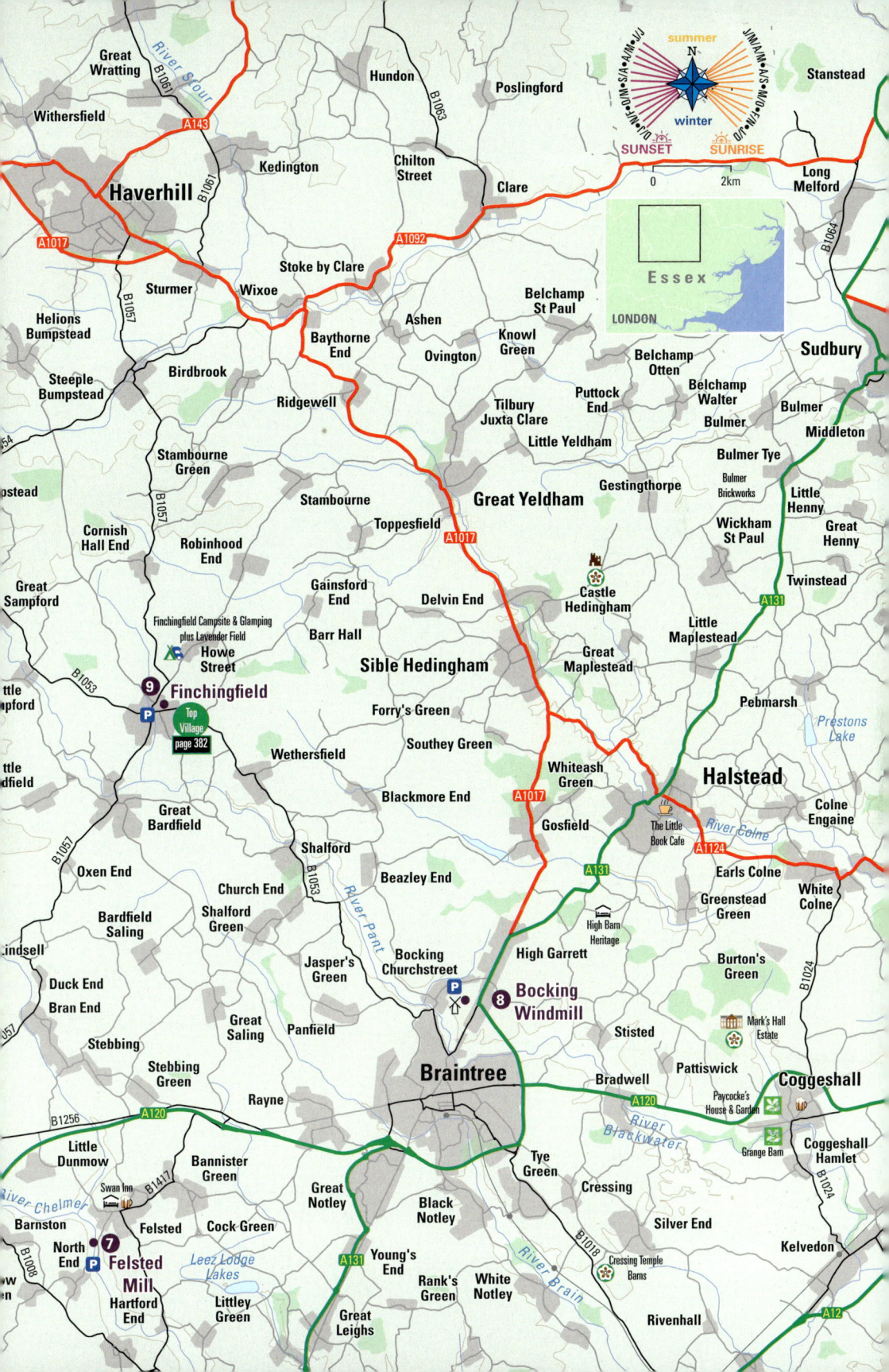

6 HATFIELD FOREST

A walk through Hatfield Forest is like stepping back in time to a medieval royal hunting forest. One of the few remaining areas of the Forest of Essex, Hatfield Forest has been managed (and still is) using the traditional methods of coppicing, pollarding and grazing for almost 1000 years and is believed to be the only surviving example of a complete royal hunting forest in Britain, if not the world.

Thousands of species of flora and fauna are to be found in this unspoiled habitat, which is designated as both a National Nature Reserve and Site of Special Scientific Interest owned and managed by the National Trust, so there is something here for landscape and wildlife photographers as well as those who just like to enjoy a wander with their camera.

What to shoot and viewpoints

Hatfield Forest covers over 400 hectares and is crossed by numerous paths. I couldn't possibly list all the points of interest, so instead what follows is a guide to a small but particularly interesting area of the forest to serve as a starting point for further exploration.

Viewpoint 1 – The meadows
Starting at the entrance car park, go through the gate beside the cattle grid and a parkland of meadows (or *wood pastures* as they are properly known) sprinkled with old trees stretches out to either side of the lane.

Head north across the meadows and this open area dotted with interesting trees and clear views to the east is a great spot for sunrise. Further north on the far side of the plain, several paths lead into the forest, all of which make a good starting point for further exploration. Aside from the areas mentioned below, the woods across this end of the forest are the most photogenic in my opinion and with clear paths are easy to navigate.

You don't actually need to wander far from the entrance lane near the car park though. Scattered within 100m or so along either side of it are some fine individual or groups of trees to photograph and the lane itself serves as a

How to get here
Hatfield Forest is close to Stansted Airport, 12 miles north east of Harlow.

Take the A414 south from Harlow and join the M11 north towards Cambridge. After 9 miles, take the A120 west exit towards Bishops Stortford and take the 5th exit at the roundabout onto the B1256. Follow the B1256 for just over two miles and just after the Green Man pub, turn right at the brown Hatfield Forest sign. The entrance to Hatfield Forest and outer car park is just over half a mile up on the right. If this car park is closed there are marked parking spaces outside the church 300m along the road. If you are visiting during opening hours (visit *nationaltrust.org.uk/hatfield-forest*) there is another car park in the centre of the forest by the lake and café.

- **Lat/Long**: 51.85972, 0.24534
- **what3words**: ///undertone.erupts.iterative
- **Grid Ref**: TL 547 202
- **Postcode**: CM22 6NG

Accessibility

There are some wheelchair-accessible areas along hard standing paths near the lake and the boardwalk; wider forest paths are grass and can be very muddy in winter.

Dogs are welcome but must be kept under close control at all times and on a lead around livestock or where signed. There are toilet facilities by the café.

Best time of year/day

There is something here all year but the highlights have to be spring and autumn. In spring the forest is fresh and green with new foliage, the Hawthorn is thick with blossom and, from mid May to early June, the meadows are alive with buttercups. Autumn brings a beautiful range of gold, russet and red to the trees as the leaves change colour.

Early in the morning is the best time of day; there are better chances of seeing wildlife in the peaceful forest before most visitors arrive and if conditions are right, which they often are in spring and autumn, there may be a veil of mist hanging over the lake and meadows.

In the winter, to reduce damage to the Forest, car parking is limited to the hard standing area only, so check the National Trust's website as you may need to book in advance.

Previous spread: *Cattle in a misty meadow (VP1). Canon 5D II, 24–105mm at 105mm, ISO 100, 1/320s at f/5.6, tripod. Oct.*

Above: *The boardwalk makes a wonderful leading line through the hornbeams (VP2). Canon 5D II, 24–105mm at 95mm, ISO 200, 1.3s at f/8, LEE polariser, tripod. Oct.*

6 HATFIELD FOREST

lead-in line through them. Of particular note are a group of ancient pollarded hornbeams in a copse just to the south of the path not far from the entrance. They can be a bit overgrown in summer but look superb in autumn.

In late spring these meadows are turned yellow by (literally) millions of buttercups which, as well as adding a splash of colour to landscape shots, make beautiful subject themselves using a macro lens or telephoto lens to isolate individual flowers. In addition, one of the herds of Red Poll cattle will usually be grazing this area from May to October adding a further element of interest to your photos. Try getting down low amongst the buttercups for an unusual angle of the grazing or resting cattle. A quick warning: while Red Poll cattle are docile (if rather inquisitive), they should be treated with respect. Avoid getting too close

or approaching them, walk around the herd rather than through it, never get between calves and adults, and remember to close any gates you pass through.

Just before the entrance lane heads into the woods, you'll see a wooden boardwalk on the left. This leads to viewpoint 2.

Top: *Buttercup detail (VP1). Canon 5D IV, 100–400mm at 400mm, ISO 200, 1/640s at f/5.6, LEE polariser, tripod. May.*

Middle: *Ancient hornbeams in spring (VP1). Canon R5, 24–105mm at 105mm, ISO 200, 1/25s at f/8, LEE polariser, tripod. May.*

Bottom: *Hawthorn blossom detail. Canon 5D IV, 24–105mm at 105mm, ISO 200, 1/4s at f/8, LEE polariser, tripod. May.*

Opposite: *Red Poll cattle in the buttercups (VP1). Canon 5D IV, 24–105mm at 55mm, ISO 200, 1/125s at f/8, LEE polariser. May.*

6   HATFIELD FOREST

Viewpoint 2 – The boardwalk ♿

The boardwalk runs through a particularly photogenic patch of woodland east of the lake but just before the boardwalk enters the woods turn right, head through the gate and walk north west across an open area that serves as a car park during the summer. On the far side is a stand of beech trees that looks spectacular in the autumn. The paths leading through it and on the far side up the slope towards it all make great lead-in lines.

Returning to the boardwalk, go through the gate into the trees and the wooden path creates the perfect lead-in line snaking through a series of hornbeams. The light can be a bit low under the trees here so a tripod is useful as is a telephoto lens to foreshorten the curves of the path and tighten the composition to avoid distractions, trees and bright areas of sky around the edges.

A path branches off to the right leading to a jetty on the lake with views across the water to the shell house on the other side. Continue along the boardwalk – where it reaches the end, a gravel path continues along the lake. Turn left instead and there's an interesting area of woodland, on the far side of which a gate leads back into the meadows and north to the entrance car park.

Viewpoint 3 – The lake ♿

The gravel path around the southern edge of the lake is a good spot from which to photograph the aforementioned boardwalk jetty emerging from the trees. The bank is lacking much in the way of foreground interest but early in the morning when the conditions are calm the reflections of the line of trees and jetty are impressive. When the sun gets high enough, it lights the tops of the trees and if you're lucky there may be mist swirling over the water. The path continues to the café and main car park; there are further views across the lake from this side although these are better towards the end of the day when the trees opposite are lit.

Above: Autumn mist over the lake (VP3). Canon 5D II, 24–105mm at 55mm, ISO 100, 1/80s at f/5.6, tripod. Nov.

Opposite Autumn in the forest **Top left**: Canon 5D II, 24–105mm at 105mm, ISO 100, 1/80s at f/11, tripod. Nov. **Right**: Canon 5D II, 70–200mm at 70mm, ISO 100, 1/500s at f/5.6, tripod. Nov. **Middle**: Canon 5D II, 24–105mm at 55mm, ISO 100, 1/80s at f/5.6, tripod. Nov. **Bottom**: Canon 5D II, 24–105mm at 50mm, ISO 100, 1/200s at f/8, tripod. Nov.

7. FELSTED MILL

Felsted Mill is a 19th-century watermill, built to replace a much older one that was destroyed by fire and although it has now been converted to housing it was a working mill up until 1960.

Tucked away in the beautiful countryside just to the south of Felsted, itself a pretty village worth exploring, there is plenty in this peaceful spot on the River Chelmer for photographers to enjoy.

What to shoot and viewpoints

A public footpath runs along the west side of the river from the parking space, follow it north and after about 400 or 500m the mill will be visible through or above the trees ahead.

The twists and turns of the narrow river work well as lead-in lines towards the mill from here and with the right camera height it should also be possible to get reflections of the mill in the water. Up until the point where the river widens into the mill pool there have only been glimpses of the mill but here the view opens up and the mill is fully visible framed by the surrounding trees.

There is more to this area than the water mill though: trees dotted along the river and up in the fields to the west (where another public footpath branches off near to the mill pool) all make effective subjects so keep your mind and eyes open. Less, as they say, is often more. Beyond this point, views are a bit limited through the trees and undergrowth on the bank.

But the footpath carries on beyond the trees alongside the river to the mill where it crosses the footbridge and goes around the mill to the road beyond. The classic shot of the mill reflected in the pool is 50m-south along the road.

Public footpaths and rights of way have been a bit of an issue here in recent years so be sure to check the OS map and stick to the public footpaths, particularly where they cross the mill property.

Opposite: Dawn at Felsted Mill. Canon 5D IV, 24–70mm at 47mm, ISO 100, 1/30s at f/11, LEE 0.6 med ND grad, tripod. Apr.

How to get here

Felsted Mill is on the River Chelmer, 7 miles west of Braintree.

Take the A120 west from Braintree and leave at the exit signposted Felsted B1417. At the roundabout take the second exit onto the B1417 and follow it for just over a mile and a half into Felsted. Turn right at the junction and, after a mile (passing the school and Swan Inn), turn left onto Mill Road. Carry on past the mill and park in the lay-by just over the bridge after the right hand bend.

- **Lat/Long:** 51.84524, 0.42245
- **what3words:** ///retiring.snug.accordion
- **Grid Ref:** TL 669 190
- **Postcode:** CM6 3PE

Accessibility

It is a short walk to the mill on a fairly even grassy path. There are wheelchair-accessible views from the roadside in front of the mill where there is also space for one or two cars to park.

At the time of writing, the footbridge by the mill is closed for repair work. It should be completed by the time of publishing but if not, rather than walking back along Mill Road where there is no footpath, it's safer to drive and park nearer the mill.

Best time of year/day

The mill faces south along the river so winter, when the sun rises and sets further south, is the best time for warm low side light on the building. The mill is in a bit of a dip in the landscape so the sun takes a while to climb high enough and that low position also means it's often misty here early in the morning. During the summer months the riverbank becomes rather overgrown with the more distant views obscured by trees.

Trees in the meadow beyond the mill. Canon 5D IV, 24–70mm at 70mm, ISO 100, 1/40s at f/11, tripod. May.

7 FELSTED MILL

Top: Detail of the mill. Canon 5D IV, 24–70mm at 24mm, ISO 200, 1/160s at f/8. Apr.

Above: Felsted Mill from above. DJI Mavic 2 Pro, 28mm, ISO 100, 1/50s at f/5.6. Apr.

The view along the stream on a cold and misty morning. Canon 5D IV, 24–70mm at 35mm, ISO 100, 1/60s at f/11, LEE 0.6 med ND grad, tripod. May.

8 BOCKING WINDMILL

How to get here

Bocking is a village on the edge of Braintree, 15 miles west of Colchester.

Leave the A12 Colchester bypass at junction 26, signposted A120 Stansted Airport. At the roundabout take the 4th exit onto the A120 and follow the road for 9.5 miles. Take the 3rd exit at the roundabout onto the A131 towards Sudbury. Follow the A131 for 1.5 miles, at the roundabout take the 2nd exit then after almost half a mile turn left onto Church Street. Follow Church Street for just over half a mile, go past Millers Close on the left and then around 250m further along, park in the lay-by on the right in front of a row of bungalows or where it is safe and legal to do so. If you see Windmill Gardens on the left you have gone too far.

Lat/Long:	51.90508, 0.56044
what3words:	///rate.defeat.scouts
Grid Ref:	TL 762 260
Postcode:	CM7 5LQ

Built in 1721, Bocking Windmill is a fully restored, grade I listed post mill. The original site of the mill was 150m further west but in 1830 it was taken down for some reason and rebuilt in its current spot complete with a new sail (bought for a whopping 6 pounds and 8 shillings). Since then the village has spread and houses have almost engulfed the mill but fortunately it still overlooks fields where, with its gleaming white paintwork, it stands out proudly.

What to shoot and viewpoints

All of the views of the windmill are from the public footpath that bisects the large fields it overlooks. The entrance to the public footpath is tucked away between the houses directly across the road from the lay-by. Follow it out into the field where the mill will soon be visible on the left.

Although the lay of the land doesn't allow for a great variety of shots, distance and choice of lens can be used for a bit of diversity. Close up with a wide-angle lens or further back with a 70–200mm or 24–70mm lens all work equally well. Do keep an eye out for modern distractions when considering your composition though; the houses to either side of the windmill and the telegraph wires that run across the field are the main culprits but both can be avoided (or cloned out).

Accessibility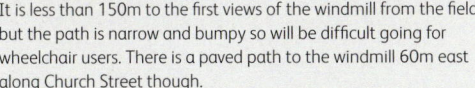

It is less than 150m to the first views of the windmill from the field but the path is narrow and bumpy so will be difficult going for wheelchair users. There is a paved path to the windmill 60m east along Church Street though.

Above: Sunrise at Bocking Windmill. Canon 5D IV, 16–35mm at 16mm, ISO 100, 1/80s at f/22, LEE 0.9 hard ND grad, tripod. June.

Best time of year/day

The sun will rise and set either side of the windmill during the summer months so that is the time to go for colour in the sky around it. The rest of the year it will be all about the first or last light side lighting the windmill, though there is always the chance of sunrise or sunset colours reflecting into the clouds as well. Wherever you shoot the windmill from, the field will feature in any foreground so the best time of year will depend largely on what crop is growing in the field.

9 FINCHINGFIELD

Picture the perfect 'chocolate box' English village – a duck pond on the village green overlooked by cottages painted in pastel colours, an old pub, a windmill and a church at the top of the hill – this is Finchingfield, a pretty village dating back to the Domesday book and said to be the most photographed in the country.

What to shoot and viewpoints

Finchingfield is a lovely village to explore with your camera. Below are some highlights to get you started but the classic view is from the village green. From the western side of the duck pond there are views looking up towards the church or from the footbridge looking towards the windmill. Stand back a bit and the footbridge actually works well as a leading line.

It is a short walk from the pond up to the church and on the way the smaller village green is often a good position from which to photograph the church while avoiding parked cars – the village sign works well as a foreground. Even if churches aren't your thing, it's worth the walk to see the adjacent 16th-century guildhall, the best views of which are through the archway and from the peaceful churchyard on the other side.

Built in 1756, Finchingfield Windmill is the oldest in Essex and is another short walk, down the hill then to the right, cutting across in front of the cottages and keeping an eye out for any interesting details along the way. Pargetting (moulding designs into the external plastering of a wall) is common here and a feature particularly associated with Essex. Views of the mill are a little limited but it can be shot from the green in front of it or from further along the road, where it can be seen behind the thatched cottages. While we are on this side of the village, about 250m along the road past the turn off to Spain's Hall (which is where Jamie Oliver lives if you are interested) is a tiny hexagonal thatched cottage known as the roundhouse for some reason. It is rather photogenic but take care on the road here as there is no footpath.

Parked cars seem to be the bane of pretty villages. Here many of them belong to residents so there is no quieter time to visit, you just have to work around them. Traffic can also be busy and between the two they will seriously test your compositional or Photoshop skills (not to mention your patience). These things are a fact of modern life but with careful composition – thinking about height and angle to hide parked cars (or better position them to clone out later) or using tighter framing to isolate groups of buildings – it is possible to minimise the intrusion.

Finchingfield in spring. Canon 5D IV, 24–105mm at 32mm, ISO 200, 1/125s at f/8, tripod. Apr.

Opposite: *Last light on the village. Canon 5D IV, 24–70mm at 33mm, ISO 100, 1/3s at f/11, LEE polariser, tripod. Feb.*

9 FINCHINGFIELD

Top: Cottage detail. Canon 5D IV, 24–105mm at 60mm, ISO 200, 1/80s at f/8. Apr.

Above: Cottage detail. Canon 5D IV, 24–105mm at 60mm, ISO 200, 1/80s at f/8. Apr.

Top right: Last light at the village pond. Canon 5D IV, 24–70mm at 31mm, ISO 400, 1/4s at f/11, LEE 0.6 med ND grad, tripod. Feb.

The guildhall entrance. Canon 5D IV, 24–105mm at 50mm, ISO 200, 1/100s at f/8. Apr.

How to get here

Finchingfield is a village 8.5 miles north west of Braintree.

Take the B1053 north from Braintree and follow it for 8.5 miles, through the villages of Shalford and Wethersfield all the way into Finchingfield. Cross the bridge over the pond, turn right just before the war memorial then left and park on the road at the top of the green. If there aren't any spaces, park wherever it's safe and legal to do so at the edge of the green.

- **Lat/Long**: 51.96792, 0.44972
- **what3words**: ///repair.bunks.surprises
- **Grid Ref**: TL 683 327
- **Postcode**: CM7 4JS

Accessibility

The village is largely wheelchair friendly. The village centre is in a dip so there are some gentle slopes and in some areas, such as towards the church, there are no footpaths along the road. Wheelchair entrance to the churchyard is on the far side in the south east corner.

Best time of year/day

The classic view of the village from the pond gets the sun rising behind it but I think it works best when bathed in the last warm light of the day. This is somewhere you can visit at any time of year. Spring and summer are perhaps best when trees are green and flowers are in bloom but Finchingfield is very popular with tourists so it's best to avoid holidays and sunny weekends.

10 THAXTED

Thaxted is a well preserved historical town tucked away in the Essex countryside, where its towering church spire and famous windmill look out over the patchwork of surrounding farmland.

The town has a connection to Dick Turpin – there is even a cottage bearing his name – but, rather disappointingly it has to be said, there is no evidence that the famous 18th-century highwayman ever lived in or even visited the town at all. Gustav Holst on the other hand definitely did live in Thaxted for several years and it was here he began work on The Planets. His house is marked with a blue plaque.

What to shoot and viewpoints

Viewpoint 1 – The town ♿
Landscape photographers will no doubt be drawn to Thaxted for its windmill but there is far more to discover by exploring the compact but pretty town centre. The highlights are the Tudor guildhall, which along with the church up on the hill behind it, dominates the northern end of Town Street. The challenge when photographing them will be avoiding parked cars so compose carefully. The three roads heading up hill from the guildhall all lead to the church and the windmill beyond, but the cobbled Stony Lane is a nice walk through the churchyard.

Viewpoint 2 – The windmill
From the top of the churchyard you'll get your first glimpse of the windmill between the rows of Almshouses. From here it's just a short walk south along the signposted path.

John Webb's Windmill stands proudly at the top of a small hill, with farmland rolling away into the distance. Perhaps the best views of the mill are from the field sloping down

Previous spread: Last light on the windmill (VP2). Canon 5D IV, 16–35mm at 30mm, ISO 100, 1/8s at f/16. July.

Top: Thaxted from the fields south of the town. Canon 5D IV, 24–105mm at 80mm, ISO 200, 1/3s at f/11, tripod. Aug.

Above: The guildhall. Canon 5D IV, 24–70mm at 24mm, ISO 100, 1/50s at f/16, LEE polariser, tripod. July.

Opposite top: Cottages on Watling Street. Canon 5D IV, 24–70mm at 60mm, ISO 200, 1/200s at f/8, LEE polariser. July.
Bottom: Thaxted windmill from the Almshouses. Canon 5D IV, 24–105mm at 32mm, ISO 400, 1/50s at f/8, LEE polariser. Aug.

How to get here

Thaxted is a small town 15 miles north west of Braintree.

Take the A120 west from Braintree towards Stansted Airport and after 7 miles take the exit onto the B184 to Great Dunmow. At the bottom of the sliproad, take the 3rd exit at the roundabout and go straight on. Take the first exit at the next roundabout onto the B1256 towards Thaxted. Keep on this road for just over a mile and at the second roundabout take the 3rd exit onto the B184. Follow this road for just over 6 miles into Thaxted and park in one of the spaces along Town Street.

	Lat/Long:	51.9536, 0.34409
	what3words:	///stands.bands.skyrocket
	Grid Ref:	TL 611 309
	Postcode:	CM6 2LA

Accessibility

Distances are small and the town is wheelchair friendly although Stony Lane is steep and bumpy. Watling Street would be a better route to the church, and Fishmarket Street a more direct route to the windmill.

Best time of year/day

The town can be photographed at any time but as it sits on the eastern side of a slope, the light is perhaps best in the morning. The end of the day is a good time to photograph the windmill when it is lit by the last low sunlight as the sun goes down over the fields to the west. There will be interest all year round but depending on the crop, the fields will look their best in spring or summer.

10 THAXTED

Thaxted's impressive church. Canon 5D IV, 16–35mm at 24mm, ISO 100, 1/60s at f/11, tripod. June.

in front of it, quite where in the field will depend on the time of day, the direction the mill is facing and how photogenic the crop in the field is. A public footpath runs around the field and both the mill and church are visible from all the way down to the bottom of the hill so explore away but please respect the crops.

The view looking across the fields from the mill itself can be rather good at sunset so as always don't forget to look behind you.

Viewpoint 3 – Distant views

The windmill and church can be seen across farmland from some of the roads coming into Thaxted, particularly the B184 south of the town and Bolford Street to the west. Parking can be problematic though and shooting from the roadside unsafe so instead I would recommend getting an OS map and exploring the footpaths in those areas, of which there are plenty.

The view from the windmill. Canon 5D IV, 16–35mm at 35mm, ISO 100, 8s at f/22, LEE Little Stopper & 0.9 hard ND grad, tripod. June.

11 SAFFRON WALDEN

A picturesque market town in the north west corner of Essex, Saffron Walden's name and historically much of its wealth came from the Saffron crocus, which was widely grown here in the Middle Ages when the saffron trade was at its peak.

Today saffron is used in cookery; back then it would have been largely used as dye by East Anglia's flourishing wool industry but as it takes thousands of flowers' stigma to produce a few grams of the finished product, saffron remains the most expensive spice in the world.

What to shoot and viewpoints

With a rich heritage, many well preserved historic buildings and a relaxed air, Saffron Walden is a wonderful place to wander with a camera. This is a short route between some of the more celebrated spots but there are lots of hidden gems to be uncovered along the town's old streets.

Beginning at the Common car park, cross the road and cut through Rose and Crown walk to the Market Place. Today most of the buildings round the square are Victorian but there has been a market held here since 1141. Of note are the library and impressive timber-frame town hall standing over a stone portico. The latter houses the tourist information centre – worth a visit if you'd like a bit more information on the town than space here allows. In the centre of the square an elaborate drinking fountain makes a great focal point in the foreground. Markets are held on Tuesdays and Saturdays so choose your day to visit depending on whether you want to photograph an empty square or the bustle of the market.

If shopping is of interest, head west along King Street to explore The Rows. Our route however, goes north up Market Hill and turning left onto Church Street. The spire of Saffron Walden's imposing church – the largest in Essex – is hard to miss from anywhere in the town but it is revealed in all its glory from Church Street where, if you can avoid parked cars, there is a great angle from which to photograph it with a row of timber-framed cottages in the foreground. Head up to the churchyard to explore further, keeping an eye out for the peregrines that nest at the base of the spire, then follow the path west onto the High Street. >>

How to get here

Saffron Walden is a small town 17 miles south east of Cambridge.

Take the M11 south from Cambridge for 8 miles and leave at junction 10 signposted A505 Saffron Walden. At the roundabout take the first exit onto the A505; at the next roundabout continue on the A505 and at the third roundabout take the 3rd exit onto the A1301. Continue on the A1301 then the B184 for almost 7 miles into Saffron Walden. Turn left in the High Street to stay on the B184/George Street, signposted Thaxted. At the roundabout take the first exit and park in the car park on the right.

	Lat/Long:	52.02406, 0.24363
	what3words:	///custard.gong.landed
	Grid Ref:	TL 540 385
	Postcode:	CB10 1LX

Opposite: First light at Castle Street. Canon 5D IV, 24–70mm at 47mm, ISO 100, 1/200s at f/8, LEE polariser, tripod. July.

Accessibility

The route is largely flat or gently sloping and wheelchair friendly with all paths being paved apart from the gravel paths in Bridge End Gardens.

Best time of year/day

Saffron Walden is worth visiting at any time of year but the gardens will be lusher and more interesting in spring and summer. Tuesdays or Saturdays are the days to visit if you want to photograph the market stalls in the square (or not if you want to avoid them).

Above: The view from Church Street at first light. Canon 5D IV, 24–70mm at 24mm, ISO 100, 1/30s at f/8, 5 shot pano, LEE polariser, tripod. Apr.

Overleaf: Colours and details of Saffron Walden.

11 SAFFRON WALDEN

11 SAFFRON WALDEN

Turn right and walk down the hill to Bridge Street; there are some lovely timber-framed buildings at the junction here and a great view down the hill but you'll need to be patient or be there early to avoid traffic. Carry on down the hill (if you like old buildings, side streets like Freshwell Street are all worth exploring) and just past the Eight Bells pub is one of the entrances to Bridge End Gardens. There is plenty to keep a photographer busy here in the peaceful rose gardens, formal gardens, walled gardens and maze (though to photograph the latter you'll first need to find your way to the raised platform in the middle).

Take one of the southern exits from Bridge End Gardens onto the charming Castle Street, lined with a colourful cluster of old cottages. Parked cars make the angles a little narrow here for wide shots along the street but not impossible and at least the parking is along the opposite side of the road so the houses aren't obscured. From Castle Street turn right onto Museum Street, passing the east end of the church before turning left onto Church Street again. At the end of the road are the castle ruins and across from them, the Common car park. While you're on the Common, one more point of interest: across the park from the car park is the turf maze (or more accurately, labyrinth). Its age and original purpose is unclear but it is the largest in the world although perhaps more interesting from a historic point of view than photographic.

For those interested in street or action photography, there's one last thing worth mentioning: the impressive One Minet Skatepark by the leisure centre to the southern edge of town on the Thaxted Road.

First light in Bridge End Gardens. Canon 5D IV, 24–105mm at 80mm, ISO 200, 0.4s at f/16, LEE polariser, tripod. June.

12 BRAGG'S MILL

Built in 1757 Bragg's Mill is a recently restored post mill near the pretty village of Ashdon, in the very north of Essex just a stone's throw from the Cambridgeshire border.

Aside from its pristine condition, the attraction for photographers is the windmill's beautiful location in a peaceful spot beside a field, high (by Essex standards anyway) on a hill overlooking the surrounding countryside.

What to shoot and viewpoints

The mill is visible from several angles, all within a short walk from the car park. The nearest is the close up view, which is a good place to start.

With no fences, visitors are able to wander around the whole perimeter of the windmill, perfect if you want to get close in with a wide-angle lens for dramatic photos looking up along the sails. It's easy for the subject to become distorted with this kind of shot so try and keep the mill central and the sails away from the corners or, if you're feeling creative, just embrace the distortion. For a bit more room for frontal views of the mill you can pop through the gap in the hedge in front of the mill to the edge of the field.

Across the lane behind the windmill, a wildflower meadow slopes gently down the hill providing an attractive foreground during the spring and summer for shots of the mill outlined from behind against the sky. A public footpath runs across the meadow, which is generally clearly mown though it may be necessary to deviate from it slightly to avoid the rather inconvenient telegraph pole spoiling the view from directly behind the mill. Wandering off to one side moves the pole out of the way, opening up a 3/4 view of the mill and makes it easier to remove the pole in processing.

Another footpath runs south past the cottages to the end of the lane and then on to the far corner of the field in front of the mill. After passing the cottages, walk along

Last light on Bragg's Mill. Canon 5D IV, 16–35mm at 20mm, ISO 100, 1/25s at f/11, LEE 0.6 med ND grad, tripod. July.

the path on the field side of the hedge and there are views back up towards the mill. It's a great angle for capturing the wider surroundings.

For those interested in a closer look, the windmill is open the second Sunday of the month between May and October.

Overleaf: The view from the wildflower meadow. Canon 5D IV, 24–70mm at 24mm, ISO 100, 1/15s at f/16, LEE polariser, tripod. June.

How to get here

Bragg's Mill is in Ashdon, a village 5 miles north east of Saffron Walden.

Take Ashdon Road east from Saffron Walden Common and after around 2.5 miles continue onto Walden Road and through the village of Ashdon. On the far side, after a sweeping bend, take the small turning on the right, signposted The Camps, Steverton End and Haverhill. Take the next right – a single lane road that climbs the half-mile up the hill. There's a small car park across the road from the mill.

- **Lat/Long:** 52.05866, 0.32506
- **what3words:** ///retrieves.streamers.else
- **Grid Ref:** TL 594 425
- **Postcode:** CB10 2JA

Accessibility

The windmill is less than 50m from the car park and all of the viewpoints are less than 200m away. The footpaths are unsuitable for wheelchairs but access is possible on the short grass around the mill itself. There are no facilities here.

Best time of year/day

With views from different angles Bragg's Mill has options at either end of the day all through the year. Frosty winter mornings are atmospheric and, during the summer, wildflowers will be in bloom in the meadows and the crop should be ripening in the fields (depending of course on which crop is being grown). The mill faces west so it is warmed by the last light of the day all year but it also catches the morning light on the sides once the sun gets over the nearby hills.

BRAGG'S MILL

Sunset at Bragg's Mill. Canon 5D IV, 16–35mm at 16mm, ISO 100, 0.6s at f/22, 2 shot HDR, tripod. June.

Top: The view across the fields from the mill. Canon 5D IV, 16–35mm at 30mm, ISO 100, 1.3s at f/16, LEE 0.6 med ND grad, tripod. July. **Middle**: The surrounding fields bathed in evening light. Canon 5D IV, 24–70mm at 59mm, ISO 100, 1/10s at f/22, LEE 0.9 med ND grad, tripod. June. **Bottom**: A distant view of the mill. Canon 5D IV, 16–35mm at 16mm, ISO 100, 1/10s at f/11, LEE 0.9 med ND grad, tripod. July.

TOWNS & VILLAGES

TOWNS & VILLAGES

With their jumbled cottages, timeless windmills, sleepy village greens and ancient churches, some of the prettiest villages in East Anglia (and indeed England) are to be found nestled amongst the patchwork of the Essex countryside.

Churchend, Foulness Island
Separated from the mainland by a network of creeks, Foulness Island is 6000 acres of farm and marshland teeming with wildlife, its tiny population of less than 200 split between two villages. You would think that the largest island in Essex and fourth largest in England would be better known but this remote rural paradise is owned by the Ministry of Defence and, from Monday to Friday, used as a testing centre for everything from grenades to guided missiles.

There is no public access to the island (other than via the Broomway when the ranges are inactive, see page 266) apart from to visit the Heritage Centre at Churchend, which is open on the first Sunday of the month between April and October. Visitors do not need to book or get permission to visit the centre. More information can be found at: qinetiq.com/en/shoeburyness/

Clavering
Clavering means 'the place where clover grows' and scattered around no fewer than seven village greens, it lives up to its name. If you are looking for pretty thatched cottages, the area around the church and Middle Street is a good place to start.

Clavering is on the B1038, 6 miles south west of Saffron Walden, CB11 4QR.

Colchester
Britain's oldest recorded town, Colchester is steeped in over 2000 years of history, the site dating back to before the Romans made it their capital of Britain in AD 49. Signs of its past can be seen everywhere but it is not just history lovers who would enjoy wandering with a camera here – there are also modern attractions for photographers, the Firstsite arts centre building, for example, makes a great long-exposure subject.

Colchester is off the A12. Town centre car park: CO3 3AA.

Previous spread: Thaxted. **Above**: Clavering. **Opposite**: Colchester.

TOWNS & VILLAGES

TOWNS & VILLAGES

Dedham
In the very north of Essex on the border with Suffolk, Dedham is a small but attractive village clustered around a High Street dominated by the 15th-century church so familiar from its appearance in many of the paintings of John Constable. Its location in some of East Anglia's most beautiful countryside makes it a must-see.

For more information see page 68.

Finchingfield
A charming village surrounding a gently sloping village green complete with duck pond, it's no surprise that Finchingfield is one of the county's most celebrated and photographed villages.

For more information see page 358.

Good Easter
Blink and you might miss Good Easter in the endless countryside, west of Chelmsford but what is hard to miss is the beautiful church and the timber barns, which date back to the Norman period.

Good Easter is 6 miles north west of Chelmsford. Parking is on the roadside where safe to do so: CM1 4RS.

Hatfield Broad Oak
Just to the south of Hatfield Forest it is not hard to imagine where this quaint village got its name and although the forest has some suitably old and wide oaks, it is unclear for which tree it is named. There are some wonderful cottages to be found along Cage End and Broad Street Green.

Hatfield Broad Oak is on the B183, 7.5 miles south east of Bishops Stortford. Parking is in the High Street: CM22 7HF.

*Top: Good Easter. **Middle**: Hatfield Broad Oak. **Bottom**: Pleshey.*

Pleshey

This quiet, well kept village of thatched and pargeted cottages gathered around the earthwork remains of Pleshey Castle in the heart of the Essex countryside must surely be one of the county's finest.

Pleshey is 8 miles north west of Chelmsford. Parking is at the church or village hall: CM3 1HA.

Saffron Walden

An ancient market town with timbered houses aplenty, a towering church and lots of green spaces, Saffron Walden is a beautiful place to explore with the camera.

For more information see page 368.

Stock

Centred around a narrow village green, Stock is a traditional but rather well heeled village with gastro pubs and posh restaurants and a recent inclusion in the Sunday Times' top 50 places to live in Britain. Which all means it is suitably well kept for photography.

Stock is on the B1007, 6 miles south of Chelmsford. Parking is at the village hall: CM4 9NF.

Thaxted

With many fine timber-framed buildings, an impressive church, a windmill and a history dating back 1000 years, the beautiful country town of Thaxted is one of the jewels in Essex's crown.

For more information see page 364.

Tillingham

Out on the quiet Dengie Peninsula, there is something timeless about Tillingham's small village green (aside from the parked cars that is). Known as The Square it is flanked by the church, an old pub, red telephone box and plenty of the white weather-boarded cottages so typical of Essex.

Tillingham is on the B1021, 7 miles north of Burnham on Crouch. Parking is on The Square: CM0 7SU.

*Top: Tillingham. **Middle**: Stock. **Bottom**: Wivenhoe.*

TOWNS & VILLAGES

Wendens Ambo
A pretty village with an unusual name. The lane leading up hill to the church, flanked to one side by picture-postcard thatched cottages is a particularly photogenic view. The unusual name originated in the 17th century when the villages of Wenden Magna and Wenden Parva were merged, Ambo being the Latin word for both.

Wendens Ambo is on the B1039, 3 miles west of Saffron Walden. Parking is at the village hall: CB11 4JZ.

Writtle
With a duck pond at one end and the church at the other, Writtle's large, tree-lined village green is very attractive. The village was the unlikely birthplace of British broadcasting when the Marconi Company, based in nearby Chelmsford, broadcast the first radio programme from an old army hut near the village green in 1922.

Writtle is off the A414, 2 miles west of Chelmsford. Car park is near the green: CM1 3DT.

Wivenhoe
On the north bank of the River Colne, just 3 miles downstream of Colchester, Wivenhoe is an old town with a history of shipbuilding, fishing and smuggling. The narrow old streets leading down to the quay are full of character (and one or two pubs).

Wivenhoe is off the A133, 4 miles south east of Colchester. High Street car park: CO7 9AZ.

Top: Wendens Ambo. **Right**: Writtle.
Opposite: Pleshey.

CHURCHES

CHURCHES

Essex boasts some of the oldest churches in the country. They range from the towering cathedral-sized medieval churches built with the wealth of the wool trade to tiny rural chapels in the remote countryside. Regardless of age or size, they make excellent subjects particularly for black and white or infrared photography, which highlights the shapes and textures of these old buildings. What follows are just a few of the most photogenic and historic.

St Peter's Church, Alresford

Destroyed by fire in 1971, the ruins of St Peter's are a wonderfully atmospheric place for photography. They are also shrouded in mystery. The site is long believed to have been used for witchcraft and continues to attract ghost hunters presumably looking for the pirate Robert Bray, who was buried at the church in 1724 in a grave away from the others, his tombstone marked with cross bones. Legend has it his ghost can be seen at night, roaming the church grounds.

There is parking for several cars by the church, near the war memorial just off Ford Lane, Alresford CO7 8AS.

St Laurence Church, Blackmore

Tucked away on the edge of a pretty village, the most striking feature of St Laurence church is the large wooden bell tower. The tower was built in 1400 but the church itself dates back to the 12th century.

There is parking in front of the church at the end of Church Street, Blackmore CM4 0RN.

St. Peter on the Wall, Bradwell-on-Sea

Built by St Cedd in 654 on the foundations of the gatehouse of a Roman fort (hence the name), this is one of the oldest churches in England still in use. Over the centuries it has survived the North Sea, fires, dissolution, World War II bombings and even being used as a cowshed.

For more information see page 218.

St Mary's Church, Broxted

A pretty church on an ancient site in beautiful Essex countryside, St Mary's has much of historic interest for photographers but it also has an interesting modern addition: two windows installed in 1991 commemorate the captivity and eventual release of John McCarthy, a journalist and resident of Broxted, who was kidnapped in Lebanon.

The church is set back from the B1051, 3.5 miles south west of Thaxted, nearest postcode CM6 2BU.

Chelmsford Cathedral

Chelmsford Cathedral was originally just a parish church but when the diocese of Chelmsford was created in 1914 it became the second smallest cathedral serving the second largest diocese in the country.

The cathedral is on New Street CM1 1TY. The nearest parking is Waterloo Lane Car Park 180m away.

St Mary's Church, Chickney

Hidden amongst the trees, the church at Chickney is a peaceful atmospheric place and one of the oldest churches in Essex, dating back to some time between AD 850 and 1000.

St Mary's is off the B1051, 4.2 miles south west of Thaxted, nearest postcode CM6 2BY. The turning is unmarked but is next to a *sharp bends ahead – max speed 20* sign. Follow the lane to the end, bearing right at the forks.

St Nicholas Chapel, Coggeshall

St Nicholas Chapel is a tiny building, originally the gatehouse chapel for Coggeshall Abbey and the most complete remaining building.

Park on Bridge Street and walk the 400m along Abbey Lane (a private road) to the chapel. It's also worth following the path further still and looping left up into the village.

Top left: St Nicholas Chapel, Coggeshall. **Middle left**: St Laurence Church, Blackmore. **Bottom left**: St Andrew's Church, Greensted. **Top right**: St Peter's Church, Alresford. **Bottom right**: Chelmsford Cathedral.

CHURCHES

CHURCHES

Top: All Saints' Church, Vange.
Above: All Saints' Church, East Horndon.

Opposite top: Copford Church.
Bottom: The Round Church, Little Maplestead.

Copford Church

Copford Church is an interesting Norman church in an idyllic location on the edge of the village tucked away amongst the trees beside the cricket pitch. The location alone makes it a great church to photograph but there are also plenty of interesting details inside and out to discover.

Copford Church has a small car park off Aldercar Road, Copford CO6 1DG.

All Saints' Church, East Horndon

Built 500 years ago in red Tudor brick, East Horndon church is an unusually shaped church with a rather spooky air. Thanks in part to its isolated position on a hilltop in a somewhat overgrown churchyard (the church has been redundant for over 50 years) but perhaps also because it is said that after her execution, supporters of Anne Boleyn smuggled her severed head (or possibly her heart) and buried it here.

Park in Thorndon Country Park South car park, CM13 3LH, walk back to the Brentwood Road and 500m south is a footpath on the right that leads to the church.

St Andrew's Church, Greensted

This pretty church, tucked away in a tiny village deep in the Essex countryside is believed to be the oldest wooden church in the world. The church has been added to over the centuries but the nave, made of split oak trunks was dated to around 1053 and archaeological evidence suggests there was a much earlier church on the site.

St Andrew's is near the end of Church Lane, Ongar CM5 9LD, where there is parking on the roadside.

Lambourne Church

This neat, white-painted and weatherboard church dates back to the 12th century although it has been much added to over the centuries. It is in a glorious rural location so peaceful that it's hard to believe the M11 is only 2km away as the crow flies.

Lambourne Church is on Church Lane, Abridge RM4 1AH around one mile off the A113 Ongar Road. There is a grass car park beside it.

CHURCHES

The Round Church, Little Maplestead
During the Crusades the church at Little Maplestead belonged to the Order of the Knights of St John of Jerusalem (known today as St John Ambulance). The current church was built in 1335 on the same site and is one of only four surviving medieval round churches in England.

The church is just along Church Road from Little Maplestead CO9 2SL but there is limited parking.

Mistley Towers
Being one of only two churches designed by Robert Adam, Mistley Towers is architecturally significant and photographically rather interesting as well. This pair of porticoed towers once sat at either end of an unusual 18th-century church but the middle was later demolished, leaving just the two towers in a small graveyard.

For more information see page 74.

All Saints' Church, Vange
The village of Vange has been swallowed up by the spread of Basildon but despite its proximity to the town, this simple medieval church at the top of a low hill feels remarkably peaceful.

All Saints' Church is signposted from the B1464 London Road SS16 4QA, where there is a small car park just off the road.

St Mary's Church, Mundon
Half hidden in the trees this timber-framed, weather-boarded church is a recently renovated grade I listed building dating back to the 14th century although its position on the pilgrims' route to St Peter's at Bradwell suggests an older church once stood here.

For more information see page 210.

Waltham Abbey Church

A magnificent Norman church which dominates the grounds of the old abbey. It is said that King Harold stopped at Waltham Abbey Church on his way to fight William of Normandy in the famous battle of Hastings in 1066. It clearly didn't do much good; when, according to legend, he returned to Waltham Abbey, it was to be buried.

Park in the Waltham Abbey Gardens car park, off the roundabout, EN9 1XQ and enjoy the abbey and gardens on the walk to the church, which is easily spotted.

St Clement's Church, West Thurrock

Famous for being one of the churches used in the film Four Weddings and a Funeral (for the funeral, if you're wondering), there has been a church on this site for over 1000 years. Today the church feels a little forlorn, surrounded by industry and literally overshadowed by a huge Procter & Gamble soap factory (cleanliness really is next to godliness), but it was in fact the company who took responsibility for the grade I listed church, rescuing it from near dereliction and fully restoring it.

St Clement's is on St Clement's Road, West Thurrock RM20 4AL in the middle of a retail and industrial area. There is a small car park on the left just past the entrance.

Willingale churches

Unusually, for a village of its size Willingale has two churches. Especially unusual is that they both share the same churchyard. There are various legends explaining why but the most likely is that during the middle ages, when the wool industry bought an increase in population (and wealth) to the village, a larger church was needed so they built a second. They are now in one parish though until 1929 were completely separate, each with its own rector.

Both churches are on The Street, Willingale CM5 0SJ, where there is limited roadside parking.

Opposite: Willingale churches. ***Top left***: Waltham Abbey Church.
Bottom left: St Clement's Church, West Thurrock.
Above: Lambourne Church.

HISTORIC BUILDINGS & GARDENS

HISTORIC BUILDINGS & GARDENS

Hundreds of years of invasions from Romans, Saxons, Vikings and Normans has shaped the history of Essex and left it with a remarkable number of historic sites to visit and photograph.

Audley End
Audley End is a magnificent Jacobean mansion near Saffron Walden. Transformed in the 18th century by Robert Adam and with grounds landscaped by Capability Brown, the original house was palatial – an incredible three times larger than it is today.

For more information visit *english-heritage.org.uk/visit/places/audley-end-house-and-gardens*

Beeleigh Abbey
Built in the 12th century, the abbey and gardens have undergone much restoration since the start of the 20th century. Beeleigh Abbey is privately owned but the grounds and gardens are open to the public several times a year.

For more information visit: *visitmaldon.co.uk/beeleigh-abbey*

Beth Chatto Gardens
In 1960, Beth Chatto took an overgrown wasteland of brambles, parched gravel and boggy ditches and over the years transformed it using plants adapted by nature to thrive in different conditions into an inspirational, informal garden. The gardens are best known for the gravel area (which is never watered) but the entire garden is a wonderful place for some floral photography.

For more information visit: *bethchatto.co.uk*

Bridge End Garden, Saffron Walden
Created in 1840 as a series of different spaces including a maze, walled garden, rose garden, wilderness and formal Dutch garden, Bridge End Garden is free to visit. It's an oasis hidden behind the old streets of Saffron Walden.

For more information see page 368.

Previous spread: Markshall Estate.

Opposite top: Beth Chatto gravel garden.
Bottom: Beeleigh Abbey.

Audley End.

HISTORIC BUILDINGS & GARDENS

St Botolph's Priory.

Bulmer Brickworks

Bulmer Brickworks is a slice of history – the Bulmer Brick and Tile company has been making bricks by hand here using the same traditional materials since the Tudor period. It isn't open to the public, although they do occasionally run tours, but a by-road running along the side of the brickworks provides excellent views of the kilns.

For more information visit: *bulmerbrickandtile.co.uk*

Colchester Castle

Set atop a hill and surrounded by parkland, Colchester Castle was built in 1076 and is the largest Norman keep in Europe, yet the site is much older. The castle was built on top of the ruins of the Roman Temple of Claudius, which dates back to 43AD, when Colchester was the first Roman capital of Britain.

For more information visit: *cimuseums.org.uk*

Colchester St Botolph's Priory

These impressive Norman ruins are set in a small peaceful park and it's a great place for long exposures under the right conditions. Sadly, it also seems to be a popular place for those who take their drinking seriously, which some may find intimidating.

For more information visit: *english-heritage.org.uk/visit/places/colchester-st-botolphs-priory*

Cressing Barns

Built in the 13th century by the Knights Templar, Cressing Barns are now amongst the oldest timber barns and some of the last remaining Templar buildings in England. Don't miss the restored Tudor walled garden.

For more information visit: *explore-essex.com/places-to-go/find-whats-near-me/cressing-temple-barns*

Opposite top: Colchester Castle. **Bottom left**: Bulmer Brickworks. **Right**: Cressing Barns.

HISTORIC BUILDINGS & GARDENS 401

HISTORIC BUILDINGS & GARDENS

Green Island Gardens
The vision of owner and garden designer Fiona Edmund, the perfectly named Green Island Gardens are 20 acres of tranquil private gardens tucked away in lush verdant woodland near Ardleigh. This is a genuine hidden gem that's worth visiting for the pond alone.

For more information visit: *greenislandgardens.co.uk*

Hadleigh Castle
Built in the 13th century on high ground overlooking the Thames estuary, Hadleigh Castle was designed as a base for defending against raids into London. Today, the ruined towers are an iconic sight up above the marshes and the views from the castle not to be missed.

For more information see page 296.

Hedingham Castle
A formidable block towering over the village of Castle Hedingham (itself worth a visit), the Norman keep is all that remains of Hedingham Castle but it is one of the best preserved in England.

For more information visit: *hedinghamcastle.co.uk*

RHS Garden Hyde Hall
Set in a beautiful area of gently rolling countryside, Hyde Hall has been transformed from what was a windswept hill in the 1950s to a jewel in the Essex landscape. The panoramic views across the countryside here are almost as impressive as the gardens.

For more information visit: *rhs.org.uk/gardens/hyde-hall*

Hylands House
A neo classical mansion house set in 574 acres of Humphrey Repton landscaped parkland near Chelmsford, Hylands House has recently been restored to its gleaming white, 19th-century splendour. Bearing more than a passing resemblance to another house the same colour in Washington DC, Hylands has twice been used as a film double for the US White House.

For more information visit: *hylandsestate.co.uk*

Top: Hedingham Castle. **Above**: Hylands House.

Opposite top: RHS Garden Hyde Hall. **Bottom**: Green Island Gardens.

HISTORIC BUILDINGS & GARDENS

Layer Marney Towers
Although the planned palatial house at Layer Marney was never built, the impressive eight-storey-high gatehouse was. It is the tallest gatehouse and surely one of the most impressive examples of Tudor architecture in the country

For more information visit *layermarneytower.co.uk*

Markshall Estate
The history of Markshall stretches back to its first mention in the Domesday Book of 1086. The house was demolished after the Second World War, and today, Markshall Estate is 2350 acres of woodland, lakes and gardens dedicated to conservation of the natural environment and a wonderful place to explore.

For more information visit *markshall.org.uk*

Paycocke's House and Garden
Thomas Paycocke was a Tudor merchant whose house in the pretty village of Coggeshall is a well preserved and impressively elaborate affair built in the 16th century with wealth from the wool trade. It's not all about the house though; the cottage garden is not to be missed.

For more information visit: *nationaltrust.org.uk/paycockes-house-and-garden*

Tilbury Fort
From when Henry VIII built the first fort on the Thames here until the Second World War, Tilbury Fort has protected London from attack from the direction of the sea.

For more information visit: *english-heritage.org.uk/visit/places/tilbury-fort/*

Top: Layer Marney Towers. *Right*: Markshall Estate. *Opposite left*: Tilbury Fort. *Right*: Paycocke's House and Garden.

NATURE RESERVES

NATURE RESERVES

Essex has many nature reserves and Sites of Specific Scientific Interest, in particular, its 350 miles of coastline holds many important sites for wintering and migrating birds. Below are just some of the nature reserves in the area but it's by no means an exhaustive list – more reserves can be found at the following websites:

Essex Wildlife Trust: *essexwt.org.uk*

RSPB: *rspb.org.uk/reserves-and-events*

National Trust: *nationaltrust.org.uk/days-out/regioneastofengland/east-of-england*

National Nature Reserves: *gov.uk/government/collections/national-nature-reserves-in-england#east-of-england-*

Abberton Reservoir

Tens of thousands of ducks, geese and swans visit this internationally important wetland site each year. Close to migration routes, the huge reservoir and surrounding pastures provide the perfect habitat for wildfowl whether resident, winter visitors or migrating visitors and a few rarities have also been known to make an appearance.

Car park postcode: CO2 0EU. For more information visit: *essexwt.org.uk/nature-reserves/abberton*

Blue House Farm

A working farm and nature reserve balancing livestock farming with good conservation practice beside the River Crouch. The combination of tidal mud flats, saltmarsh and grazing pastures attracts a number of wildfowl and wading birds as well as hares, otters, water voles and dragonflies.

Car park postcode: CM3 6GU. For more information visit: *essexwt.org.uk/nature-reserves/blue-house-farm*

*Opposite top left: Beardet tit **Right**: Abberton Reservoir. **Middle left**: Wallasea Island. **Right**: Brown hare. **Bottom**: Fox in an Essex meadow. **Previous spread**: Avocets at Northey Island.*

Fingringhoe Wick

Acquired in 1961, Fingringhoe Wick was Essex Wildlife Trust's first nature reserve. Since then they have turned a barren site overlooking the Colne Estuary into a rich variety of habitats – grassland, gorse heathland, reed beds, ponds, meadows and scrub so there is something of interest all year round.

Car park postcode: CO5 7DN. For more information visit: *essexwt.org.uk/nature-reserves/fingringhoe*

Langdon

With over 500 acres of wildflower meadows, ponds and ancient woodlands spread across a ridge of hills to the south of Basildon, Langdon Nature Reserve is Essex Wildlife Trust's largest inland nature reserve. Home to hundreds of species of wildflowers, many butterflies, badgers, foxes, turtle doves, nightingales and woodcock, it plays an essential role in preserve habitat for once common wildlife that is suffering due to intensive farming and urban sprawl.

Car park postcode: SS16 6EJ. For more information visit: *essexwt.org.uk/nature-reserves/langdon*

Northey Island

A tranquil island in the Blackwater Estuary accessed at low tide by a causeway, Northey Island is a haven for wading birds and wildfowl, which can either be seen from the river wall on the mainland or on the island itself.

Car park postcode: CM9 5JQ. Northey Island may be closed at certain times of year and access is at low tide only, please check: *www.nationaltrust.org.uk/visit/essex-bedfordshire-hertfordshire/northey-island*

Old Hall Marshes

Home to breeding species including avocet, lapwing, redshank, pochard, shoveler and bearded tit, Old Hall Marshes is a landscape of grazing marshes, reed beds, saltmarsh and islands. During migration, marsh harriers, wheatears, whinchats and waders can also be seen.

Car park postcode: CM9 8TP. For more information visit: *rspb.org.uk/reserves-and-events/reserves-a-z/old-hall-marshes*

NATURE RESERVES

Rainham Marshes
On the very edge of Essex, a stone's throw from London, Rainham Marshes is an ancient, low-lying grazing marsh in the Thames Estuary. The reserve is a haven for reptiles, amphibians and invertebrates as well as breeding waders and wintering wildfowl.

Car park postcode: RM19 1SZ. For more information visit: rspb.org.uk/reserves-and-events/reserves-a-z/rainham-marshes

Stour Estuary
A nature reserve incorporating woodland and mudflats along the River Stour Estuary. Highlights include the thousand of waders and wildfowl that flock to the estuary in winter. In spring, the woods are full of wildflowers and you may even hear a nightingale.

Car park postcode: CO12 5ND. For more information visit: rspb.org.uk/reserves-and-events/reserves-a-z/stour-estuary

Stanford Wharf
Stanford Wharf was created to replace habitat on the Thames Estuary that was lost due to the London Gateway Port development. The reserve was developed in particular as a feeding and roosting site for wintering and passage water birds, including shelduck, teal, wigeon, avocet, ringed plover, dunlin, grey plover, black-tailed godwit and redshank.

Car park postcode: SS17 0EE. For more information visit: rspb.org.uk/reserves-and-events/reserves-a-z/stanford-water

Wallasea Island
The site covers 1800 acres in a remote corner of Essex, most of which has been transformed from arable farmland into a landscape of newly created saltmarsh, mudflats and lagoons. Species include avocets, hen harriers, peregrines, common seal and water voles.

Car park postcode: SS4 2HD. For more information visit: rspb.org.uk/reserves-and-events/reserves-a-z/wallasea-island

Top: Waders at the Stour Estuary. Above: Little egret.

Waders in the Blackwater.

ABOUT THE AUTHOR – JUSTIN MINNS

Biography

Although Justin Minns is well-known for his atmospheric images of East Anglia, he travels extensively to fulfil his passion for photography and the outdoors. For this, his second fotoVUE volume after *Photographing East Anglia*, Justin didn't have to travel far from his home in Suffolk to bring us this beautiful work about the county of Essex. Perhaps a surprising subject for landscape photography, but as you can see, a worthy one.

A Fellow of the Royal Photographic Society, Justin is a full-time professional photographer, and one of the best in the UK. His work has won awards in numerous photographic competitions including Landscape Photographer of the Year, Outdoor Photographer of the Year and International Garden Photographer of the Year.

He works closely with the National Trust with other clients including English Heritage, BBC, British Museum, Starling Bank and he has even photographed a remote corner of Saudi Arabia for NEOM, the planned community of the future. Justin is also an ambassador for LEE Filters and f-Stop bags.

If you would like to learn from Justin, he is an experienced photography tutor running 1-2-1 and group workshops in East Anglia and the rest of the UK including photography workshops for the National Trust, Forestry Commission and the Royal Photographic Society. Further afield he leads several photography tours a year to stunning locations around the world including Iceland, Madeira and Namibia.

"The joy of landscape photography for me is being there. Being a part of nature and witnessing its wonders. Those wonderfully unpredictable conditions and fleeting moments of light that make the heart beat a little faster. The thrill of watching the first light of the day creep over the frozen stillness of a wintry landscape, while the air and my fingers tingle with the cold, and the challenge of capturing the atmosphere of moments like this is what it is all about."

You can find out more about Justin and see more of his work at:
www.justinminns.co.uk

Camel in the desert, Saudi Arabia.
Canon 5D IV, 70–200mm at 200mm,
ISO 200, 1/400s at f/16.

ABOUT FotoVUE

If you are a keen photographer or want to take the best photos when out and about or on holiday, fotoVUE guidebooks show you where and how to take photographs in the world's most beautiful places. fotoVUE photographer-authors use their local knowledge to show you the best locations to photograph and the best times to visit.

Order at: www.fotovue.com and use code: ESSEX at checkout to get: 20% off all books

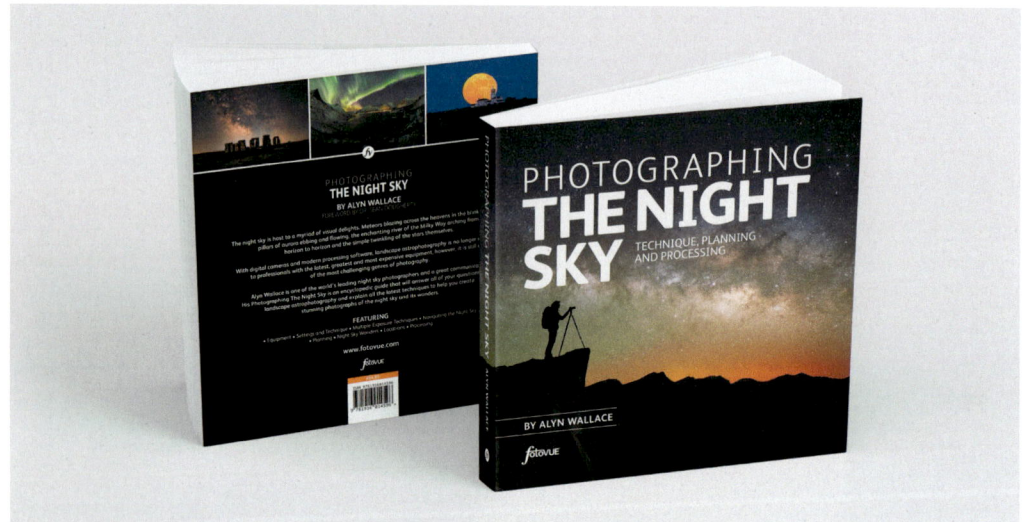

What people say about fotoVUE photo-location and visitor guidebooks

"The best photographer guidebooks by a mile."
"The quality of product is surpassed only by the attention to highly relevant detail."
"This could be the best location-oriented photoguide I have yet to come across."
"A fantastic book and an amazing travel guide."
"The template for all photography location guides."

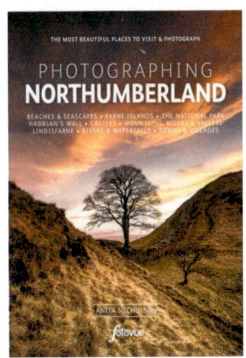
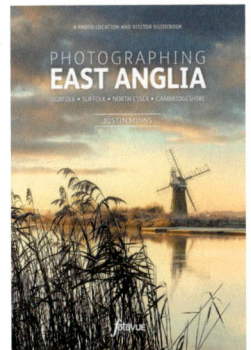
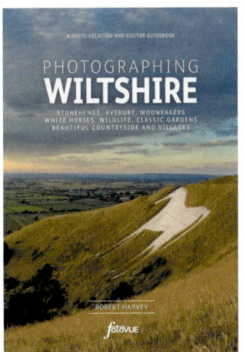

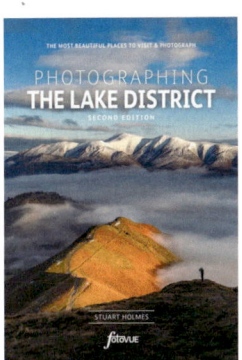
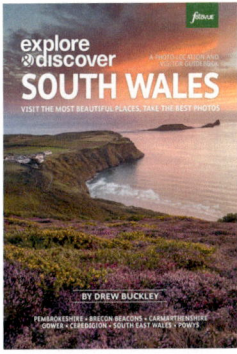
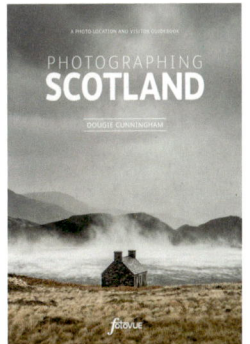
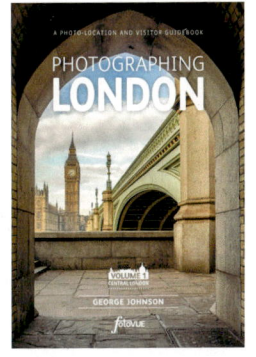

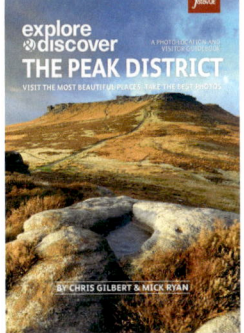
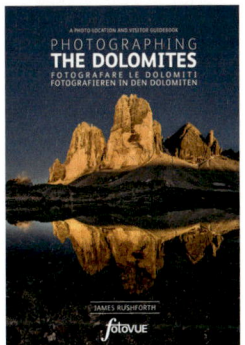
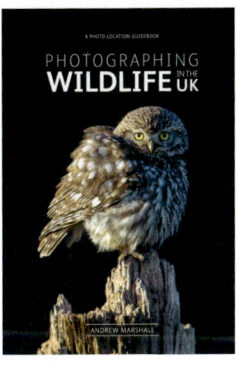

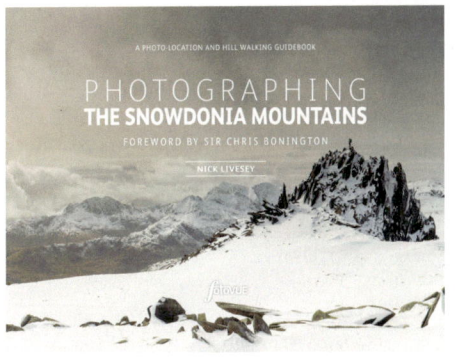

LOCATION INDEX

A

Alresford Creek 144

B

Barlinghall Creek 262
Battlesbridge 232
Beeleigh Falls 190
Bocking Windmill 356
Bradwell-on-Sea 218
Bragg's Mill 374
Brightlingsea 134
Bures 56
Burnham-on-Crouch 246

C

Chalkney Woods 46
Chappel Viaduct 50
Clacton-on-Sea 114
Coalhouse Point 300
Colne Point 120

D

Danbury Common 204
Dedham 68

E

Epping Forest 322

F

Felsted Mill 352
Finchingfield 358
Fingringhoe 150
Frinton-on-Sea 108

H

Hadleigh Castle 296
Hamford Water 94
Harwich & Dovercourt 86
Hatfield Forest 346
Heybridge Basin 178
Hillhouse Woods 62
Hoe Mill Lock 196

L

Leigh-on-Sea 286
Lion Wharf 252

M

Maldon 184
Manningtree 74
Mersea Island 158
Mountnessing Windmill 318
Mundon Oaks 210

N

North Fambridge 242

P

Paglesham 258
Point Clear 132

R

Red Sands Fort 272

S

Saffron Walden 368
Sandford Mill 200
Shoeburyness 276
South Woodham Ferrers 238
Southend-on-Sea 282
St Osyth Creek 126
Stansgate 216

T

Temple Hill 328
Thaxted 364
The Broomway 266
The Stort Navigation 336
Thorrington Tide Mill 140
Tollesbury 172
Two Tree Island 290

W

Walton-on-the-Naze 104
Warley Place 312
Wrabness 80